Supermarket Retailing in Africa

This book surveys the landscape of supermarket retailing in Africa, showing how this expanding part of the retail sector is changing consumerism on the continent.

Drawing on research covering retail formats, consumer behaviour, strategies, operation research, ICT, relationship marketing, and market linkage, the book investigates the many factors impacting the growth of supermarkets in Africa. The contributors employ theories, concepts, and methods in order to help us to understand changing consumer behaviour, the strategies used by suppliers to access supermarkets, the role of service suppliers in the growth of the sector, and ultimately how supermarkets can assist in making the market linkage between producers and consumers in Africa. The chapters provide a comprehensive exploration of modern retail, discussing its growth and future, identifying consumer preferences, as well as suggesting solutions to the challenges that retailers and suppliers on the continent face in developing the sector.

This book will be of interest to scholars and students of the retail sector and retail management in Africa.

Felix Adamu Nandonde is a Lecturer in Marketing at the Sokoine University of Agriculture, Morogoro, Tanzania.

John L. Stanton is a Professor in Food Marketing at Saint Joseph's University, Philadelphia, USA.

Routledge Contemporary Africa Series

Implementing the Sustainable Development Goals in Nigeria
Barriers, Prospects and Strategies
Edited by Eghosa O. Ekhator, Servel Miller and Etinosa Igbinosa

Indigenous Elites in Africa
The Case of Kenya's Maasai
Serah Shani

Media and Communication in Nigeria
Conceptual Connections, Crossroads and Constraints
Edited by Bruce Mutsvairo and Nnamdi T Ekeanyanwu

The Zimbabwean Crisis after Mugabe
Multidisciplinary Perspectives
Edited by Tendai Mangena, Oliver Nyambi and Gibson Ncube

Postcolonial Agency in African and African Diasporic Literature and Film
A Study in Globalectics
Lokangaka Losambe

Inequality in Zambia
Edited by Caesar Cheelo, Marja Hinfelaar and Manenga Ndulo

Supermarket Retailing in Africa
Edited by Felix Adamu Nandonde and John L. Stanton

Sexual Humour in Africa
Gender, Jokes and Societal Change
Edited by Ignatius Chukwumah

Combatants in African Conflicts
Professionals, Praetorians, Militias, Insurgents, and Mercenaries
Simon David Taylor

Popular Protest, Political Opportunities, and Change in Africa
Edited by Edalina Rodrigues Sanches

For more information about this series, please visit: https://www.routledge.com/Routledge-Contemporary-Africa/book-series/RCAFR

Supermarket Retailing in Africa

Edited by Felix Adamu Nandonde and
John L. Stanton

LONDON AND NEW YORK

First published 2022
by Routledge
4 Park Square, Milton Park, Abingdon, Oxon OX14 4RN

and by Routledge
605 Third Avenue, New York, NY 10158

Routledge is an imprint of the Taylor & Francis Group, an informa business

© 2022 selection and editorial matter, Felix Adamu Nandonde and John L. Stanton; individual chapters, the contributors

The right of Felix Adamu Nandonde and John L. Stanton to be identified as the authors of the editorial material, and of the authors for their individual chapters, has been asserted in accordance with sections 77 and 78 of the Copyright, Designs and Patents Act 1988.

All rights reserved. No part of this book may be reprinted or reproduced or utilised in any form or by any electronic, mechanical, or other means, now known or hereafter invented, including photocopying and recording, or in any information storage or retrieval system, without permission in writing from the publishers.

Trademark notice: Product or corporate names may be trademarks or registered trademarks, and are used only for identification and explanation without intent to infringe.

British Library Cataloguing-in-Publication Data
A catalogue record for this book is available from the British Library

Library of Congress Cataloging-in-Publication Data
Names: Nandonde, Felix Adamu, editor. | Stanton, John L., editor.
Title: Supermarket retailing in Africa/edited by Felix Adamu Nandonde and John L. Stanton.
Description: Abingdon, Oxon; New York, NY: Routledge, 2022. |
Series: Routledge contemporary Africa | Includes bibliographical references and index.
Identifiers: LCCN 2021048895 (print) | LCCN 2021048896 (ebook) |
ISBN 9780367408350 (hardback) | ISBN 9781032221489 (paperback) |
ISBN 9780367854300 (ebook)
Subjects: LCSH: Supermarkets–Africa. | Retail trade–Africa.
Classification: LCC HF5469.23.A352 S87 2022 (print) |
LCC HF5469.23.A352 (ebook) | DDC 381/.456413096–dc23/eng/20211006
LC record available at https://lccn.loc.gov/2021048895
LC ebook record available at https://lccn.loc.gov/2021048896

ISBN: 978-0-367-40835-0 (hbk)
ISBN: 978-1-032-22148-9 (pbk)
ISBN: 978-0-367-85430-0 (ebk)

DOI: 10.4324/9780367854300

Typeset in Times New Roman
by Deanta Global Publishing Services, Chennai, India

FELIX ADAMU NANDONDE – I dedicate this book to my wife, Pamela John Liana

JOHN L. STANTON – This book is dedicated to my wife, who has helped me through every stage of my writing. She is my angel

Contents

Editor bios ix
Contributors bios x
Acknowledgements xiii
Supermarket retailing in Africa: An introduction xiv

1 Understanding performance of retail formats in Africa 1
JOHN L. STANTON AND FELIX ADAMU NANDONDE

2 Consumer shopping patterns and pricing considerations for BOP consumers: The case of Madagascar 16
ARILOVA A. RANDRIANASOLO

3 Factors motivating consumers to visit supermarkets in Tanzania: Case of Dar es Salaam and Arusha Regions 36
FRANCIS MUYA, MAUREEN KABUGUMILA, FRANCIS MOSES, AND DEUS SHATTA

4 Understanding consumers' preference of purchasing items from supermarkets as opposed to traditional markets in Ghana 52
EMMANUEL KOJO SAKYI

5 ICT usage in supermarkets in East Africa: Benefits, challenges, and way forward 70
M. KAGOYA SUMAYA AND A. R. MUSHI

6 Assessing the technological relevance of South African supermarkets in the face of changing consumer behaviour 91
TENDAI CHIGUWARE

7 Operations research contribution to the performance of supermarkets in East Africa 104
A. R. MUSHI AND SUMAYA M. KAGOYA

8	Strategies used by local food suppliers to increase participation in modern food retailing in Tanzania FELIX ADAMU NANDONDE	129
9	Exploring the relationships between supermarkets and local suppliers in developing countries: Evidence from Tanzania DANIEL WILSON NDYETABULA	151
10	Understanding the role of service providers on the development of supermarkets in Africa EDWARD A. N. DAKORA	170
11	Supermarket retailing in Africa: Lessons learnt FELIX ADAMU NANDONDE AND JOHN L. STANTON	187
	Index	193

Editor bios

Felix Adamu Nandonde is a Lecturer in Marketing at the Sokoine University of Agriculture, Morogoro, Tanzania. Felix has graduated with a PhD in Business Economics from Aalborg University in Denmark, an MSc from Newcastle University-upon Tyne, UK, and a Bachelor's in Business Administration from Mzumbe University, Tanzania. He teaches courses on Agribusiness Strategy Management and Quantitative and Qualitative Data Analysis for PhD Agribusiness and Management Strategy for MBA Evening. He also teaches International Marketing of Agribusiness Products for MBA-Agribusiness. His research works have appeared in the *Journal of African Business, Transnational Corporation Review, British Food Journal, Emerging Economies Cases Journal, FIIB Business Review, Journal of Global Business,* and *Organization Excellence and International Journal of Retail & Distribution Management.* Felix has published eight book chapters and authored a Business Communication Skills handbook with the Mzumbe Book Project, Morogoro, Tanzania. Mr Nandonde is a co-founder of a GMF consultancy firm (www.gmf.co.tz) based in Morogoro, Tanzania. Before academia, he worked with the National Bank of Commerce (NBC), Tanzania Limited as a Sales Consultant Business Banking, and Ministry of Livestock and Fisheries as a Director of Production and Marketing.

John L. Stanton has a PhD in Marketing from Syracuse University and has been in the food industry for about 40 years. He is currently a professor and previously held the endowed chair in the Food Marketing Department at Saint Joseph's University in Philadelphia. Dr Stanton was elected to the European Retail Academy Hall of Fame and the Private Label Manufacturers Hall of Fame. Besides academia, Dr Stanton has also worked in the food industry. Dr Stanton was a senior Fulbright Scholar in Tanzania and made numerous speaking turns throughout Africa and around the world, including Mexico, Russia, Germany, France, Argentina (Argentine Grocery Association, Denmark (AC Nielsen conference), Uruguay, Taiwan, Japan, Singapore (Retail leadership conference), Sri Lanka, Brazil, Kenya, and many others. Dr Stanton has published over 100 peer-reviewed articles and 12 books. He has been regularly quoted in the media, both the food trade and general media, such as CNN

Contributors bios

Tendai Chiguware has a PhD from Fort Hare University in South Africa. He holds an MPhil in Social Studies from the University of Zimbabwe and an undergraduate degree from Midlands State University in Zimbabwe. Formerly he was at the Agricultural and Rural Development Research Institute (ARDRI) in South Africa. His articles have appeared in the *African Studies Quarterly*, *Journal of Human Ecology*, and *Africa's Public Service Delivery & Performance Review*. He is a member of Anthropology Southern Africa (ASnA) and the Association for Research on Nonprofit Organizations and Voluntary Action (ARNOVA)

Edward A. N. Dakora is a Senior Lecturer in the Department of Management Sciences at Sol Plaatje University in Kimberley, South Africa. He has a DTech in Marketing, a Master's degree in Retail Business Management and a Bachelor of Technology in Retail Business Management from the Cape Peninsula University of Technology in Cape Town, South Africa. He has published several articles in peer-reviewed journals. He served on the Advisory Board of Retail Congress Africa in 2015, a gathering of industry leaders to discuss retail market opportunities and challenges in Africa. He is a member of the Wholesale and Retail Sector Education and Training Authority's (W&RSETA) Higher Education Group (an advisory body to the W&RSETA).

Maureen Semu Kabugumila is a Lecturer in Business Studies at the National Institute of Transport in Tanzania. Ms Kabugumila is currently pursuing a PhD in Business Management from the Open University of Tanzania. She holds a Master's degree in commerce from the University of Madras India and a Bachelor's degree in Commerce with Computer Applications from Madurai Kamaraj University, India. Her research papers have appeared in the *Uongozi Journal of Management and Development Dynamics*, *Journal of Logistics, Management and Engineering Studies*, *American Journal of Service Science and Management*, and *International Journal of Business and Social Science*.

Sumaya, M. Kagoya is a Lecturer in the Faculty of Computing and Informatics, Department of Applied Computing and IT, at Makerere University Business School in Uganda. She holds an undergraduate degree in Computing and a postgraduate Diploma in Education. She has a Master's in Information

Technology, a Master's in Business Administration and a Master's of Science in Project Planning and Management. She is currently finalising her PhD in operations research in E-government implementation at the University of Dar-es-Salaam, Tanzania.

Allen R. Mushi is an Associate Professor in the Department of Mathematics, University of Dar-es-Salaam. He holds a BSc (Education), a Master's degree in Management Science, and a PhD in Mathematics, specialising in operations research. He has researched and published in the areas of academic time-tabling, industrial scheduling, and multi-criteria decision analysis, exact and heuristic solutions to complex optimisation problems, municipal solid waste management systems optimisation, and recently on agricultural irrigation systems optimisation. He has been teaching both undergraduate and postgraduate students in operations research for more than 23 years.

Francis Frederick Muya is a Lecturer in Business Administration at the National Institute of Transport. Mr Francis is a PhD candidate at Mzumbe University and has an MSc in International Trade from the University of Dar-es-Salaam and a Bachelor's degree in Business Administration from Mzumbe University, Tanzania. His research works have appeared in *African Review Journal*, *Makerere Journal of Higher Education*, *Uongozi Journal of Management Studies*, *International Journal of Social Sciences & Educational Studies*, *American Journal of Service Science and Management*, and *Journal of Logistics, Management and Engineering Studies*. His research interests lie in marketing, trade, entrepreneurship, and management. Mr Francis is a Registered Technical Teacher in Business Administration with the National Council of Technical Education (NACTE).

Francis Moses Mwaisaka is an Assistant Lecturer in Business Studies and Marketing, Sales Management and Advertising at the National Institute of Transport (NIT) in Tanzania. Mr Francis has a Master's degree in Business Administration (MBA), specialising in Marketing, from St Augustine University of Tanzania, and a Bachelor's degree in Public Relations and Marketing from the St Augustine University of Tanzania. His research lies in marketing, management and consumer behavioural studies.

Daniel Wilson Ndyetabula is a Senior Lecturer and Head of the Department of Agricultural Economics and Agribusiness at the Sokoine University of Agriculture (SUA), Tanzania, specialising in agricultural finance and investment appraisal. He is also a Visiting Lecturer at the Department of Agricultural Economics, Extension, and Rural Development at the University of Pretoria, South Africa, where he has been teaching finance and investment appraisal-related courses under the UP-AERC collaborative Master's program. He serves as a member of the Academic Advisory Board (AAB) of the African Economic Research Consortium (AERC) and member of the accreditation subcommittee of the AERC.

Arilova (Lova) Randrianasolo is an Assistant Professor of Marketing at Butler University's Lacy School of Business. He holds a Bachelor's of Science degree in international business and entrepreneurship from Saint Louis University, a Master's degree in Music Business from New York University, and a doctorate in International Business and Marketing from Saint Louis University. His work has been published in academic journals such as the *Journal of Global Marketing, Journal of Brand Management, Journal of International Marketing, Journal of International Consumer Marketing, Journal of Consumer Marketing, International Journal of Music Business Research*, and *Madagascar Conservation & Development*. He has presented papers at international conferences such as the Academy of International Business, the American Marketing Association's and the Academy of Marketing Science.

Emmanuel Kojo Sakyi is an Associate Professor of Public Administration and Management at the Department of Public Administration and Health Services Management, University of Ghana Business School. He obtained his PhD from the University of Manchester. He is currently the Academic Consultant for the Master's of Public Administration (MPA) programme at the Euro-Mediterranean University, Slovenia. He is the immediate past Vice-Chancellor of the Ho Technical University. He has edited two collections, and his research articles have appeared in the *Journal of Applied Research in Higher Education, Public Organization Review, OIDA International Journal of Sustainable Development, Politics & Policy*, and *African Social Science Review*.

Deus Nichodemus Shatta is a Principal Instructor in Procurement and Supply Chain Management at the National Institute of Transport. Mr Shatta is a PhD candidate at the Open University of Tanzania and holds an MSc in Procurement and Supply Chain Management from Mzumbe University, Tanzania, a Post Graduate Diploma in Scientific Computing from the University of Dar-es-Salaam, Tanzania, a Post Graduate Diploma in Education from the University of Arusha, Tanzania, and a CPSP (T). Mr Shatta has published three papers in the *International Academic Journal of Procurement and Supply Chain Management, International Journal of Applied Research in Management and Economics*, and *American Scientific Research Journal for Engineering, Technology, and Sciences (ASRJETS)*. Mr Shatta is an Authorized Member of the Procurement and Supplies Professionals and Technicians Board (PSPTB) based in Tanzania.

Acknowledgements

We understand that without the tireless effort of the individuals who helped us achieve the objective of putting this book together, our dream of writing this book would not have been possible. Our thanks first go to our living GOD. Second, we thank the 11 contributors who are based in different countries in Africa and the USA. We would also like to take this opportunity to thank our reviewers for taking their precious time to assist us in the process of reviewing submitted works at different stages in the preparation of this book; the list is below:

Arilova A. Randrianasolo, *Butler University, USA*
Daniel Wilson Ndyetabula, *Sokoine University of Agriculture, Tanzania*
Edward Dakora, *SPU University, South Africa*
Emmanuel Chao, *Mzumbe University, Tanzania*
Moses Wandera, the *Cooperative University of Kenya, Kenya*
Reena das Nair, *University of Johannesburg, South Africa*
Richard Adu-Gyamfi, *International Trade Centre, Geneva*
Simplice Asongu, *the African Governance and Development Institute, Cameroon*
Tolu Olarewaju, *Staffordshire University, UK*

We are grateful to our families – Nandonde and Stanton, who have been affected in one way or another during the process of writing this book. In a very special way, we would like to thank the Routledge publishing team headed by Leanne Hinves, Helena Hurd, and Matthew Shobbrook for their encouragement and patience.

Finally, we apologies for any errors or omissions that may appear in any of the pages of this book; no harm was intended to anyone.

Thank you all!

Felix Adamu Nandonde
Morogoro, Tanzania
John Stanton
Pennsylvania, USA

Supermarket retailing in Africa
An introduction

Africa has seen the transformation of fast-moving consumer goods in its supermarket retailing landscape in cities and in some countries even in villages. This transformation has awakened the interest of researchers, policymakers, consumers, manufacturers, and producers in understanding the future of the modern retail industry on the continent. In general, the retail business on the continent was dominated by African companies operating in different countries on a small scale until early 2001, when the internationalisation of retail started to be common in Africa. This phenomenon was fuelled by the end of Apartheid in South Africa in 1994, which led to South African retail firms such as Shoprite, Pick n Pay, Massmart (Nandonde and Kuada, 2016).

Retailers from outside the African continent also joined the race to transform the African supermarket retail business. For example, Sainsbury, a UK supermarket that operated in Egypt, collapsed in 2001 after two years of operations. Similarly, Carrefour, which operated and failed in Algeria, has recently engaged in re-internationalisation and has been expanding into the East African market with 12 stores in Kenya, two stores in Uganda, and four stores in Tanzania since 2016, when it started its operations in the region (Otieno, 2021). Casino, a French retail firm dominating the Francophone countries, is also doing well (see Chapter 1).

Despite these changes in the supermarket business on the continent, there are no formal statistics that show the number of supermarket stores available in Africa, excluding those in South Africa, and how much the industry contributes to the continent's economy. Therefore, little is known about the contribution of supermarket business to both direct and indirect employment in the continent. For example, when Nakumatt supermarket, a Kenyan retailer, collapsed in 2017, it was revealed that the retailer had 67 stores and employed 6,700 people directly in Kenya, Rwanda, Tanzania, and Uganda (Nandonde, 2020). Such a number of people being employed by one retailer alone suggests that the industry is very important for the future of social and economic development. Also, there is a consensus that the supermarket business is on the rise in Africa.

The approach to studying supermarket operations in academic literature in Africa has been dominated by development thinking that focuses on the importance of the industry on smallholder farmers and poverty reduction (see Anderson et al., 2015; Haantuba, H. and de Graaf, J., 2012;, Van der Heijden et al., 2013).

With the rise of South African retailers, business approach emerged; however, a lot of literature is still available in grey literature such as newspapers, dissertations/theses and commissioned jobs. Journalists working on newspapers in Kenya and South Africa have done a great job in documenting the economic and social effects of the supermarkets business on the continent (see www.businessdaily.com, www.eastafrican.com, www.financialtimes.com). This is because the industry is more advanced in those countries compared to other countries in sub-Saharan Africa.

Recently, business researchers have joined the race. These studies have paid attention to understanding consumer visitations to supermarkets and strategies used by retailers (see Dadzie and Nandonde, 2018, das Nair 2017, Nandonde, 2019, Chapter 5). However, it seems that the development approach will dominate the supermarket business in Africa for some years to come. Although we understand the efforts made by previous studies on documenting the supermarket business in Africa, we argue that what is happening in the continent needs academic insight from different backgrounds to unearth the future of supermarket retailing on the continent. Researchers have made previous efforts in isolation, but the challenges the modern retailing industry faces on the continent need a holistic approach. This is due to the nature of the supermarket business and its impact. Researchers from different backgrounds such as law, organisational behaviour, human resources, operations management, finance, accounting, marketing, development, human nutrition, economics, urban planning, geography, agricultural economics, agribusiness, sociology, and psychology, just to mention a few, can uncover the way modern retailers sustain themselves in Africa. This multidisciplinary approach will also enable interconnections across academic specialisations. It will also inform practitioners and academicians better about the investments and scope of the supermarket business in Africa and enable investors to decide on a business model that will make their business sustainable.

Our main aim of compiling this book is first to highlight the changing nature of the supermarket retail business in Africa and the need for engagement in academia and by practitioners for the growth of the industry. Second, the supermarket business needs special attention since it touches all areas of life. We have attracted academicians from Ghana, South Africa, Tanzania, Uganda, and the USA, who have addressed many sectorial issues of interest in this book.

Problems surrounding supermarket retailing in Africa are many, but we argue that understanding consumer needs provides more knowledge to investors interested in capturing the emerging retail business on the continent. Supermarkets are being closed in Africa, and many people are losing jobs, and suppliers are failing to claim their money from these collapsed stores. In general, this is a financial loss. For example, the closure of Uchumi supermarket in Tanzania left more than 300 suppliers with a narrow chance of reclaiming their supplies that amounted to US$3.8 million during its closure in 2015 (The Citizen, 2015). This indicates that although there are opportunities for supermarket businesses to grow in Africa, we need to understand more about the barriers that threaten the sustainability of supermarket retailing in Africa.

Based on what is happening in African supermarket retailing, there is strong ground to suggest that considerable research remains for academic considerations with a holistic approach. Academic research can be conducted on three levels of analysis that include macro, meso, and micro. However, there must be a combination of practices and academics for any research to be meaningful and helpful to investors. This observation does not mean we undermine the contributions from academia, but we want to have something of value that combines practice and academia to help the retail business to grow. In this book, we are delighted to integrate contributions from various disciplines such as marketing, public administration, agriculture economics, sociology, mathematics, and operation management.

Crucially, chapters discuss issues related to the development of supermarket retailing in Africa, focusing on business within a wider social context. This is based on the fact that the supermarket business is part of a broader relationship that interweaves with other academic insights. Collectively, we hope that this book is of importance to a more pervasive, extensive, and interdisciplinary academic contribution to the knowledge of the supermarket business in Africa.

Sections of the book

The book has 11 chapters that connect with the book's aim and trends of what is happening in the African supermarket retailing business, namely retail formats, consumer behaviour, consumer visitations to supermarkets versus traditional markets, application of ICT, and operations management in retail research and the supplier–retailer relationship. Chapter 1 focuses on the formats of the modern stores available on the continent and their performance. Stanton and Nandonde present the impact of retail formats, which seem to be imported to Africa by international retailers. The chapter demonstrates the current revenue collections and future performance of retailing and suggests what should be done to control market failure of the introduced retail formats. Randrianasolo's study on the shopping patterns of the bottom of the pyramid (BOP) consumers in Madagascar is presented in Chapter 2. The study shows the current shopping patterns and pricing considerations in Madagascar, and provides a more holistic understanding of why multinational retailers have not reached the majority of the Malagasy population. In Chapter 3, Muya, Kubugumila, Moses, and Shatta examine consumers' supermarket visits in Tanzania. The authors show how social and economic factors influence consumers to visit supermarkets in Tanzania. Chapter 4 presents Sakyi's work on the potential of consumers to purchase in supermarkets versus in traditional retail stores with a focus on Ghana. The chapter examines the impact of shopping malls (within the Ho Municipal Assembly) on the consumer choice of shopping location, shopping behaviour, and preference of where to buy specific household items. The results of the study reveal that the ambience of shopping malls, neatness, and packaging of goods in the malls attract more customers.

The potential usage and challenges of ICT in the supermarket business in East Africa are discussed by Kagoya and Mushi in Chapter 5. They show that although there is some use of ICT in supermarkets in the region, some important processes for the business are still done manually. Chiguware's work in Chapter 6 shows that the South African supermarket industry has been consistent with global changes and innovations and has embraced ICT usage to attract consumers. The chapter presents some of the ICT services, including online shopping, various click and collect delivery models, and loyalty programmes that offer savings to consumers. Chiguware shows that supermarkets face challenges at the macro level, which limit them as ICT oriented.

Nandonde in Chapter 8 explores the strategies used by local food suppliers to increase their participation in modern food retailing in developing economies, in this case Tanzania. The study shows that some of the strategies used by food suppliers to access supermarkets include outsourcing (contract farming), social networks, business relationships, innovation, employment of experienced foreign staff, sales support, and the production of a wide range of products.

In Chapter 9, Ndyetabula sheds light on the relationship between suppliers and retailers in the fresh produce business. The chapter indicates the impact of relations on the inclusion or exclusion of farmers through the lenses of the growing power of retailers in the supply chain and in changing agri-food systems in Tanzania. In Chapter 10, Dakora unveils the contribution of service providers to supermarket expansion in Africa. The chapter illustrates the role of key stakeholders (support service providers) in the value chain of South African supermarkets and presents how such a role enabled the expansion of their operations into the rest of Africa.

Mushi and Kagoya in Chapter 7 show the importance of operations research (OR) for supermarket retailing research in Africa. The chapter reviews OR supermarket applications around the world, collects data on specific features of the East African market, and proposes measures suitable to the regional markets. Lastly, in Chapter 11, Nandonde and Stanton conclude the lessons learnt on supermarket retailing in Africa by indicating five proposals for growth: setting appropriate retail formats, facilitating the use of ICT technologies, strengthening the related supported industry for the growth of supermarket retailing in Africa, promoting the use of operation research tools in research, and strengthening the supplier–retailer relationship. Despite this, no single policy can be formed to work in all countries in Africa; however, we argue that researchers, policymakers, and investors need to consider these factors for the growth of the sector.

References

Andersson, C. I., Chege, C. G., Rao, E. J., & Qaim, M. (2015). Following up on smallholder farmers and supermarkets in Kenya. *American Journal of Agricultural Economics*, 97(4), 1247–1266.

Dadzie, S. H. and Nandonde, F. A. (2018). Factors influencing consumers' supermarket visitation in developing economies: the case of Ghana. In Byrom and Medway (eds), *Case Study in Food Retailing and Distribution*, 1st ed., 53–67, Elsevier.

das Nair, R. (2017). The internationalization of supermarkets and the nature of competitive rivalry in retailing in South Africa. *Development Southern Africa*, 35(3), 315–333.

Haantuba, H., & de Graaf, J. (2012). Linkages between smallholder farmers and supermarkets: lessons from Zambia. In Ellen B. McCullough, Prabhu L. Pingali and Kostas G. Stamoulis (eds), *The Transformation of Agri-Food Systems*, 231–248. London: Routledge.

Nandonde, F. A. (2019). A PESTLE analysis of international retailing in the East African Community. *Global Business and Organizational Excellence*, *38*(4), 54–61.

Nandonde, F. A. (2020). In the desire of conquering East African supermarket business: what went wrong in nakumatt supermarket. *Emerging Economies Cases Journal*, *2*(2), 126–133.

Nandonde, F. A., & Kuada, J. (2016). International firms in Africa's food retail business-emerging issues and research agenda. *International Journal of Retail & Distribution Management*, *4*(4), 448–464.

Otieno, B. (2021). Carrefour opened second store in Kampala. *The EastAfrican*, 16 March, Accessed on 19 August 2021 at https://www.theeastafrican.co.ke/tea/business/carrefour-opens-second-store-in-kampala-3324464

The Citizen (2015). Why Uchumi exits Tanzania and Uganda. 21 October, Accessed on 20 September, 2019 at https://www.thecitizen.co.tz/tanzania/news/business/why-uchumi-exits-tanzania-uganda-2536002

Van der Heijden, T., & Vink, N. (2013). Good for whom? Supermarkets and small farmers in South Africa-a critical review of current approaches to increasing access to modern markets. *Agrekon*, *52*(1), 68–86.

Websites

www.businessdaily.com
www.eastafrican.com
www.financialtimes.com

1 Understanding performance of retail formats in Africa

John L. Stanton and Felix Adamu Nandonde

Introduction

Africa has witnessed a rapid increase in supermarkets as a market channel for convenient consumer goods. There are many factors that have accelerated the growth of the retail supermarket business on the continent, and these include the swelling of the middle class, an increase in income, urbanisation, and macro policy changes that attract foreign direct investment (FDI). As a result of these factors, international retailers such as Carrefour, Walmart, and Sainsbury's have successfully opened stores in various African countries. Similarly, African retailers such as Shoprite and Game (South African retailers), Tuskys, Uchumi, and Nakumatt (Kenyan retailers) have followed suit and opened stores in many countries on the continent. However, the supermarket business terrain is not a smooth ride for retailers operating in Africa.

Despite this positive trend of supermarket emergence across the continent, strong signals of the failure of African retailers began to manifest in the initial stages of the operations of such retailers. For example, Shoprite, a South African retailer, closed its operations in Tanzania and Uganda as early as 2017 (see Nandonde, 2019 for details). Further, the retailer planned to exit from a number of African countries such as Nigeria and Ghana on the grounds of poor performance. Furthermore, the retailer is closing many stores in its home market (South Africa). In this respect, it is important to understand the business environment of African retailers for the future sustainability of the supermarket sub-sector on the continent. There is a need to investigate where people buy their food and who the major players are in each market.

Following the rise of retail distribution in Africa, different structures have emerged, such as hypermarkets, superstores, discount stores, supermarkets, and convenience stores. It is crucial to understand the extent to which the African retail business environment favours all these forms of business. Accordingly, this study is intended to understand the performance of various retail formats on the continent and suggest which forms are suitable for growth of the retail business in Africa. In this chapter, the definition of supermarkets is not based on space but rather on self-service, whereby consumers can select his/her preferred items from an assortment of items in the form of self-service.

DOI: 10.4324/9780367854300-1

Previous studies on retail formats in developing economies have paid significant attention to China (Goldman, 2001), more specifically on the manner in which international retailers change the formats of their stores in these developing economies. The studies, however, have paid little attention to consumer purchases in these stores. Therefore, the current study tried to understand the kinds of products consumers purchase in the cited stores to determine how these emerging retail businesses can remain competitive and grow sustainably in developing economies.

There are various types of retail format that are emerging in Africa. This chapter argues that it is very important to understand the business environment and culture of the host country before starting to operate in any of the retail formats. Literature shows that many retail formats that exist in developed countries are shifting to developing economies.

One should not expect to have every format available in every market. In cases where there was only one modern chain in the country, figures were excluded in the interests of space. We should also note that we did not include every country in Africa. This is not to suggest that those not included are less important, but rather that the countries in general are meant as examples of how modern African retailers function.

To achieve its objective, the study relied on the information from the webstore Planet Retail. This website was used to collect the information below, but this is only a small amount of the material that can be gained from their data. The study used data on sales, consumer spending, and a number of different retail formats in different countries in Africa. We understand that the data used in the study is not representative, as some stores were not presented in the database. Furthermore, we relied on the available data from 2014. In this respect, the information provided will enable the reader to get an overview of what each market is like.

Algeria

Currently, there is only one type of market structure in place in Algeria, besides the local markets, which is the hypermarket/superstore format. There are only two hypermarkets in this country, which are owned by French retailer Carrefour. The retailer re-entered the Algerian market in 2013 after its failed operation in 2009, following its first foray in the country in 2006. Rising incomes and underdevelopment of the retail sector attracted investors to this country (Vidalon, 2015). The amount of sales increased from 2014 to 2019. From 2014 to 2015, there was a spike in sales from 0 to US$12 million. From 2015 to 2019, there was a huge increase in sales, which reached US$22 million.

The projected sales for 2020 to 2024 show a steady increase to US$25 million. Visitors spent on edible grocery. Retailers saw a slight decrease in sales in 2015 and 2018. Consumer spending per capita initially decreased from 2014 to 2015. From 2015 to 2024, spending per capita increased slowly, but the amount never expected to reach the level of 2014. In 2014, the spending per capita was about US$780, and the expected amount in 2024 is US$700.

By 2014, there was only two supermarket-format retailers in Algeria, Inditex and Yves Rocher. Inditex had superior sales at the value of US$11 million; Yves Rocher had a value of US$5.1 million. Yves Rocher's sales decreased from 2014; the forecasted sales for 2024 are 4.9 million. In 2015, two more retailers, Carrefour and Intersport International, entered the competitive landscape in Algeria. Carrefour entered the market generating US$11.2 million in sales. Carrefour steadily increased its sales from 2015 to 2019. It is projected to generate US$25 million in 2024, while Inditex is forecasted to generate US$15 million. The increase can partly be attributed to the development of society and partly to consumers increasingly using the modern grocery channel.

Yves Rocher is considered the leader in terms of the number of stores; it started with 13 outlets in 2014 and increased to 16 stores in 2016. The retailer is forecasted to have 19 outlets by the year 2024. From 2015 to 2019, Carrefour had steady sales in their one location, and they are projected to still be at only one location by the year 2024. Inditex started with three outlets in 2014 and then increased to six outlets in 2016. Inditex is projected to have 11 outlets by 2024. Intersport had one outlet in 2015, which steadily increased throughout 2019 to six outlets. By 2024, they will have 11 outlets.

Angola

Angola is characterised by four store formats: hypermarkets, superstores, supermarkets, and convenience stores. In 2020, the wholesale and retail business was estimated to contribute 18% of the GDP and employ 1.7 million people. The formal retail business was estimated to control 30% of the annual sales of the retail business in the country in 2019, and this increased by 5% in 2000 (www.researchandmarkets.com).

Generally, each business banner, such as Shoprite, operates in different formats, such as supermarkets and discount stores, in Angola. There are two retailers, Kero and Nosso Super, owned by the Angolan government that operates as hypermarkets and superstores. In 2004, Kero's sales were at US$520 million, and this increased to US$590 million in 2005. From 2005 to 2019, the sales decreased to US$190 million. This is projected to increase steadily to US$230 million by 2024.

Nosso Super was estimated to have annual sales of US$180 million in 2014. However, their annual sales decreased to US$125 million in 2016, and then increased to US$170 million in 2019. There are several reasons for this change in sales in Angola, which had an impact on retail income. It is projected that retail sales will reach US$250 million by 2024. Shoprite started in 2014 with US$100 million in sales; sales are projected to be US$90 million by 2024. Kero had US$49 million in sales in 2014, which steadily fluctuated through to 2019; sales are projected to be US$39 million in 2024. Fruit & Veg City had the lowest amount of sales of all the retailers in this category. They started at US$10 million in sales and this fluctuated through to 2019; they are projected to see a decrease in sales from 2020 to 2024, with sales finishing at US$7 million.

Shoprite is the only retailer operating in the discount store format in Angola. In 2014, it started at US$19 million in annual sales. In 2016, Shoprite reached US$25 million in sales. However, the retailer is confident that sales will increase in the future due to changes in consumer lifestyles and the attractive business environment generated by the Angolan government. In 2016, the retailer announced it would invest US$517 million in the Angola market following the government announcement that it was removing some of the business hurdles for South African retailers (www.supermarket.co.za).

In both, consumer spending is on edible groceries. For consumer spending, in 2014, total spending was US$38 billion. For consumer spending per capita, in 2014, the spending was US$1,400. There was a surge in income spent on groceries in 2017, with consumer spending at US$45 billion and consumer spending per capita at US$1,600. The spending overall decreased from 2018 to 2019. In 2024, consumer spending is projected to decrease to US$34 billion and consumer spending per capita to US$1,250.

The leading retailers are Kero, Nosso Super, Shoprite, Fruit & Veg City, and Yum! Brands. For Kero, sales were US$597 million in 2014 and they reached an all-time high in 2015 with US$605 million. The sales plummeted in 2019 but are projected to be US$230 million in 2024. Nosso Super started with US$190 million, which decreased in 2016, but then increased steadily soon afterwards. The projected sales for 2024 are US$260 million. Shoprite's sales in 2014 were US$185 million. Throughout the years, their sales fluctuated and reached an all-time high during 2017 with US$190 million. Sales have continued to go up and down and are projected to do the same through 2020 to 2024. In 2024, their projected sales are US$150 million. In 2014, Fruit & Veg City had US$1 million in sales; however, the retailer closed in 2019. For Yum! Brands, sales started in 2015 with US$950,000; sales have remained the same and are projected to be US$950,000 in 2024.

The retailer with a largest number of outlets is Shoprite: The retailer started with 40 outlets in 2014 and employed 4,000 people (www.shoprite.co.ao). Shoprite is projected to have 69 outlets by 2024. In 2014, Nosso Super had 32 outlets. These have slowly increased and are projected to reach 48 outlets by 2024. Kero had 13 outlets in 2014 and this increased to 18 in 2015. Kero is projected to have 13 outlets by 2024, which will be a decrease.

Benin

Since 2014, the Benin market has witnessed the emergence of hypermarkets and superstores. Systeme U, a French retailer, has the only hypermarket and superstore in Benin. Their sales were consistent from 2014 to 2019 with around US$15 million; sales from 2020 to 2024 are projected to increase by a large margin moving up to US$30 million by the year 2024.

Just like the hypermarket and superstore categories, there is only one retailer in Benin in the supermarket and in the neighbourhood store category. Another French retailer, Casino, also enjoyed fairly consistent sales from 2014 to 2019, sitting at around US$1.3 million sales. These sales are projected to remain consistent until the year 2023, when sales are expected to jump up to US$1.8 million. It will remain on the rise throughout the year 2024, capping out at about US$2.1 million.

Casino remains the only retailer in the discount store category in Benin. Although their discount stores are doing better in total sales, ranging from US$2.8 to 2.1 million, these stores are following the same patterns as their supermarkets. Sales remained consistent from 2014 to 2022 and sales are projected to spike in 2023. These sales increases are expected to be bigger than the sales in their superstore category, where discount stores are projected to almost double their sales in 2023, and almost triple their current sales in 2024. In general, the Benin market is dominated by French retailers.

Edible grocery spending is among the top-selling items in retail in Benin. Retailers saw a slight decrease in sales in 2015 and 2016. Since then, sales and consumer spending per capita have been gradually increasing and eventually surpassing their 2014 sales and consumer spending per capita in 2019. Both categories will continue to increase slowly through the years 2020 to 2024 in edible grocery spending. Consumer spending is expected to be around US$4 billion in 2024, and consumer spending per capita is expected to be about US$400 spending per person.

Although Systeme U only has stores in the hypermarket category, it is the top retailer in Benin when it comes to dollar sales. Sales by Systeme U's remained at US$12 to15 million from 2014 to 2019; whereas Casino was consistent with around US$4.9 million sales. In 2021, Systeme U was projected to increase their sales up to US$20 million and up to about US$30 million in 2024. Casino retail sales are expected to remain the same from 2019 to 2022 and have a slight increase in 2023 and 2024, reaching around US$8 million. In this respect, Casino has more outlets in Benin than Systeme U. Systeme U has only one hypermarket in Benin, where Casino has three stores in total including their supermarkets and discount stores. In 2021, Systeme U is expected to add another outlet, whereas in 2023 Casino is expected to add two more outlets.

Botswana

Shoprite, a South African retailer, has the only hypermarket in Botswana. Dollar sales in Botswana were on a steady increase from 2014 to 2019, where sales were only a tad down from 2018. Dollar sales are projected to increase in 2020 to about US$37 million; the sales are expected to increase even higher to almost US$50 million from 2021 to 2024.

In the supermarket category, the Botswana market is more competitive since there are five different retailers competing. Leading in dollar sales in this category is Choppies, followed by SPAR (a South African firm), Shoprite, Pick n Pay, and Fruit & Veg City. In 2014, Choppies started very inconsistently until 2017, when it remained fairly consistent in dollar sales, and it is expected to remain consistent at around US$500 million in dollar sales.

SPAR has a trend in dollar sales similar to that of Choppies except that Choppies is expected to remain consistent with sales of US$500 million from 2021 to 2024. SPAR is projected to see a steady increase in sales from US$300 million in 2019 to almost US$400 million in 2024. Shoprite may be leading in the hypermarket category, but in the supermarket category the firm has fallen back into third place with sales of less than US$100 million from 2014 to 2024. The sales of Pick n Pay are expected to increase from around US$20 million in 2021 to US$40 million in 2024, and Fruit & Veg City have been constant at around US$10 million sales from 2021 to 2024.

Shoprite is the only retailer in the discount category operating in Botswana. Its sales in 2014 were about US$20 million but this increased to US$35million in 2020. Sales are projected to reach a peak of about US$37 million in 2024.

Consumer spending per capita shows that edible grocery spending is once again top in this category; in 2014, spending was just short of US$4 billion in Botswana. Spending remained the same until 2017, when it increased slightly. Since then, spending has been increasing steadily, and the trend is expected to reach US$4.5 billion by 2024. It should be noted that all consumer spending saw a significant increase from 2016 to 2017 and between 2017 and 2018. Consumer spending per capita decreased from 2014 to 2015 and from 2015 to 2016. In 2017, consumer spending increased once again and surpassed the 2014 sales and then increased again in 2018. From 2018 onwards, spending per capita was expected to increase to about US$ 4,235 in 2024, and edible grocery spending is the leading category.

Choppies is the leading retailer in the Botswana market by a large margin, with sales reaching over US$500 million in 2020, but sales are projected to decrease slightly in 2024 to US$500 million. By the year 2024, SPAR (South Africa) is expected to compete in sales with Choppies, with sales reaching over US$420 million. Walmart and Shoprite are in the middle in this category, with both retailers' sales remaining constant at about US$300 million since 2017. The lowest in this category is Woolworths, a South African firm, whose sales have never been or projected to exceed US$100 million.

Choppies is the leading retailer in the number of outlets category. In 2014, the retailer had almost 80 stores and these are projected to increase steadily to almost 100 stores in 2024. This is followed by SPAR, which started with 60 stores in 2014, and these are projected to reach 80 stores in 2024. Shoprite and Walmart follow closely in terms of the number of stores, both with around 40. Yum! Brands is last with less than 20 stores from 2014 to 2020, but they are expected to reach 20 stores by 2024.

Burkina Faso

Burkina Faso does not have any retailers in the hypermarket or discount store category, but Casino does run in the supermarket and the neighbourhood store category. Sales started with about US$500 million in 2014 and fell slightly to around US$400 million in 2016, and these are projected to increase to above

US$500 million in 2022. In 2023, Casino is expected to increase its sales from US$400 milion to almost US$800 million, and then to over US$1billion in 2024.

Total consumer spending in 2014 was over US$6 billion, and this has been and will increase steadily to about US$11 billion in 2024. Edible grocery spending contributes a huge proportion of consumer spending. In 2014, consumers in this category spent US$4 billion. The spending reached a peak between 2015 and 2017, but will continue increasing from 2018 to 2024. Foodservice spending is the second leading domain in this category, followed by clothing, footwear, and jewellery.

Consumer spending per capita shows that individual consumers spent almost US$400 in 2014, but this decreased to almost US$100 in 2016 through 2017. The trend in spending started to increase in 2018, and this is expected to increase to US$500 by 2024. More than half of consumer spending per capita is spent on edible groceries followed by foodservices, clothing, footwear, and jewellery.

There are two retailers leading in sales in this category, namely Total and Casino. In 2014, Total started with over US$1.5 million in banner sales but this decreased significantly to almost US$900K in 2015. This trend is expected to remain constant until 2024. Casino's banner sales were around US$600K but this is expected to increase to US$800K and US$1 million in 2023 and 2024, respectively.

Total is the leading retailer in terms of the number of outlets, almost 18 in 2014, but this decreased to about ten in 2015. The retailer closed one more store in 2018, but is not expected to have any more or less by 2024. Casino had only one store in 2014 and is not expected to increase this until 2023.

Cameroon

Cameroon does not have any retailers in the hypermarket category, but SPAR International runs in the supermarket and neighbourhood store category. Sales started at about US$11.7 million in 2014 but increased to above US$40 million in 2020. The forecasted sales by 2024 are US$90 million. Casino is the other retailer in the supermarket category, and has maintained sales of about US$1 million for ten years from 2014; this is not expected to increase by 2024.

The discount store format that is owned by Casino is the only retailer in this category in Cameroon. In 2014, it started with US$4.75 million in sales, which dropped in 2015 and then increased through to 2017. After 2017, the sales plummeted, falling to US$1.2 million by 2019. Sales are forecasted to increase to about US$2.6 million by the end of 2024.

The top retailers by banner sales are SPAR International and Casino. SPAR International started with US$5 million in sales, which remained consistent for a couple of years but increased in 2019. The forecasted sales for 2024 are US$93 million. In 2014, Casino had US$6 million in sales and this has remained stagnant. The forecasted sales for 2024 are US$6 million.

SPAR International is the leading retailer with the largest number of outlets, starting in 2014 with one store and then steadily increasing; they are projected to reach nine outlets by 2024. Casino remained consistent from 2014 to 2017 with five outlets. SPAR International closed one outlet in 2018, and they are forecasted to continue with four outlets until 2022; however, it is forecasted to see an increase to six outlets by 2024.

Egypt

In Egypt, there are three retailers, Spinneys, Carrefour, and Panda, in the hypermarket category. Spinneys started in 2014 with US$200 million in sales, and this increased to US$490 million in 2016; sales are projected to further increase from 2016 to 2019, and the forecasted sales for 2024 are US$1.32 billion. In 2014, Carrefour's sales were US$600 million, but these declined to US$400 million in 2017 and increased afterwards. The sales are forecasted to reach US$625 million in 2024. In 2014, Panda did not have any sales, but they are forecast to increase steadily to US$190 million in 2024.

There are three retailers, Al Othiam, Carrefour, and Metro, in the supermarket category. Al Othiam started in 2014 with no sales, but the retailer's sales increased to US$ 19 million in 2018. From 2016 to 2019, sales increased gradually. The forecasted sales for 2024 are US$980 million. In 2014, Carrefour's sales were US$100 million, but these declined to US$97 million in 2017 and increased afterwards. Sales are forecasted to be US$300 million in 2024. In 2014, Metro had US$230 million sales and this decreased to US$98 million in 2017. The forecasted sales for 2024 are US$85 million.

There are two retailers, BIM and Metro, in the discount category. In 2014, BIM's sales were US$50 million but this increased to US$175 million in 2017. The sales are forecasted to reach US$325 million in 2024. In 2014, Metro had US$165 million but this decreased to US$98 million in 2017. The forecasted sales are US$85 million for 2024.

The majority of spending comes from groceries. More than half of the money is consumer spending, whose per capita is on groceries. In 2014, consumer spending was US$75 billion with a per capita figure of US$880. In both cases, spending decreased from 2014 to 2017, and then increased after 2017. The forecasted spending on groceries is US$70 billion by 2024 with the spending per capita remaining constant at US$750.

The leading retailers by banner sales in Egypt are Spinneys, Carrefour, Al Othaim, BIM, and Metro. Spinneys started with US$190 million this is expected to reach US$1.35 billion by 2024. Carrefour had US$700 million sales in 2014, but these decreased to US$580 by 2017. After 2017, sales increased and are expected to reach US$995 million by 2024. In 2016, Al Othaim had US$180 million sales and this has increased, and are expected to reach US$990 million by 2024. BIM started with US$90 million sales, and this has slightly increased throughout the years. Sales are expected to reach US$370 million by 2024. Metro started with US$400 million in sales, but this decreased to US$210 in 2017. Sales increased in 2019, but are expected to decrease to US$210 million by 2024.

There are five retailers, Yum! Brands, McDonald's, Total, BIM, and Metro in the convenience store format. Yum! Brands started with 210 outlets in 2014, and this amount has increased slightly; they are expected to reach 275 outlets by 2024. McDonald's started with 95 retailers in 2014 and this will increase through to 2024. They are expected to have 120 outlets by 2024. Metro started with 100 outlets in 2014 and are expected to reach 130 outlets by 2024. Total started with 75 retailers in 2014 and this has slightly increased; they are expected to have 90 outlets by 2024. BIM started with 75 outlets in 2014 and this has increased exponentially; they are expected to reach 425 outlets by 2024.

Gabon

There is only one store, Casino, within the category of hypermarket in Gabon. In 2014, the retailer had US$3.45 million in sales, which decreased to US$2.87 million in 2015. Throughout the next eight years, sales are expected to increase slightly, and are expected to reach US$3.75 million by 2024.

Similarly, there is only one store, Casino, in the supermarket and neighbourhood store category. In 2014, the retailer had sales of US$3.5 million, but this decreased to US$3.1 million in 2015. Over the next eight years, the sales are expected to increase slightly to US$5 million by 2024.

The majority of spending comes from groceries. About half of the money for consumer spending and consumer spending per capita is on groceries. In 2014, consumer spending was US$2.5 billion, and spending per capita was US$125,000. In both cases, spending decreased from 2015 to 2017. In 2018, spending slightly increased, and spending on groceries and spending per capita are forecasted to reach US$3.4 billion and US$150,000, respectively, in 2024.

There are four retailers, Casino, Total, L'Occitan, and Yves Rocher, that are considered to be leading the retailing industry in Gabon. Casino started with US$7 million, but this decreased in 2015. From 2016 to 2024, sales slowly increased, and they are expected to reach US$9 billion by 2024. Total had US$5.9 million in sales in 2014, and these have been slightly increasing and are expected to reach US$7 million by 2024. In 2017, L'Occitan had US$500K in sales, which have been increasing and are expected to reach US$990K by 2024. Yves started with US$500K in sales and this slightly increased throughout the years, and are expected to reach US$750K by 2024.

There are four retailers in Gabon, namely Casino, Total, L'Occitan, and Yves Rocher. Total started with 39 outlets but this decreased to 36 outlets in 2017. From 2018 to 2024, the number of outlets are expected to remain constant with 36 stores. In 2019, Casino had four outlets and this is expected to increase slightly to five stores in 2024. In 2017, L'Occitan had one outlet and this is expected to increase to five outlets by 2024. In 2014, Yves Rocher started with three outlets and this has increased slightly throughout the years and is expected to reach four by 2024.

Ghana

In Ghana, there are four retailers, namely Shoprite, Walmart, Total, and Woolworths. Shoprite started its operations in Ghana in 2007; they started with US$62 million sales in 2014, but this dropped to US$42 million in 2016. After 2016, sales slowly increased through to 2021 and are projected to decrease slightly by 2024; their expected sales are US$51 million in 2024. In 2014, Walmart had US$11 million in sales, and this will increase exponentially through to 2024, where they are expected to reach US$61 million. In 2016, Total had US$10.6 million in sales and this has slightly decreased; they are expected to reach US$10 million by 2024. Woolworths started with US$4 million in sales in 2014 and this has increased slightly throughout the years. The sales are expected to reach US$7 million by 2024.

The majority of spending comes from groceries. About half of the money for consumer spending and consumer spending per capita is on groceries. In 2014, consumer spending and spending per capita was US$12 and US$440 billion, respectively. In both cases, spending is forecasted to slightly increase through to 2024. Spending on groceries and spending per capita are expected to reach US$580 billion and US$18, respectively, by 2024

In Ghana, there are five retailers, namely Shoprite, Walmart, Total, and Woolworths, and Yum! Brands. Total started with 122 outlets and will increase exponentially through to 2024. The expected number of outlets is 170 by 2024. In 2014, Walmart did not have any locations, but by 2024, the number of outlets is expected to reach nine. In 2016, Shoprite had nine outlets and this will remain constant through to 2024. Woolworths started with one outlet in 2014 and this has increased slightly throughout the years and is expected to reach five outlets by 2024. Yum! Brands started with ten outlets in 2014, this has slightly increased; they are expected to reach 32 outlets by 2024.

Kenya

There are five retailers, Naivas, Carrefour, EastMatt, Cleanshelf, and Nakumatt, using the formats of hypermarkets and superstores in Kenya. In 2014, Naivas had sales of US$200 million and it maintained this through to 2018. Throughout the next several years, it is expected to increase and reach sales worth US$490 million by 2024. In 2014, Cleanshelf had sales of US$50 million, and these have slightly increased and are expected to reach US$99 million by 2024. In 2014, EastMatt had sales of US$60 million, and these have slightly increased and are expected to be US$110 million in 2024. In 2014, Carrefour did not have any sales, but this will increase through to 2024, when it is expected to have sales worth US$200 million. In 2014, Nakumatt had US$399 million in sales, and it maintained this through to 2018. After 2018, the retailer's sales decreased exponentially, and they are expected to be worth US$20 million by 2024.

There are five retailers that operate in the supermarket and neighbourhoods store format in Kenya, namely Tuskys, Carrefour, Chandarana Foodplus,

Choppies, and Uchumi. In 2014, Tuskys had sales worth US$405 million, but these decreased slightly in 2015. After 2015, the sales increased, and by 2024 the sales are expected to reach US$995 million. In 2014, Carrefour did not have any sales, but these have been increasing, and by 2024 sales are expected to reach US$190 million. In 2014, Chandarana had sales worth US$10 million and these have slightly increased and are expected to reach US$75 million by 2024. In 2014, Choppies did not have any sales, but these have been increasing slightly and are expected to reach US$5 million by 2024. In 2014, Uchumi had sales worth US$100 million, but these decreased slightly through to 2018. After 2018, the sales remained consistent, but they are expected to be worth US$5 million by 2024.

The majority of spending in Kenya comes from groceries. About half of the money for consumer spending and consumer spending per capita is on groceries. In 2014, consumer spending was worth US$15 billion, and spending per capita was US$380. In both cases, spending is expected to slightly increase through to 2024. The forecasted spending for groceries in 2024 is US$29 billion, and spending per capita is US$500.

In 2014, Naivas had sales worth US$200 million, and these remained constant through to 2018. Sales are expected to increase to US$490 million by 2024. In 2016, Carrefour had US$5 million in sales, and these have slightly increased and are expected to reach US$38 million by 2024. EastMatt started with US$10 million in sales in 2014, and these have slightly increased throughout the years. The sales are expected to reach US$45 by 2024. Chandarana started with US$7 million in sales in 2014, and these have been increasing and are expected to reach are US$40 million by 2024.

There are five retailers in Kenya: Total, Tuskys, Naivas, Shell and Choppies. Total started with 158 outlets, but these decreased slightly through to 2015; their projected outlets by 2024 is 122. In 2014, Tuskys had 41 locations, and these have been slightly increasing and it is expected to reach 90 outlets by 2024. In 2014, Naivas had 38 outlets and this has slightly increased and is expected to reach 64 by 2024. Shell started with 58 outlets in 2014 and this has decreased throughout the years, and is projected to reach 24 outlets by 2024. Choppies started with nine outlets in 2016, and this has slightly increased and is expected to reach 39 by 2024. However, the retailer exited the Kenyan market in March 2020 due to loss-making in foreign market operations.

Morocco

There are two stores, SNI and Carrefour, within the hypermarket and superstore category in Morocco. In 2014, SNI started with US$1.35 billion in sales. Sales increased through to 2015 and are forecasted to remained steady through to 2024, where they are expected to reach US$1.78 billion by that year. In 2014, Carrefour had US$100 million worth in sales. This remained constant until 2018, when they increased to US$299 million in 2019. The sales are projected to remain the same until 2022, after which they will increase to US$305 million by 2024.

In the supermarket and neighbourhood store category, there are two retailers, namely SNI and Carrefour. In 2014, SNI started with US$299 million in sales, which increased in 2015 but decreased in 2016, and then increased after 2016. The expected sales for 2024 are US$480 million. Carrefour started with US$320 million in sales in 2014, which decreased in 2015, but then steadily increased afterwards. The projected sales for 2024 are US$488 million.

The majority of spending comes from groceries, whereby about half of the money for consumer spending and consumer spending per capita is on groceries. In 2014, consumer spending was US$25 billion, and spending per capita was US$750. In both cases, spending decreased in 2015 but remained constant through to 2017. Also, spending slightly increased after 2017 through to 2024, where spending for groceries is expected to be US$25billion and spending per capita to be US$750 in 2024.

There are five retailers, SNI, Carrefour, Ikea, BIM, and Inditex, who are leading through their banner shops. In 2014, the sales for SNI were US$1.65 billion, but this spiked in 2015 and then decreased in 2016. After 2016, sales steadily increased. By 2024, the sales are projected to be US$2.25 billion. In 2014, Carrefour had US$1.2 billion in sales, which decreased in 2015 and then steadily increased. By 2024, the expected sales will be US$1.95 billion. Ikea started with US$320 million sales in 2016. Then sales exponentially increased in 2017 but remained constant through to 2024. By 2024, the expected sales are US$1 billion. In 2014, BIM had US$160 million in sales, which slowly increased through to 2024. In 2024, the expected sales are US$400 million. In 2014, Inditex had US$90 million in sales, which then slowly increased. By 2024, the expected sales are US$150 million.

There are five retailers, BIM, Total, SNI, Yum! Brands, and Carrefour, leading in terms of the number of outlets. In 2014, BIM had 210 outlets, which exponentially increased to 490 in 2019; this will slowly increase through to 2024, when the expected number of locations is 525. Total started with 100 outlets in 2014 and barely increased through 2024. By 2024, the expected number of outlets is 115. In 2014, SNI started with 80 outlets and this increased in 2015. The number of outlets decreased in 2016, but will slightly increase by 2024 to 80 outlets. In 2014, Yum! Brands started with 60 outlets, and by 2024 the expected number of outlets is 95. In 2014, Carrefour started with 70 outlets and has maintained this number. By 2024, the expected number of outlets is still 70.

Senegal

In Senegal, retailers operate in the supermarket and neighbourhood store formats, and there are two retailers, Auchan and Casino, in this category. In 2014, Auchan had US$2.5 million in sales; this will increase exponentially by 2024, when the expected sales are US$39 million. In 2014, Casino had US$4.5 million in sales. The sales slightly decreased through to 2024. By 2024, the expected sales are US$3 million.

The majority of spending comes from groceries. About half of the money for consumer spending and consumer spending per capita is on groceries. In 2014, consumer spending was US$5 billion, and spending per capita was US$350. In both cases, spending decreased in 2015 and was then maintained through to 2017. Also, after 2017, spending in both cases is expected to increase through to 2024. The forecasted spending for groceries in 2024 is US$9 billion and spending per capita is US$550.

Total, Auchan, Lagardère Services, Casino, and Yves Rocher are the top five retailers by banner stores in Senegal. In 2014, Total had US$5 million in sales, and this is expected to continue to increase by 2024. By 2024, the expected sales are US$31 million. In 2014, Auchan had US$2.5 million in sales, and the sales increased through to 2024. By 2024, the expected sales are US$38.5 million. In 2018, Lagardère Services had US$10 million in sales. The sales then exponentially increased through to 2024. By 2024, the expected sales are US$58 million. In 2014, Casino had US$5 million in sales, and the sales then increased in 2015. From 2015 to 2017, the sales decreased to US$4 million, and after 2017 sales remained stagnant. By 2024, the expected sales are US$3.5 million. In 2014, Yves Rocher did not have any sales, and this has remained stagnant. The sales are expected to slowly increase to US$1 million by 2024.

There are five retailers, Total, Auchan, Lagardère Services, Casino, and Yves Rocher, which are leading in terms of the number of outlets in Senegal. In 2014, Total had 24 outlets, which had exponentially increased to 68 retailers by 2015. After 2015, outlets continued to increase though slowly and there are expected to be 88 outlets by 2024. In 2014, Auchan had three outlets, which continued to increase and they are expected to have 32 outlets by 2024. In 2014, Casino had seven outlets, which slowly decreased through to 2021. However, the number of outlets is expected to increase to nine by 2024. In 2016, Lagardère Services had two outlets, and the number has increased over time and is expected to be 12 by 2024. In 2014, Yves Rocher had one outlet open, but this is expected to reach ten by 2024.

South Africa

There are two retailers, Shoprite and Pick n Pay, operating in hypermarket and superstore formats in South Africa. In 2014, Shoprite had US$3.4 billion in sales, but these sales decreased through to 2016. After 2016, sales increased to reach US$4 billion in 2020, and these are expected to reach US$4.4 billion by 2024. In 2014, Pick n Pay had US$1.4 billion in sales, which decreased through to 2016, and remained constant afterwards. The sales are expected to reach US$1.2 billion by 2024.

There are five retailers that operate in the supermarket and neighbourhood store format, which are SPAR, Shoprite, Pick n Pay, Walmart, and Woolworths. SPAR, Shoprite, and Pick n Pay have followed a similar model of sales for some time. In 2014, each retailer had annual sales of above US$4billion but these decreased and reached the lowest level of sales of US$3.7 billion in 2016 for Pick n Pay. After 2016, sales increased for all retailers and they became the leading retailers by sales; SPAR reached annual sales of US$6 billion in 2019. from

US$5.8 billion in sales in 2014, the expected sales for SPAR are US$6.8 billion by 2024.

Shoprite started with US$5.1 billion in sales in 2014, and these are expected to reach US$6.1 billion by 2024. In 2014, Pick n Pay had US$4.5 billion in sales, which are to reach US$4.95 billion by 2024. In 2014, Walmart had US$996 million in sales, which increased with time and are expected to reach US$1.96 billion by 2024. In 2014, Woolworth had US$1.5 billion in sales, which is expected to remain consistent through to 2024.

The majority of spending, about half of consumer spending and consumer spending per capita, is on groceries. In 2014, consumer spending and spending per capita was US$990 and US$50 billion, respectively. In both cases, spending decreased in 2015; through to 2017 spending increased and is expected to reach US$55 billion for groceries in 2024 and remain the same at US$990 for spending per capita.

There are five top retailers in South Africa, namely SPAR, Shoprite, Pick n Pay, Walmart, and Steinhoff International, in this category. All five retailers have followed a similar model for their sales for some time. In 2014, SPAR had US$7 billion in sales, but this is expected to increase to US$9.95 billion by 2024. Shoprite started with US$9.95 billion in 2014, but this is expected to increase to US$12 billion by 2024. In 2014, Pick n Pay had US$6.3 billion in sales, which are expected to reach US$7.9 billion by 2024. In 2014, Walmart had US$6.8 billion in sales, which are expected to reach US$9.95 billion by 2024. In 2014, Steinhoff International had US$3.97 billion in sales, which are expected to reach US$6 billion by 2024.

Tanzania

There is only one retailer, Nakumatt, that operates as a hypermarket or superstore, and in 2014 the retailer had annual sales estimated at US$39.5 million. However, the sales decreased to about US$9.6 million in 2017. The retailer exited the Tanzania market in 2017 on the grounds of logistic challenges that limited the flow of goods from Kenya to Tanzania (See Nandonde, 2019).

Other retailers, namely Walmart (Game) and Choppies, in 2014, were also operating in Tanzania in the supermarket format. Walmart (Game) had US$12 million in sales, but this decreased to around US$9.2 million in 2017. The firm is expecting to increase its sales to US$22 million by 2024. In 2016, Choppies had less than US$1 million in sales, and this has continued to increase with time and reached US$9 million in November 2019 when it exited the Tanzania market.

Conclusion and way forward

In general, this chapter shows that supermarkets and neighbourhood stores dominate the grocery business on the continent. Also, retailers that operate in Africa but who originate from Anglophone countries invested heavily in the same countries in Africa. This is the same for French retailers such as Casino who invested heavily in French-speaking countries. Recently, however, we have seen Carrefour investing in English-speaking countries, such as Kenya and Tanzania.

The supermarket format is doing better in Africa compared to other formats such as hypermarkets and discount stores. Although neighbourhood stores can do good in Africa, many retailers seem to be ready to invest in supermarket formats. The supermarket format seems to be leading in terms of revenue generation. This is contrary to European countries where the discount format is preferred (Zentes et al., 2011). In some countries, including Tanzania, Walmart, operating under the Game business banner, is not prepared to open more stores, as they have had one supermarket for more than ten years of doing business in the country.

The performance of the supermarket format in some developing countries is attributed to such reasons as an increase in income and changes in lifestyle, which brought the need for consumers to buy consumer goods in modern stores, including supermarkets (Nandonde, 2016; Wang, 2011). However, these findings need to be treated with caution because the data was based on secondary information, and many of the retailers/firms found in African countries were not included in the database where we extracted data for this study.

References

Goldman, A. (2001). The transfer of retail formats into developing economies: the example of China. *Journal of Retailing*, 77, 221–242.

Nandonde, F. A. (2016). Integrating local food suppliers in modern food retail in Africa: The case of Tanzania. Non-published PhD thesis submitted to Aalborg University, Denmark.

Nandonde, F. A. (2019). A PESTLE analysis of international retailing in the East African Community. *Global Business and Organization Excellence*, 38(4), 54–61.

Vidalon, D. (2015). French retailer Carrefour returned to Algeria, 19th March. Retrieved October 2019 from https://www.reuters.com/article/us-carrefour-algeria/french-retailer-carrefour-returning-to-algeria-source-idUKKBN0MF14P20150319

Wang, E. (2011). Understanding the 'retail revolution' in urban China: a survey of retail formats in Beijing. *The Service Industry Journal*, 13(2), 169–194.

Zentes, J., Morschett, D. and Schramm-Klein, H. (2011). Retail formats-general merchandise. In *Retail Strategic Management*. Springer, 49–69.

Website

www.researchandmarkets.com
www.shoprite.co.ao
www.supermarket.co.za

2 Consumer shopping patterns and pricing considerations for BOP consumers

The case of Madagascar

Arilova A. Randrianasolo

Introduction

Literature shows that consumers in developing economies face low levels of consumption adequacy and higher consumption restrictions, which lead to overall lower levels of life satisfaction (Randrianasolo, 2017). According to scholars (i.e. Prahalad and Hammond, 2002; Prahalad, 2010), multinational enterprises can simultaneously participate in profit-seeking activities while addressing the problems many consumers face in developing economies, often referred to as the bottom of the pyramid (BOP). The BOP refers to the world's poorest markets and stems from the conceptualisation that the largest sector of the world's population consists of the poorest and least developed markets (Prahalad, 2010). Conversely, at the top of the pyramid are markets with the highest amounts of wealth but the smallest number of people (Randrianasolo, 2018).

In their seminal paper, Prahalad and Hammond (2002) suggest that multinational enterprises can contribute to the economic and social development of BOP markets through profit-seeking activities. BOP strategies, however, require multinationals to not only understand the realities that many BOP consumers face, but also to adapt their marketing mix appropriately. BOP consumers face realities such as consumption inadequacy that stems from poverty, low access to education, poor infrastructure, and lack of access to healthcare (Kuo, Hanafi, Sun, and Robielos, 2016; Randrianasolo, 2017).

In the retail industry in Africa, numerous multinational retailers have largely failed to realise and consider the realities of BOP consumers and have thus struggled to grow because of it. For example, to enter the South African market in 2011, Wal-Mart acquired the majority shareholding in Massmart, a South African firm, but yet struggled to increase profits after the acquisition (Phillip, 2019). Similarly, the world's largest retailer of speciality coffee, Starbucks, failed to make a profit in South Africa (Browdie, 2019). This chapter focuses on one country, Madagascar, to highlight the shortcomings of many retailers in terms of understanding consumer shopping patterns and pricing considerations in an African BOP market.

DOI: 10.4324/9780367854300-2

Previous studies indicate that understanding these two factors (shopping patterns and pricing considerations) can determine retail success (Bolton and Shankar, 2018; Xia, Chatterjee, and May, 2019). Multinational retailers such as Shoprite entered the Malagasy market with grocery stores in 2002 (Shoprite, 2002). However, these retailers failed to serve a large portion of the Malagasy population due to a lack of consideration for pricing and shopping patterns. For example, Shoprite, Africa's largest retailer (Smith, 2015), only has locations in four Malagasy cities as of 2020: Antananarivo, Antsirabe, Toamasina, and Mahajanga (Shoprite, 2020). This is alarming since these cities represent only three of the six Malagasy provinces (Antsirabe and Antananarivo are in the same province). As of 2021, Shoprite has left Madagascar (Savana, 2021).

Despite being in the country for nearly two decades, Shoprite failed to expand to other large cities such as Toliara, Fianarantsoa, Antsiranana, Fort Dauphin, and Sainte Marie, and eventually closed all operations in Madagascar in 2021. Also, Leader Price, a French grocery retail company, only has nine stores in Madagascar, six of which are in the capital Antananarivo, one in Nosy Be, one in Toamasina, and another in Mahajanga (Trendtype, 2019). Similar to grocery retailers, although small apparel retailers exist, no company has been able to serve the Malagasy population with a supermarket for clothes.

The objective of this chapter therefore is to (1) review the current shopping patterns and pricing considerations in Madagascar, and (2) to provide recommendations for multinationals intending to enter the retailing industry in African countries with large BOP markets such as Madagascar. The research question here is: *How can multinational retailers reach and serve BOP markets better in Africa?* To answer this research question and achieve these objectives, this chapter reviews the concept of BOP, discusses distribution, shopping patterns and pricing considerations for BOP consumers in one BOP market in Madagascar, and finally makes recommendations for multinationals intending to enter the retailing industry in BOP markets.

Review of the BOP concept

As previously mentioned, the BOP concept stems from the view that the world is composed of an economic pyramid where the majority of the world's population, roughly two thirds, rests at the bottom of this pyramid with the least amount of wealth (Randrianasolo, 2018). The BOP is composed of roughly 4.6 billion people at the bottom of the economic pyramid with respect to wealth distribution in the world (Subhan and Khattak, 2016). These people have been underserved by multinational corporations and comprise the untapped market potential (Randrianasolo, 2018).

The BOP concept has been used in research to investigate topics such as social business orchestrators in less developed markets (Gold, Chowdhury, Huq, and Heinemann, 2020), the role of hybrid organisations in scaling social innovations in underdeveloped markets (Vassallo, Prabhu, Banerjee, and Voola, 2019), and the success of multinational enterprises' (MNEs') socially responsible initiatives in developed markets (Randrianasolo, 2018) among other phenomena. These studies categorise BOP markets as those markets comprising some of the world's poorest consumers in the least developed economies.

In his seminal works, Prahalad brought forth this concept to propose that the sheer size of these markets present opportunities for multinationals to tap into large consumer populations while simultaneously eradicating poverty. The author spent his career investigating and proposing business models for BOP markets concerning areas such as product innovation, distribution models, and pricing considerations (Prahalad and Hammond, 2002; Prahalad, 2010; Prahalad, 2012). Consumers in BOP markets face poverty-induced realities that are vastly different from other market types, which is why firms seeking to penetrate BOP markets must consider new innovative products and business models to reach these consumers. The main message from Prahalad's work is that the BOP presents large market opportunities, but to effectively tap these markets, multinationals must reconfigure and revise traditional models of products, processes, pricing and distribution. This chapter focuses on pricing and distribution in BOP markets to highlight the shortcomings of the retail industry in Madagascar. Madagascar's GDP per capita in 2018 was $432, 77% of the population lived under less than $2 per day, and was (and still is) considered as the 8th poorest country in the world (Macri, 2019; Trading Economics, 2020). Thus, Madagascar represents a BOP market.

Innovations in distribution models are just as crucial to firm success in BOP markets as product and process innovations (Duarte, Macau, e Silva, and Sanches, 2019). Multinationals often focus on large resources for adapting products to fit BOP markets, yet they fail to innovate on distribution models, resulting in limited access and availability for their products in these markets. However, to be successful in BOP markets, there must be a paradigm shift in distribution models. Some companies have found success in the BOP by shifting paradigms in distribution models. For example, Aakar Innovations employed a micro-enterprise distribution model in India, where individual people were employed to sell and distribute compostable sanitary pads for women at low cost to BOP populations (Monitor Deloitte, 2017). Similarly, Envirofit partnered with non-governmental organisations and retailers in Africa, Asia, and Latin America to help finance and distribute fuel-efficient cook-stoves to BOP market segments (Monitor Deloitte, 2017). Although there are numerous examples of BOP success by employing micro-distributors or direct distribution, many of the world's poor are still underserved due to information asymmetries and lack of access to goods and services (Knizkov and Arlinghaus, 2019). As discussed below, this statement is especially true for the retail industry in African countries such as Madagascar.

Distribution and shopping patterns in Madagascar

To understand the shortcomings of the retail industry in reaching BOP consumers in Madagascar, it is important to first understand the shopping patterns in this country. A shopping pattern is defined here as the way consumers acquire goods with respect to timing, amount, and frequency (Ma, Sharpe, Bell, Liu, White, and Liese, 2018). The following paragraphs discuss the patterns of grocery shopping and apparel shopping in Madagascar.

Grocery shopping: In developed countries such as the United States or Canada, consumers are accustomed to heading to the grocery store typically once a week or once every two weeks to shop for groceries that may last for a week or two until it is time to go to the grocery store again. These consumers purchase groceries and store them in a refrigerator within their homes until they are consumed. This is not the case for most Malagasy households. A typical Malagasy family consumes food bought each day from a local open-air market called a "*tsena*", where individual local sellers serve the population within the area with groceries. This is so because people do not have refrigerators; they also use this time for social gatherings and connecting with sellers. *Tsena* is literally translated as "market" in English. In the nation's capital and in the larger cities throughout the country, there is a *tsena* in every region of each respective city. For example, the Mahazo region in Antananarivo has the Mahazo *tsena*. In smaller towns throughout the country, there may be just one or two *tsenas* serving the town's population. This shopping pattern of buying daily needs in open-air markets such as the *tsena* in Madagascar is consistent with shopping patterns in many developing economies (Wertheim-Heck, Vellema, and Spaargaren, 2015).

In many Malagasy households, someone goes to the *tsena* before breakfast to either buy the daily bread, eggs, or rice needed for breakfast that day. An hour or two after breakfast, another trip to the *tsena* is necessary to buy the "*laoka*" for lunch and dinner. Malagasy meals are based on rice. The meat and vegetables that are eaten with rice are known as the *laoka* and change daily, but lunch and dinner always include rice. The *laoka* for lunch and dinner is usually not purchased before breakfast because the meat and vegetable merchants do not typically set up their merchandise until mid-morning. That means that two trips to *tsena* are required per day. The point here is that most Malagasy households buy their breakfast and *laoka* daily at the local *tsena* rather than relying on weekly trips to grocery stores.

As previously mentioned, shopping patterns are the way consumers acquire goods with respect to timing, amount, and frequency (Ma et al., 2018). The grocery shopping pattern of Malagasy consumers can thus be described as daily trips, sometimes twice a day (frequency) to the *tsena* to buy one day's worth of food (amount) and is usually done in the mornings (timing). This shopping pattern should be understood by grocery retailers seeking to serve the Malagasy population. However, rather than innovate or adapt to the market, foreign retailers have made efforts to shift this shopping pattern and appeal to Malagasy people to go shopping at their large grocery stores. This is problematic because shifting consumer behaviour in poor areas is one of the most difficult tasks a multinational can face (Simanis and Duke, 2014).

Apparel shopping: Shopping for clothes in one of the world's least developed countries is not a straightforward task. Where customers in developed countries may visit large department stores such as Target or Macy's when searching for new clothes, Malagasy consumers tackle this same task with two main options. First, the Malagasy people can go to small retailers where merchandise may be new, but many are counterfeited versions of popular brands. The problem with these counterfeited brands is that they are normally of low quality (Priporas, Kamenidou, Kapoulas, and Papadopoulou, 2015). This is especially problematic in BOP markets because consumers in these markets have a heightened level of concern for the quality and longevity of products due to low-income levels (Oodith and Parumasur, 2017). These stores can sell counterfeited merchandise due to weak intellectual property protections in the country. In fact, the Property Rights Alliance ranked Madagascar as 114th out of 129 ranked countries in the world in 2018 in their International Property Rights Index (Property Rights Alliance, 2019). With such weak property rights protection, many stores openly sell counterfeit products.

Second, to buy clothes, Malagasy consumers have the option of going to second-hand open-air clothing markets called "*friperie*" or "*fripe*" for short. There are designated areas in the large cities allocated for *fripe* markets. For example, in Antananarivo, there is a popular *fripe* market called "fripe'ny Mahamasina" in the Mahamasina area. In smaller towns, people can set up *fripe* markets on roadsides or even next to the town's *tsena*. People who run *fripe* markets get merchandise from overseas, so these are typically not counterfeit products, but rather they are used apparel that have been donated or bought for cheap and re-sold in the Malagasy market.

It is important to note that smaller scale Malagasy retailers with their own Malagasy brands do exist throughout the country, but their prices and distribution points do not meet the needs of most BOP consumers in this market. For example, the Maki Company is a Malagasy retailer that offers apparel for men, women, and children (Maki Company, 2020); however, they only have locations in large cities (particularly touristic cities) and are not a viable option for regular Malagasy consumers. As previously mentioned, pricing considerations must also be considered in serving the Malagasy BOP consumers. The next section discusses this concept.

Pricing considerations for BOP consumers in Madagascar

Madagascar is on the UN's least developed countries list with 80% of the population living on less than just $1.25 per day and over 90% surviving on less than just $2 per day (United Nations, 2018). Although the population has low purchasing power, this does not mean that consumers do not exist. As previously mentioned, Malagasy consumers participate in purchasing activities every day in large aggregate amounts, yet foreign retailers have failed to tap into this market. It is a common belief that BOP consumers do not have much purchasing power, and therefore they do not offer attractive market segments for foreign investors. However, researchers (Pitta, Guesalaga, and Marshall, 2008) found that more than 50% of the purchasing power in developing countries comes from BOP segments. In fact, low purchasing power does not necessarily mean that the market is unattractive for retailers. The next section presents the methodology for the study.

Methodology

Data collection: This empirical study was conducted to provide evidence that purchasing power does not necessarily determine market attractiveness for retailers. To collect data for this empirical study, ATKearney's 2017 Global Retail Development Index (GRDI) was used (ATKearney, 2019). These data were collected because this index ranks the top 30 developing countries in terms of retail investment attractiveness and considers market attractiveness, country risk, market saturation, and time pressure (ATKearney, 2019). This index provides an aggregated "GRDI" score for each of the 30 countries.

Independent and dependent variables: This study used the GRDI score as the dependent variable because it represents market attractiveness. To examine if a country's purchasing power influences retail attractiveness, the purchasing power parity score of each country, taken from the World Bank, was used as the independent variable (World Bank, 2019a).

Control variables: Several control variables that may influence the investigated relationship were also collected. First, the size of the retail market in the countries may influence retail attractiveness; therefore, national retail sales (in $ billions) were collected and included as a control variable. These data were provided by ATKearney's (2019) index. Second, the national population may also influence a country's retail attractiveness; therefore, the country population was included as another control. Data for this were also collected from ATKearney (2019). Third, the unemployment rate in terms of the percentage of unemployed in the total labour force of each country was collected from the World Bank (2019b) database because the unemployment rate may influence retail attractiveness. Finally, since infrastructure may influence retailer distribution, a country's logistical distribution systems represented by the World Bank's (2019c) logistics performance index was used as a control variable. Table 2.1 displays the demographic information of the countries in the study.

Analysis and results: A hierarchical linear regression analysis in SPSS 25 was conducted to predict the GRDI score based on the country's purchasing power parity score. This statistical analysis was used because it displays the manner in which independent variables explain the variance in the dependent variables after accounting for all control variables. In other words, within the hierarchical regression, a model of the influence of control variables on the dependent variables is first estimated (Model 1), then a model that includes the independent variable is estimated so a change in the variance explained can be examined (Model 2). In Model 1 of the hierarchical regression, the control variables (national retail sales, national population, logistic performance index score, unemployment) were included as predictors of GRDI, and showed a significant model [R-Squared $=.46$, $F\,(1,\,29) = 4.89$, $p <.005$]. Although the overall model was significant, none of

Table 2.1 Descriptive statistics of countries used in empirical study

	Min.	Max.	Mean	Std. deviation
Unemployment %	0.70	27.30	6.69	5.58
Logistics performance index score	2.36	3.96	2.95	0.37
Ease of doing business score	12.00	157.00	75.30	41.83
GRDI score	37.80	71.70	50.04	8.75
PPP	0.32	7792.72	575.87	1632.64
Countries	India, China, Malaysia, Turkey, United Arab Emirates, Vietnam, Morocco, Indonesia, Peru, Colombia, Saudi Arabia, Sri Lanka, Dominican Republic, Algeria, Jordan, Kazakhstan, Cote D'Ivoire, Philippines, Paraguay, Romania, Tanzania, Russian Federation, Azerbaijan, Tunisia, Kenya, South Africa, Nigeria, Bolivia, Brazil, Thailand			

the control variables had a significant influence on GRDI. The regression equation for Model 1 is:

$$GRDI\ Score = .04 - (.10)\ National\ Retail\ Sales + (.59)\ National\ Population$$
$$+ (.23)\ Logistics\ Performance\ Index\ Score$$
$$- (.17) Unemployment$$

In Model 2 of the regression analysis, purchasing power parity was included as a predictor of GRDI, and the change in R-Squared (.001) was not significant. Also, none of the predictors in this model were significant. These results show that purchasing power is not a predictor of retailing attractiveness in a market. Table 2.2 displays the results of the hierarchical regression. The equation for Model 2 is as follows:

$$GRDI\ Score = .04 - (.08)\ National\ Retail\ Sales + (.60)\ National\ Population$$
$$+ (.23)\ Logistics\ Performance\ Index\ Score$$
$$- (.15) Unemployment + (.09)\ Purchasing\ Power\ Parity$$

However, even with these results, the question still remains: how can retailers be profitable with a population of such low individual spending power levels? As proposed by Prahalad (2010), when dealing with BOP markets, firms must

Table 2.2 Hierarchical regression results of the influence of purchasing power parity on global retail development index

	Model 1			Model 2		
Independent variables	B	S.E.	β	B	S.E.	β
National retail sales	−.10	.34	−.10	−.08	.35	−.08
National population	.59	.33	.60	.59	.34	.60
Unemployment	−.17	.16	−.17	−.15	.16	−.15
Logistics performance index score	.23	.17	.23	.21	.18	.21
Purchasing power parity	–	–	–	.09	.16	.09
Change in R-Squared	–	–	.46*	–	–	.001
F for Change in R-Squared	–	–	4.89	–	–	.32

*$p < .01$

re-examine their "price–performance relationship." Specifically, "this is not about lowering prices; it is about altering the price–performance envelope" (Prahalad, 2010, p. 52). To understand the price–performance relationship in terms of retailing in Madagascar, it is important to understand what price means to BOP consumers in this country. Price is more than what is written on a product's price tag at the grocery store, which is usually already too high for the consumers. There is also the price of time and effort. For example, in the nation's capital, Antananarivo, there is a large problem with traffic. At certain times of the working day, it may take up to two hours to travel 5 kilometres. This problem is exponentially worse for those who do not own vehicles and rely on the public transport system. Going to a grocery store in the town centre, therefore, requires lots of time and effort for the poorest consumers, and therefore getting daily groceries at a local *tsena* is the more affordable option with respect to time and effort. It is important here to highlight that affordability is the primary concern of BOP consumers, not just cheaper prices (Kotler, Kartajaya, and Setiawan, 2010). In other words, price encompasses total purchasing cost rather than just what is on the price tag of a product (D'Andrea and Herrero, 2007). In Madagascar, BOP consumers face the problem of high product prices in large grocery stores as well as the hassle of getting to and out of these stores from home.

Although the total purchasing cost is discussed above, it is worth considering the need to hit the BOP consumer price point. In terms of the actual "price tag," many BOP consumers in Madagascar cannot afford the products from these stores. In a large grocery store in Antananarivo, one can find laundry detergent sold in a jug, vinegar sold in 16- or 20-ounce bottles, or cigarettes sold in packs. This sounds like a normal grocery store in developed countries, but it is not commensurate with the BOP consumers' price points. Specifically, people surviving on $2 per day cannot afford to buy a $5 jug of laundry detergent or a $2 bottle of vinegar. Instead, these consumers have become accustomed to purchasing unbundled products. In the town of Vatomandry, it is customary to buy cooking oil by going to the *tsena* with their own re-usable bottle and buying an eighth of a litre of oil, just enough for cooking needs of that day. Many who smoke cigarettes are accustomed to buying unbundled individual cigarettes rather than a pack of cigarettes. Rather than buying a $2 bottle of vinegar at the grocery store, many BOP consumers would buy vinegar in small plastic packets just slightly larger than ketchup packets from McDonald's for a fraction of the price for a $2 bottle. Similarly, rather than buying a $5 jug of laundry detergent, consumers are accustomed to purchasing small packets of laundry detergent about the size of a small bag of M&Ms for a fraction of the price of the jug.

These unbundled products can be found at small street-corner vendors who buy large packets and unbundle the products themselves, or vendors at the *tsena* who create their own small packaging for products that they buy in bulk. The point here is that to reach the BOP consumers who do not have high spending power, products have to be unbundled to meet the consumer price points.

Many scholars have highlighted the need to unbundle products to be able to reach BOP consumer affordability (e.g. Kotler et al., 2010). Understanding how to unbundle a pack of cigarettes, however, is much simpler than unbundling retail stores. The following section presents the study recommendations.

Recommendations for retailers intending to expand into the BOP

As mentioned earlier, large foreign retailers have failed to reach many BOP consumers in Madagascar due to a lack of understanding of consumer shopping patterns and the inability to meet the BOP consumer price point. Employing the findings from previous research, three recommendations are made for retailers intending to tap into the Malagasy BOP market: (1) adapt distribution models to fit the consumers, (2) unbundle products to meet consumer price points, and (3) adopt micro-franchising models in the market.

Adapting distribution models and emphasising quality

In order to successfully reach BOP consumers in countries such as Madagascar, retailers must adapt their distribution models. This means that for grocery retailers, the paradigm must shift from large grocery stores in city centres to smaller and more specialised stores, located in the *tsena* markets of each city. For example, if a foreign retailer intends to enter Madagascar through the Antananarivo market, then he/she should establish one distribution centre that serves many small specialised stores located throughout the various *tsena* markets in the city. Small stores in the *tsena* markets should specialise primarily in rice, meats, and vegetables as these products would serve the daily needs of Malagasy BOP consumers.

To serve the apparel market, foreign retailers are advised to establish small, specialised retail outlets in areas close to the aforementioned "*fripe*" within the cities. These smaller retail stores should focus on supplying products with the value proposition of providing high quality at a price point that BOP consumers can afford. This is the challenge of effectively penetrating a BOP market, providing high-quality products at affordable prices to BOP consumers. It has been stated that BOP consumers are more concerned with quality than are the consumers from developed markets because of the low spending power of the former (Nakata and Weidner, 2012). In other words, these consumers want the most bang for their buck because they must use the little money they have as efficiently as possible (Polak and Warwick, 2013). As previously discussed, however, BOP markets are plagued with counterfeit and low-quality products (Petrescu and Bhatli, 2013). Therefore, to create a sustainable competitive advantage in this market, foreign retailers must include high quality within their value propositions. With this stated, keeping a high-quality level at affordable BOP prices remains a challenge. This challenge has been extensively discussed in BOP research (e.g. Kaplinsky, 2011; Polak and Warwick, 2013; Prahalad, 2012). Most research in this area recommends that in order to achieve affordability in BOP markets without sacrificing quality, the marketing mix and value chain processes have to be adapted to the market (Polak and Warwick, 2013; Prahalad, 2010). From this perspective, it is recommended that apparel retailers seeking to enter Madagascar's market must source their products locally to keep costs low and ultimately make prices affordable to BOP consumers.

Although sourcing the product locally can be a tool of keeping costs low in the supply chain and ultimately allowing companies to keep product prices low, it does little to communicate quality perceptions to consumers. In order to communicate that products have a high level of quality in developing countries, companies may employ strategies that suggest the globalness of the company's brand. Specifically, research (i.e. Randrianasolo, 2017) shows that in developing countries, perceived brand globalness positively influences perceived brand quality. This means that foreign companies seeking to signal high-quality levels to BOP consumers can do so with globally oriented advertising strategies. One such strategy is called global consumer culture positioning (GCCP) strategy. GCCP strategies are positioning strategies that communicate to consumers that the brand is a symbol of the global consumer culture, and purchasing the brand can reinforce a consumer's membership in the global community (Okazaki, Mueller, and Taylor, 2010; Westjohn, Singh, and Magnusson, 2012). Consumers in BOP markets admire products and lifestyles that represent the global community because consumers in these markets are likely to seek global citizenship (Strizhakova, Coulter, and Price, 2008). This need for global citizenship stems from poverty, which psychologically influences individual people in less developed markets to participate in upward social comparison (Randrianasolo, 2017). In other words, poverty causes people to socially compare their lives to the lives of those around the globe, which in turn causes a need for global citizenship, and ultimately the perception that global brands are of high quality (Randrianasolo, 2017). Therefore, it can be stated that to signal quality in the Malagasy market, retailers should employ globally oriented marketing strategies such as GCCP strategies.

In sum, apparel retailers are recommended to establish small retail stores in the *fripe* areas of the cities in Madagascar, and the apparel should be sourced locally to adopt a value proposition that ensures consumer affordability and high quality.

Unbundling products to meet consumer price points

As previously discussed, consumers in BOP markets are accustomed to purchasing unbundled products that can reach their price point (e.g. cigarettes sold in units of 1 cigarette rather than in packets; vinegar sold in small plastic packets rather than bottles). Thus, it is recommended here that both grocery retailers and apparel retailers should unbundle products to meet Malagasy BOP consumer price points.

With respect to grocery retailers, unbundling products require understanding the Malagasy consumer's daily grocery needs. For example, eggs should be sold in single units rather than packages of 8 or 12 eggs; meat should be packaged in a way that reflects the average amount of meat needed for the average Malagasy family's daily *laoka*; and vegetables should be sold by the gram rather than in pre-packaged plastic wrapping. These unbundled products may ultimately have higher per-unit prices than bundled products but are packaged in a more affordable manner than the larger bundles.

In terms of apparel retailers, every product should be sold in individual units to meet consumer price points. For example, socks should not be packaged in bundles of three, six, or ten pairs, but instead should be sold by the pair. Similarly, undergarments should be sold individually rather than in bundled packs.

In sum, it is recommended that for retailers to reach affordable BOP consumer price points effectively, they must unbundle products to match consumer spending habits in these markets.

Adopting micro-franchising models

In their research conducted in BOP markets in Malaysia, Hassan, Rom, Ashikin, and Said (2016) found value in micro-franchising models for BOP populations. Similarly, Fairbourne (2007) emphasise that micro-franchising models provide solutions to three main problems that people in BOP markets face: lack of skills needed to grow a successful organisation, high unemployment due to lack of jobs, and lack of resources, goods, and services. In this respect, it is proposed that micro-franchising models benefit BOP constituents and are an effective tool for retailers intending to enter BOP markets.

As defined by Fairbourne (2007), the 'micro' in micro-franchising refers to mini or small, and franchising 'involves systematising an operation, paying close attention to each and every aspect of a business until it is a turn-key operation, then replicating it to scale' (Fairbourne, 2007, p. 9). It is important to note, as Fairbourne (2007) emphasises, that a key to the sustainability of micro-franchising in BOP markets is keeping it micro, meaning that the franchisee investment should be kept at a level that BOP entrepreneurs and investors can afford. Keeping things 'micro' has proven successful in the micro-finance industry in developing countries. This model has contributed to poverty reduction in many underdeveloped markets, while also positively contributing to other factors such as empowerment of women (Develtere and Huybrechts, 2005; Jose and Buchanan, 2013). Thus, micro-investments are a key strategy for success in BOP markets.

Employing a micro-franchising strategy would not only be beneficial to BOP constituents, but it would also aid in the franchisor firm's quest to gain organisational legitimacy, or social acceptance in the BOP market. Multinational companies entering BOP markets often face a high level of institutional distance between their home countries and the host BOP markets, which result in high liabilities of foreignness (LOF). LOF are the inherent costs that foreign companies face when entering and adjusting to the host markets (Randrianasolo, 2018). In order to overcome, reduce or offset LOF, companies must gain organisational legitimacy (Randrianasolo and Arnold, 2020). One method of boosting organisational legitimacy is to employ local workforces in the host country (Forstenlechner and Mellahi, 2011). Thus, adopting a micro-franchising model for retailers seeking to enter Madagascar's BOP market would not only prove sustainable, but it would also help to reduce LOF by gaining legitimacy in the environment.

Summary of recommendations

In sum, the recommendations here suggest that companies seeking to enter the retail industry in Madagascar should employ a micro-franchising strategy model of strategically placed small retail outlets that sell locally sourced unbundled products. Figure 2.1 displays the suggested model for grocery retailers, and Figure 2.2 displays the suggested model for apparel retailers.

Retailers should employ these models in order to adapt their marketing mix to the Malagasy BOP market. Specifically, as displayed in Figure 2.1, grocery retailers should adopt small grocery outlets strategically placed within *tsenas* and supplied by a central city distribution centre. Similarly, as displayed in Figure 2.2, apparel retailers should adopt small retail outlets placed in the *fripe* areas throughout the cities in Madagascar sourced by locally produced products.

The models proposed in Figures 2.1 and 2.2 are appropriate for franchising models in Madagascar; however, another perspective holds that multinationals when entering BOP markets could benefit from strategic alliances with local organisations (Remmen and Ravn, 2009). Particularly, when faced with high liabilities of foreignness, partnerships with local organisations such as local non-governmental organisations can offset this cost because these local organisations usually are socially embedded into informal networks and are rich in social knowledge (Webb, Kistruck, Ireland, and Ketchen, 2010). Therefore, multinationals may want to opt for a strategic alliance entry mode over a franchise model. In such cases, the model in Figure 2.3 may be more appropriate than the models proposed in Figures 2.1 and 2.2.

Figure 2.3 displays a model appropriate for both grocery and apparel retailers. In this model, it is proposed that multinational retailers seeking partnerships with local organisations that may have more knowledge and social embeddedness in the BOP should do so with strategic alliances. Within the alliance, the local organisation should contribute by taking on pricing and distribution decisions in the marketing mix, since these organisations have more knowledge and embeddedness, which would not only allow them to understand pricing better, but would

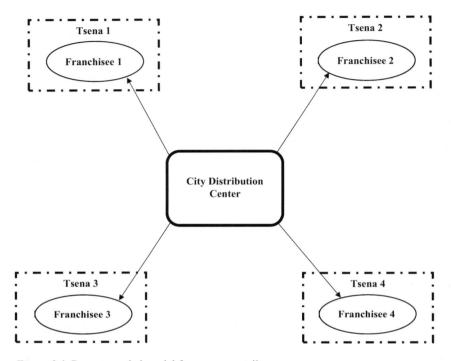

Figure 2.1 Recommended model for grocery retailers.

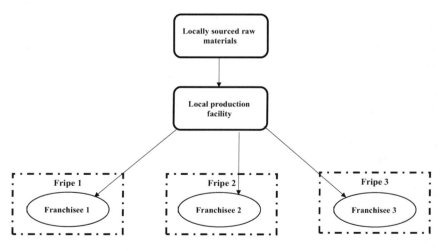

Figure 2.2 Recommended model for apparel retailers.

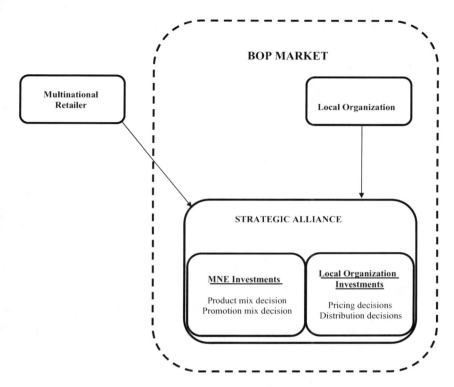

Figure 2.3 Recommended model for multinational retailers seeking strategic alliances.

also have better access to distribution channels. The multinational retailer in this instance should take on product mix and promotion mix decisions. The multinational retailer should take on the former because the retailer has expertise in this area. They should take on the latter because, as previously stated, promotions should reflect a high level of globalness to indicate quality (Randrianasolo, 2017). These recommendations provide practical and theoretical implications to companies intending to enter African retail markets, as discussed in the next section.

Implications for African retail markets

Globally, the BOP represents a $5 trillion market (BOP Innovation Centre, 2019). Of this $5 trillion market, $429 billion is accounted for in Africa (World Resource Institute, 2019). This large market, however, is still largely untapped as it not only offers valuable consumers, but it also enables entrepreneurs, workforces, diverse suppliers, retail partners, and producers who are employed to boost economic gain (BOP Innovation Centre, 2019). In the previous sections of this chapter, one aspect of BOP penetration within retail in Madagascar was discussed. The

Theoretical contributions

Theoretically, the arguments in this chapter can be summarised based on institutional theory, which states that institutions provide meaning and structure to actions and processes (Carnidale, 2018; Scott, 2013). Institutions create societal spheres of accepted and expected behaviour and can be described as the force behind behavioural systems (Scott, 1987). in this regard, the institutional environment in countries such as Madagascar influences the shopping behaviours of BOP consumers in such markets. In order for retailers to serve BOP consumers in Madagascar and in other African BOP markets effectively, it is imperative that they not only understand the institutional environments of these markets, but they should also adjust their existing models and processes to the markets. In this present chapter, two aspects of such suggested adjustments are discussed.

Within the Malagasy market's institutional environment, the institutional norm is that consumers shop for groceries at *tsenas* and shop for clothes in *fripe* markets. Therefore, rather than trying to lure consumers to grocery stores or large department stores, multinational enterprises seeking to enter the retail industry in Africa should adhere to the institutional norms in such environments by complementing the institutional norms through the adaptation of distribution models.

Similarly, the institutional environment in Madagascar is composed of BOP consumers with very low-income levels. Understanding this, firms should adhere to this reality and unbundle products to meet the consumer price point. This requires the adaptations of product packaging and bundling. Overall, according to the institutional theory, institutions are the "rules of the game" that companies must abide by in order to thrive within a given environment (Gertler, 2010). In order to thrive within the retail industry of Africa's BOP markets, companies must first understand the rules of the game and play by them. These theoretical contributions induce several practical implications, as discussed below.

Practical implications

The African continent holds many open-air markets such as the *tsena/fripe* in Madagascar, the Karatina Market in Kenya, the Merkato Market in Ethiopia, the Kejetia Market in Ghana, the Khan El Khalili Market in Egypt, and the Onitsha Market in Nigeria (Babatunde, 2017). These open-air markets show how many BOP consumers purchase groceries and apparel. This chapter suggests specific strategies to aid multinational firms in penetrating these markets and adapting for Africa's BOP markets. First, it is suggested that multinational corporations seeking to enter BOP markets should seek the markets within the cities they are penetrating and establish their presence in these markets. For example, grocery retailers should establish their smaller stores within the *tsenas* in Madagascar rather than building larger stores and attempting to lure consumers to these larger stores. Similarly, apparel retailers should establish their stores in the *fripe* areas in Madagascar rather than building large department stores that are inaccessible to BOP consumers. It is important to note that these recommended stores within the *tsenas* or *fripes* are recommended to carry unbundled products that meet BOP consumer price points.

Second, it is suggested that companies employ a micro-franchising model when implementing the aforementioned distribution strategy. It is important that the "micro" is emphasised to keep the investment affordable for BOP franchisees. This model would achieve several objectives. First, it would help reduce the liability of foreignness. Multinationals intending to enter BOP markets are typically headquartered in developed nations. This typically means that there is a large amount of institutional distance between the firm's home country and the host BOP market. Institutional distance is positively related to the liability of foreignness, and therefore multinationals from developed countries intending to enter BOP markets face high levels of this liability due to high levels of institutional distance (Randrianasolo, 2018). Research reveals that selecting a franchising model in the host countries can increase social acceptance or legitimacy, which in turn decreases the liability of foreignness (Gauzente and Dumoulin, 2010). Second, selecting a franchising model reduces the risk for the firm in a foreign country. Rather than opting for equity-based investments such as a wholly owned subsidiary or a joint venture, multinationals can employ a contract-based franchising entry mode. Finally, a micro-franchising model would boost economic development in BOP markets. BOP markets have entrepreneurs and can employ a workforce ready to boost production and stimulate the economy, yet many BOP markets do not have the opportunity to do so (Prahalad, 2010). Therefore, micro-franchising opportunities would allow for greater economic stimulation and development of BOP markets.

Finally, it is suggested that as multinationals employ these models within BOP markets such as Madagascar, they should employ marketing campaigns that educate consumers on new shopping habits related to the franchised stores the multinational retailers implement. Research reveals that BOP consumers must be educated on new innovations and models introduced to their markets (Danse, Klerkx, Reintjes, Rabbinge, and Leeuwis, 2020). Therefore, it is suggested that multinationals should educate consumers through informative advertising in their marketing campaigns. These practical implications are aimed at not only aiding companies in penetrating retail markets in Africa but also in boosting development in these markets.

Conclusion

The BOP corporate concept is focused on adapting the marketing mix to implement profit-seeking activities that appropriately fit BOP constituents. In this chapter, the case of retailing in Madagascar was employed to demonstrate that although scholars have investigated and recommended appropriate strategies for being successful in the BOP for nearly two decades, many industries are still plagued with companies that fail to properly implement these strategies. Specifically, a lack of understanding of consumer shopping patterns and pricing considerations still leads to having large pockets of BOP consumers who are underserved in the retailing industry in Madagascar. This problem in retailing is not unique to Madagascar, as many African nations still have large BOP markets. Therefore, the models proposed in this chapter seeks to provide strategic implications not only to companies intending to enter the retail industry in Madagascar but also to companies intending to expand into other African nations. The goal here is to invest in the BOP through retailing in search of profits and in boosting development in these markets.

References

ATKearney (2019). The age of focus: the 2017 global retail development index. Retrieved from: https://www.atkearney.com/global-retail-development-index/article?/a/the-age-of-focus-2017-full-study. Accessed 1 November 2019.

Babatunde, M. (2017). Africa's 5 largest open-air markets. *Face2Face Africa*. Retrieved from: https://face2faceafrica.com/article/african-markets. Accessed 10 October 2019.

Bolton, R. N., & Shankar, V. (2018). Emerging retailer pricing trends and practices. In Gielens, K. & Gijsbrechts, E. (Eds), *Handbook of Research on Retailing*, 104–131. Edward Elgar Publishing, Cheltenham, UK.

BOP Innovation Center (2019). Base of the pyramid. Retrieved from: http://bopinnovationcenter.com/what-we-do/base-of-the-pyramid. Accessed 10 October 2019.

Browdie, B. (2019). Starbucks has failed South Africa so far but it is set for a do over. *Quartz Africa*. Retrieved from: https://qz.com/africa/1741804/starbucks-has-failed-in-south-africa-but-wants-a-do-over/. Accessed 10 October 2019.

Cardinale, I. (2018). Beyond constraining and enabling: toward new microfoundations for institutional theory. *Academy of Management Review*, *43*(1), 132–155.

D'Andrea, G., & Herrero, G. (2007). Understanding consumers and retailers at the base of the pyramid in Latin America. In Rangan, V. K., Quelch, J. A., Herrero, G., & Barton, B. (Eds.), *Business solutions for the global poor: Creating social and economic value*, 25–40. San Francisco, CA: Jossey-Bass.

Danse, M., Klerkx, L., Reintjes, J., Rabbinge, R., & Leeuwis, C. (2020). Unravelling inclusive business models for achieving food and nutrition security in BOP markets. *Global Food Security*, *24*, 100354. doi.org/10.1016/j.gfs.2020.100354

Develtere, P., & Huybrechts, A. (2005). The impact of microcredit on the poor in Bangladesh. *Alternatives*, *30*(2), 165–189.

Duarte, A. L. D. C. M., Macau, F., e Silva, C. F., & Sanches, L. M. (2019). Last mile delivery to the bottom of the pyramid in Brazilian slums. *International Journal of Physical Distribution & Logistics Management*, *49*(5), 473–491.

Fairbourne, J. S. (2007). Why microfranchising is needed now: introduction and book overview. In Fairbourne, J. S., Gibson, S. W., & Dyer, W. G. (Eds), *Microfranchising: Creating Wealth at the Bottom of the Pyramid*, 1–17. Cheltenham, UK: Edward Elgar Publishing.

Forstenlechner, I., & Mellahi, K. (2011). Gaining legitimacy through hiring local workforce at a premium: the case of MNEs in the United Arab Emirates. *Journal of World Business*, *46*(4), 455–461.

Gauzente, C., & Dumoulin, R. (2010). Franchise as an efficient mode of entry in emerging markets: a discussion from the legitimacy point of view. In Singh, S. (Ed.), *Handbook

of *Business Practices and Growth in Emerging Markets*, 255–272. Hackensack, NJ: World Scientific Publishing Co.
Gertler, M. S. (2010). Rules of the game: the place of institutions in regional economic change. *Regional Studies*, *44*(1), 1–15.
Gold, S., Chowdhury, I. N., Huq, F. A., & Heinemann, K. (2020). Social business collaboration at the bottom of the pyramid: the case of orchestration. *Business Strategy and the Environment*, *29*(1), 262–275.
Hassan, N. M., Rom, M., Ashikin, N., & Said, A. M. A. (2016). Micro-franchising for people at the Bottom of Pyramid (BOP) in Malaysia. *Advanced Science Letters*, *22*(12), 4564–4567.
Jose, S., & Robert Buchanan, F. (2013). Marketing at the bottom of the pyramid: service quality sensitivity of captive microfinance borrowers. *Journal of Consumer Marketing*, *30*(7), 573–582.
Kaplinsky, R. (2011). 'Bottom of the Pyramid Innovation' and pro-poor growth. The World Bank. Retrieved from: http://documents.worldbank.org/curated/en/435351468325278859/Bottom-of-the-pyramid-Innovation-and-pro-poor-growth. Accessed 23 October 2019.
Knizkov, S., & Arlinghaus, J. C. (2019). Is co-creation always sustainable? Empirical exploration of co-creation patterns, practices, and outcomes in bottom of the pyramid markets. *Sustainability*, *11*(21), 6017.
Kotler, P., Kartajaya, H., & Setiawan, I. (2010). *Marketing 3.0: From Products to Customers to the Human Spirit*. John Wiley & Sons, Westford, MA.
Kuo, T. C., Hanafi, J., Sun, W. C., & Robielos, R. A. C. (2016). The effects of national cultural traits on BOP consumer behaviour. *Sustainability*, *8*(3), 272.
Ma, X., Sharpe, P. A., Bell, B. A., Liu, J., White, K., & Liese, A. D. (2018). Food acquisition and shopping patterns among residents of low-income and low-access communities in South Carolina. *Journal of the Academy of Nutrition and Dietetics*, *118*(10), 1844–1854.
Macri, R. (2019). Here's to you little one. *The American Journal of Tropical Medicine and Hygiene*, *101*(2), 283.
Maki Company. (2020). A propos de la companie. Retrieved from: http://maki-company.com/index.php?id_cms=6&controller=cms. Accessed 3 January 2020.
Monitor Deloitte (2017). Reaching deep in low-income markets: enterprises achieving impact, sustainability, and scale at the base of the pyramid. Retrieved from: https://www2.deloitte.com/content/dam/Deloitte/us/Documents/process-and-operations/us-cons-reaching-deep-in-low-income-markets.pdf. Accessed 20 December, 2019.
Nakata, C., & Weidner, K. (2012). Enhancing new product adoption at the base of the pyramid: a contextualized model. *Journal of Product Innovation Management*, *29*(1), 21–32.
Okazaki, S., Mueller, B., & Taylor, C. R. (2010). Global consumer culture positioning: testing perceptions of soft-sell and hard-sell advertising appeals between the US and Japanese consumers. *Journal of International Marketing*, *18*(2), 20–34.
Oodith, P. D., & Parumasur, S. B. (2017). Brand Consciousness of BOP Consumers in South Africa. *Journal of Economics and Behavioral Studies*, *9*(3), 82–100.
Petrescu, M., & Bhatli, D. (2013). Consumer behaviour in flea markets and marketing to the Bottom of the Pyramid. *Journal of Management Research*, *13*(1), 55–63.
Phillip, X. (2019). The curious case of Walmart's foray into Africa. *The Africa Report*. Retrieved from: https://www.theafricareport.com/15186/the-curious-case-of-walmarts-foray-into-africa/Accessed 19 December 2019.

Pitta, D., Guesalaga, R., & Marshall, P. (2008). Purchasing power at the bottom of the pyramid: differences across geographic regions and income tiers. *Journal of Consumer Marketing*, 25(7), 413–418.

Polak, P., & Warwick, M. (2013). *The Business Solution to Poverty: Designing Products and Services for Three Billion New Customers*. Berrett-Koehler Publishers, San Francisco, CA.

Prahalad, C. K. (2010). *The Fortune at the Bottom of the Pyramid, Revised and Updated 5th Anniversary Edition: Eradicating Poverty Through Profits*. Wharton School Publishing, Upper Saddle River, NJ.

Prahalad, C. K. (2012). Bottom of the pyramid as a source of breakthrough innovations. *Journal of Product Innovation Management*, 29(1), 6–12.

Prahalad, C. K., & Hammond, A. (2002). Serving the world's poor, profitably. *Harvard Business Review*, 80(9), 48–59.

Priporas, C. V., Kamenidou, I., Kapoulas, A., & Papadopoulou, F. M. (2015). Counterfeit purchase typologies during an economic crisis. *European Business Review*, 27(1), 2–16.

Property Rights Alliance (2019). International property rights index: Madagascar. Retrieved from: https://www.internationalpropertyrightsindex.org/country/madagascar. Accessed 18 December 2019.

Randrianasolo, A. A. (2017). Global brand value in developed, emerging, and least developed country markets. *Journal of Brand Management*, 24(5), 489–507.

Randrianasolo, A. A. (2018). Organizational legitimacy, corporate social responsibility, and bottom of the pyramid consumers. *Journal of International Consumer Marketing*, 30(3), 206–218.

Randrianasolo, A. A., & Arnold, M. J. (2020). Consumer legitimacy: conceptualization and measurement scales. *Journal of Consumer Marketing*, 37(4), 385–397.

Remmen, A., & Ravn, J. (2009). access2innovation–a strategy to fight climate change? *IOP Conference Series: Earth and Environmental Science*, 6(41), 412039 (1–2).

Savana, A. (2021). Distribution: South African group Shoprite (also) leaves Uganda and Madagascar. *Kapital Afrik*. Retrieved from: https://www.kapitalafrik.com/2021/08/23/distribution-south-african-group-shoprite-also-leaves-uganda-and-madagascar/. Accessed 21 November 2021.

Scott, W. R. (1987). The adolescence of institutional theory. *Administrative Science Quarterly*, 32(4), 493–511.

Scott, W. R. (2013). *Institutions and Organizations: Ideas, Interests, and Identities*. Sage, Thousand Oaks, CA.

Shoprite (2002). Shoprite enters Madagascan market. Retrieved from: https://www.shopriteholdings.co.za/articles/Newsroom/2002/shoprite-enters-madagascan-market.html. Accessed 4 April 2020.

Shoprite (2020). Trouver un magasin. Retrieved from: https://www.shoprite.com.mg/trouver-un-magasin.html. Accessed 4 April 2020.

Simanis, E., & Duke, D. (2014). Profits at the bottom of the pyramid. *Harvard Business Review*, 92(10), 86–93.

Smith, A. (2015). Top 5 biggest retailers in South Africa. Retrieved from: https://buzzsouthafrica.com/biggest-retailers-in-south-africa/. Accessed 4 April 2020.

Strizhakova, Y., Coulter, R. A., & Price, L. L. (2008). Branded products as a passport to global citizenship: perspectives from developed and developing countries. *Journal of International Marketing*, 16(4), 57–85.

Subhan, F., & Khattak, A. (2016). What constitutes the Bottom of the Pyramid (BOP) market. In *Institute of Business Administration International Conference on Marketing*

(IBA-ICM). Kuala Lumpur, Malaysia. Retrieved from: https://www.researchgate.net/profile/Amira-Khattak/publication/315744411_What_Constitutes_the_Bottom_of_the_Pyramid_BOP_Market/links/58e15806a6fdcc41bf944d30/What-Constitutes-the-Bottom-of-the-Pyramid-BOP-Market.pdf. Accessed 21 November 2021.

Trading Economics (2020). Madagascar GDP per capita. Retrieved from: https://tradingeconomics.com/madagascar/gdp-per-capita. Accessed 5 April 2020.

Trendtype (2019). Leader Price adds its ninth store in Madagascar. Retrieved from: https://www.trendtype.com/news/leader-price-anosizato/. Accessed 4 April 2020.

United Nations (2018). List of least developed countries (as of March 2018). Retrieved from: https://www.un.org/development/desa/dpad/wp-content/uploads/sites/45/publication/ldc_list.pdf. Accessed 4 April 2020.

Vassallo, J. P., Prabhu, J. C., Banerjee, S., & Voola, R. (2019). The role of hybrid organizations in scaling social innovations in bottom-of-the-pyramid markets: insights from microfinance in India. *Journal of Product Innovation Management, 36*(6), 744–763.

Webb, J. W., Kistruck, G. M., Ireland, R. D., & Ketchen, Jr, D. J. (2010). The entrepreneurship process in base of the pyramid markets: the case of multinational enterprise/nongovernment organization alliances. *Entrepreneurship Theory and Practice, 34*(3), 555–581.

Westjohn, S. A., Singh, N., & Magnusson, P. (2012). Responsiveness to global and local consumer culture positioning: a personality and collective identity perspective. *Journal of International Marketing, 20*(1), 58–73.

Wertheim-Heck, S. C., Vellema, S., & Spaargaren, G. (2015). Food safety and urban food markets in Vietnam: the need for flexible and customized retail modernization policies. *Food Policy, 54*, 95–106.

World Bank (2019a). PPP conversion factor, GDP. Retrieved from: https://data.worldbank.org/indicator/pa.nus.ppp Accessed 20 December 2019.

World Bank (2019b). Unemployment, total (% of total labour force) (modelled ILO estimate). Retrieved from: https://data.worldbank.org/indicator/SL.UEM.TOTL.ZS. Accessed 20 December 2019.

World Bank (2019c). Logistics performance index. Retrieved from: https://datacatalog.worldbank.org/dataset/logistics-performance-index. Accessed 20 December 2019.

World Resource Institute (2019). BOP market by income segment: Africa – $429 billion. Retrieved from: https://www.wri.org/resources/charts-graphs/bop-market-income-segment-africa-429-billion. Accessed 20 December 2020.

Xia, F., Chatterjee, R., & May, J. H. (2019). Using conditional restricted Boltzmann machines to model complex consumer shopping patterns. *Marketing Science, 38*(4), 711–727.

3 Factors motivating consumers to visit supermarkets in Tanzania
Case of Dar es Salaam and Arusha Regions

Francis Muya, Maureen Kabugumila, Francis Moses, and Deus Shatta

Introduction

Africa has witnessed the rise of supermarkets driven by South African and Kenyan retailers. In this respect, many studies have been done on the different aspects related to supermarkets on the continent. However, most previous studies have paid attention to the effects of supermarkets on smallholder farmers (Emongor and Kirsten, 2009), the linkage of agri-food processors to supermarkets (Nandonde and Kuada, 2016) and factors motivating consumers to visit supermarkets (Dadzie and Nandonde, 2019). Despite the plethora of previous studies, little attention, if any, has been paid to the motivation behind consumers' visiting supermarkets in Africa.

Despite the rise of supermarkets in Africa and particularly in Tanzania, retail firms are collapsing. International retailers such as Nakumatt, Uchumi, and Shoprite have collapsed in Tanzania (Nandonde, 2019). Domestic retailers also have closed their operations in different countries in Africa. For instance, eight Ukwala outlets across Kenya were involved in a takeover by Botswana based company Choppies in the year 2016 (The Daily Nation, 2016). Four years later, Choppies scaled down operations to only two stores in Kenya (The East African, 2020). All these developments indicate that the business environment is not favourable for retailers in the region. In that regard, given the rise of supermarkets, we argue that it is very important to understand the factors motivating consumers to visit supermarkets in Africa, focusing on the Tanzania market.

Although the environments that supermarkets operate in face a lot of turmoil, the supermarket business seems to still be among the growing business opportunities in large African cities. However, whether the business environment will contribute to the growth and flourishing of this kind of business in Africa is still uncertain. The retail business depends on the buyer's initiative to visit these outlets, but a multitude of factors influence this decision (McGuire, 1976; Prince, 1990: Khan, Chelliah, and Ahmed, 2017; Dadzie and Nandonde, 2019). What specific factors drive buyers to a supermarket and to what extent it is something worth researching.

Much research on the factors influencing consumer behaviour and choices has been carried out; however, most of these studies were either in countries other

DOI: 10.4324/9780367854300-3

than Tanzania (Wong and Yu, 2003; Reardon and Hopkins, 2006; Mai and Zhao, 2004; Toiba, 2015), or were carried out in different sectors other than retail (Khan, Chelliah, and Ahmed, 2017). Some of the studies were also done a long time ago; thus, the passage of time may have had some influence on the business environment (McGuire, 1976; Prince, 1990). Further to this, the studies utilised different methodologies; thus, their conclusions cannot be generalised. It should be noted that factors influencing consumer' to visit an outlet like a supermarket cannot be generalised across countries, sectors, or even time periods. Thus, a study dedicated to investigating the factors influencing consumers to visit supermarkets in selected regions of Tanzania becomes critical.

Supermarkets in Tanzania

Retailing is one of the oldest forms of trade in Tanzania, where the majority of Tanzanians obtain different products to meet their daily needs. Several economic restructuring initiatives have been embarked on between 1996 and 2006 in Tanzania. Some of these initiatives include the privatisation and reform of parastatals, liberalisation of the financial sector, creation of the market-oriented regulatory framework, trade reform, regional integration, reversal of fiscal dominance of monetary policy, fiscal consolidation, and sizeable finance assistance from donors (Mandalu, Thakhathi, and Costa, 2018). Through these economic restructuring initiatives, the country has experienced significant growth of different types of business, including retail. Following these reforms, the country has witnessed large scale and giant multinational retailers, including supermarkets, entering the traditional retail markets with all the benefits of exceptional economies of scale, advanced technology, and globally established brand names. The majority of these retailers expanded internationally to move beyond mature and saturated home markets, among other major reasons. Through their superior information systems and buying power, these giant retailers offered better merchandise selections, good services, and big savings to consumers. Over the years, several giant US retailers, such as McDonald's, KFC, Gap, Toys 'R' Us, and Wal-Mart have become prominent in countries around the world, including Tanzania, as a result of their large marketing power (Kotler, Wong, Saunders, and Armstrong, 2005).

The Dar es Salaam and Arusha regions are among the major two urban centres in Tanzania hosting different supermarkets. The introduction of new malls/shopping centres in Dar es Salaam (such as Mlimani City Mall, Quality Centre, Palm Village Mall, Shoppers Plaza, Mayfair Plaza, Mkuki House, and Msasani City Mall, etc.) has attracted multiple multinational retailers and domestic retailers, such as Shoprite, Game, Nakumatt, Uchumi Supermarket, Village Supermarket, Mkwabi Supermarket, Choppies, TSN Supermarket, Imalaseko, Maisha Supermarket, and others into the Tanzanian market. In Arusha, Tanzania, for example, supermarkets such as Sanawari Supermarket, Village Supermarkets, Clock Tower Supermarket, Ussoke Supermarket, Sakina Supermarket, and Tumaini Supermarket are household names. All of these are important shopping destinations for local residents as well as tourists and expatriates living in the country. Until 2018, the contribution of retail and other activities such as wholesale and repairs on the shares of gross domestic product reached 9.12% (United Republic of Tanzania, 2019). In the current era, the Tanzania government is determined to improve the business environment by providing a wide range of appropriate incentives and support to unleash the creativity of the private sector and other stakeholders in harnessing Tanzania's comparative advantages.

Despite the eagerness, retailers have found that store retailing is proving difficult to transfer across national frontiers. In the year 2000, the country witnessed many supermarket retail chains exiting the industry due to reasons such as failure to pay rent and possibly due to lacking the knowledge of the formal retail shopping culture in Tanzania. For example, it is estimated that up to 90% of food sales occur through traditional small stores, street vendors, and unregulated markets (Shand, 2017). Despite these challenges, there have been some positive prospects to investors in this industry as the rate of urbanisation in Tanzania will almost double from 28.6% in 2015 to 50.0% in 2050. The number of urban consumers will more than double over the same period, from 15 million in 2015 to 64.6 million in 2050 (Market Research.Com, 2016). Given this situation, understanding the key factors that influence customers to visit supermarkets will help multinational and domestic retailers to realise high profits in their businesses.

Literature review

In order to understand the factors influencing consumers to visit supermarkets, this study used the theory of planned behaviour (TPB) by Ajzen (1991). Originally, this theory was designed to predict and explain human behaviour in specific contexts. According to this theory, perceived behavioural control, together with behavioural intention, can be used directly to predict behavioural achievement. A central factor in the theory of planned behaviour is the individual's intention to perform a given behaviour. Intentions are assumed to capture the motivational factors that influence a behaviour; they are indications of how hard people are willing to try and how much effort they are planning to exert in order to perform the behaviour. As a general rule, the stronger the intention to engage in a behaviour, the more the likelihood of performing the behaviour. In perceived behavioural control, the importance of actual behavioural control is self-evident. The resources and opportunities available to a person must, to some extent, dictate the likelihood of behavioural achievement. Of greater psychological interest than actual control, however, is the perception of behavioural control and its impact on intentions and actions. Perceived behavioural control plays an important part in the theory of planned behaviour. In fact, the theory of planned behaviour differs from the theory of reasoned action due to additional aspects in the former of perceived behavioural control.

The theory of planned behaviour postulates three conceptually independent determinants of intention. The first is the attitude toward the behaviour and refers to the degree to which a person has a favourable or unfavourable evaluation or appraisal of the behaviour in question. The second predictor is a social factor termed subjective norm, which refers to the perceived social pressure to perform or not to perform the behaviour. The third antecedent of intention is the degree of perceived behavioural control, which, as we saw earlier, refers to the perceived ease or difficulty of performing the behaviour, and it is assumed to reflect past experience as well as anticipated impediments and obstacles. As a general rule, the more favourable the attitude is, and subjective the norm is towards a behaviour, the greater the perceived behavioural control and the stronger the individual's intention to perform the behaviour under consideration.

McGuire (1976), in a paper on 'Some Internal Psychological Factors Influencing Consumer Choice', divided the internal psychological makeup of the consumer into the directive aspect and the dynamic aspect of personality. The directive aspect involves structural characteristics of one's personality that channel the information processing of one's own experiences and of communications from other people through a number of successive steps. The steps range from exposure to information, perception of the information received, comprehension of what consumer perceives, agreement of what he/she comprehends, retention of what is accepted, information search and retrieval, the decision among the available options to the ultimate purchasing act, and consumption behaviour. The dynamic aspects of personality include the energising components of human personality, which are the motivational forces that activate and sustain information processing and account for its termination. Consumer motives are divided into cognitive and affective motivation, including consistency, attribution, categorisation, objectification, autonomy, stimulation, teleological, utilitarian, reinforcement, assertion, affiliation, identification, and modelling. These motives show that a consumer is induced by both internal and external motives. Although McGuire's paper was written almost 43 years ago, it gives a comprehensive guide to what factors sellers in different industries such as the retail industry in Tanzania must take into account in order to turn buyers into continued users of their products.

Elsewhere, Prince (1990) did a survey using visitors and non-visitors on the factors influencing consumer intention of visiting museums. In this study, the author found that visits to museums are heavily influenced by the socio-demographic background of potential visitors. He also found that differences in the socio-demographic background are manifested in the frequency of museum visits and in the other types of leisure/recreational destinations chosen. Other factors identified as important in influencing visitors choice of destinations include proper presentation of museum images, prior knowledge about a museum, longer opening hours, and increasing rates of advertising. The key area identified as a visit-stimulator was the provision of workshops where visitors could see people making and doing things. This study provides important findings on the factors that can influence consumers' decisions. Prince's study was, however, carried out many years ago and in outlets different from supermarkets and outside Tanzania. Due to the difficulty of generalising findings across different time periods, case studies, and countries, the current study is highly justifiable.

Davies et al. (2001) used a neural network approach to predict the supermarket shopping behaviour of consumers in the UK. The study findings revealed that the most satisfied and high-spending customers in supermarkets tend to be those with incomes that enable them to take full advantage of the choice and quality offered. Other customers are more concerned with the reasonability of prices and availability of discounts, although their satisfaction is also linked with store atmosphere. Using Structural Equation Modelling Partial Least Square, the current study established the relationships between some selected factors and consumers' intention to visit supermarkets.

Mai and Zhao (2004) conducted a survey examining the characteristics of supermarket shoppers in Beijing using a structured questionnaire from a sample of 200 respondents who were randomly selected. The findings revealed that Chinese consumers have the custom of making small and frequent shopping trips to the supermarkets. It was also noted that the majority of shoppers carry a limited amount of items because they walk to the supermarkets. In addition to shopping in supermarkets, Beijing shoppers also shop in other areas, especially traditional markets. When asked to explain why and where they shopped, shoppers cited proximity to homes, satisfactory product assortment, good quality, and reasonable price as key reasons. Though the study was carried out in a developed country, its findings are very helpful in discerning the factors which influence consumer visits to supermarkets in developing countries. While the study dwelt on shoppers' characteristics, the current study in Tanzania was intended to analyse if such characteristics are crucial in shoppers' decisions to visit supermarkets.

In the course of identifying the socio-demographic profiles of consumers associated with shopping in each retail format, especially supermarkets, hawkers, and open-air markets in Ghana, Meng et al. (2014), using ordinal logit estimation, revealed that demographic factors such as marital status, age, and household structure as well as socio-economic factors such as income, occupation, level of education attained, and location have a statistically significant effect in determining food shopping frequency in retail outlets. The results, however, revealed only marginal effects of the key factors associated with food purchase frequency for each of three outlet types, that is, supermarket, open-air market, and hawkers. The authors in the current study, therefore, aimed at establishing whether the results cited here can be applied to the Tanzania environment using Structural Equation Modelling Partial Least Square.

In another study, Toiba (2015) analysed the relationship between modern food retail penetration and changes in food shopping behaviour and dietary patterns in Indonesia. The results of the analysis, based on 1,180 surveyed households, revealed that the majority of consumers visit traditional food retailers most frequently. The results revealed further that consumers who shopped more frequently at modern food retailers tended to have higher incomes, high education, more assets, credit cards, and higher concerns about nutrition information labels and food safety, while price-sensitive consumers were more likely to shop at traditional food retailers. The results of the econometric analysis confirmed that consumers who had the highest probability of spending more on food in modern food retailers were consumers with children under 5 years of age, high income, more education and assets, and who were more concerned about safety. On the other hand, sensitive-price consumers were more likely to patronise traditional food retailers. Though the study was carried out in Indonesia, the results provide a strong foundation for understanding factors influencing consumers to visit to supermarkets.

The departure for this study was offered in a study by Dadzie and Nandonde (2019) that was carried out in Ghana. The scholars found that demographic and social factors influence consumers' decisions when purchasing commodities from supermarkets. The study cited here was carried out in Ghana, a country with a social, economic, and even technological environment that is different from that which exists in Tanzania; the current study was therefore undertaken in a different context. Data in the current study were analysed using Structural Equation Modelling Partial Least Square, which offers many opportunities for testing data validity and reliability as well as establishing a relationship between exogenous and endogenous variables. From the theory and empirical review of literature, the following hypotheses were tested, as shown in Figure 3.1.

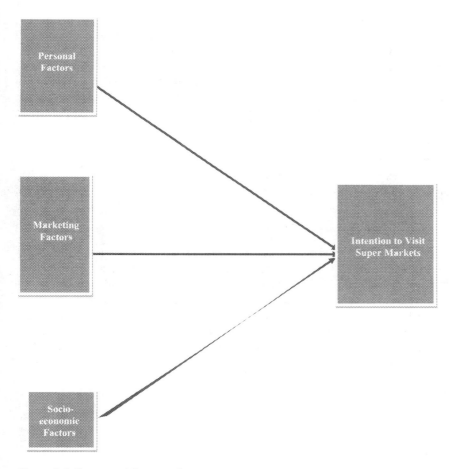

Figure 3.1 Conceptual framework.

H1: There is a positive relationship between socio-economic factors and the decision to visit a supermarket.

H2: There is a positive relationship between marketing factors and the decision to visit a supermarket.

H3: There is a positive relationship between personal factors and the decision to visit a supermarket.

Methodology

Research design

The study was carried out in two regions of Arusha and Dar es Salaam using a cross-sectional research design. As stated earlier, the two regions are among the major urban centres in Tanzania, hosting a large number of supermarkets. Dar es Salaam has the highest population, which is estimated at 5,147,070 people, which is equivalent to 9.8% of the total population of the Tanzania mainland (URT, 2013b). The Dar es Salaam region has the highest population because of, among other things, the availability of basic social and economic services, which lead to an increased number of immigrants from other regions. The region hosts different types of businesses, and has the largest port facilities in Tanzania, including JKN international airport. According to URT (2019), Arusha has an estimated population of 1,999,907 people. The market offered by the local population in the Arusha region is boosted by a large number of tourists who visit the region each year. The population for this study included all residents of the two regions. It was the belief of the authors that the urban population has shopping habits unlike those of the rural population; hence, the authors expected to get information that could be generalised in other urban areas of Tanzania mainland.

Sample and sampling procedures

A convenient sampling procedure was used in this study. Using this procedure, selecting the sample and eliciting the participation of the respondents become very easy (Salkind, 2012). The questionnaire was physically administered in the streets close to supermarkets in the cities of Arusha and Dar es Salaam. Data were collected from 300 participants, but only 284 (95%) questionnaires were usable as other questionnaires were left out due to the possibility of response bias in the form of the consistency motif and social desirability (Podsakoff, MacKenzie, Lee, and Podsakoff, 2003).

Measurement and variables

The exogenous variables in this study are the factors motivating consumers to visit supermarkets, which were divided into marketing factors, socio-economic factors, and personal factors. A five-point Likert scale ranging from 1 to 5 (where

1 stands for not influential at all and 5 stands for extremely influential) was used to ascertain the level of influence of the selected variables on the decision to visit a supermarket. These variables were adopted from previous studies (i.e. Dadzie and Nandonde, 2019; Davies et al., 2001; Martinez, Vadell, and Ruiz, 2010; Meng et al., 2014; Toiba, 2015). The endogenous variable in this study was the intention to visit supermarkets, which was measured using three items of frequency on an ordinal scale: visits to a supermarket, action taken at the supermarket, and the amount of money spent at the supermarket.

Study results

Demographic characteristics of the respondents

A total of 284 respondents participated in this study, whereby 59.5% were from the Dar es Salaam region, and 40.5% were from the Arusha region. Out of these, 61.3% were males, and 38.7% were females. With regards to their marital status, 51.1% were married, 37.3% were not married, 9.2% were living together, and 2.5% were divorced. The majority (44%) of the respondents were aged between 20 and 30 years of age, 43.3% were between 31 and 40 years of age. This age distribution reflects the nature of shopping habits in Tanzania, where the majority are the youth in the entire population (United Republic of Tanzania, 2013a). With regards to their nationality, 85.2% were Tanzanian and 14.8% were non-Tanzanians. On their level of education, the majority (35.9%) of the respondents had a bachelor's degree and 17.3 had a master's degree. These results are in line with the findings reported in a study by Schmidt and Nandonde (2019), who found that educated people dominate supermarket visits in developing economies. Out of 284 respondents, 48.2% were employed, 43% were self-employed, and 8.8% were students. The study results revealed further than 40.8% of the respondents visit supermarkets using their own means of transport, 35.6% use public transport, especially minibuses, 13% use taxis, and 10.6% use motorcycles. The demographic characteristics of the respondents are presented in Table 3.1. The majority of respondents (93%) reported visiting supermarkets at least three times per month. About 68% of the respondents had an income of above TZS 2 million per month.

Data analysis process and the use of SmartPLS3

Partial Least Squares Structural Equation Modelling (PLS-SEM) was used in the course of analysing data for this study. SEM is a modern analysis technique, which is differentiated from covariance-based Structural Equation Modelling (CB-SEM). There is widespread usage of SEM due to its ability to handle complex models with many paths, constructs, and even indicators without imposing distributional assumptions on the data (Hair et al., 2018). SmartPLS3 software was employed in this study because of its benefits. The software provides guidelines, which are very clear for data analysis in the application of PLS-SEM. One

Table 3.1 Demographic characteristics of the respondents

Characteristics		n = 284	%
Region	Dar es Salaam	169	59.5
	Arusha	115	40.5
Sex	Male	174	61.3
	Female	110	38.7
Marital status	Married	145	51.1
	Never Married	106	37.3
	Living Together	26	9.2
	Divorced	7	2.5
Age	20–30	125	44
	31–40	123	43.3
	41–50	0	0
	51–60	32	11.3
	Over 60	4	1.4
Nationality	Tanzanian	242	85.2
	Non-Tanzanian	42	14.8
Education	Certificate of Primary Education	12	4.2
	Ordinary Certificate of Secondary Education	40	14.1
	Advanced Certificate of Secondary Education	3	1.1
	Certificate	34	12
	Diploma	30	12
	Bachelor Degree	102	35.9
	Postgraduate Diploma	10	3.5
	Master's Degree	49	17.3
	PhD Degree	4	1.4
Occupation	Employee	137	48.2
	Self-employed	122	43
	Students	25	8.8

of the benefits of the SmartPLS3 software is that it has few limitations with sample size requirements as compared to other SEM software such as AMOS (Hair et al., 2018). Also, the SmartPLS3 software does not require linearity and normality conditions (Hair et al., 2018). The following section shows the procedures employed in the SmartPLS3 software.

Importing data files in SmartPLS3 software

Before drawing the path model in the SmartPLS3 software, the collected data were taken to the data file format of.csv for the purpose of creating a new SmartPLS3 SEM project.

Drawing the theoretical path model in SmartPLS3 software

To draw the theoretical path model in the SmartPLS3 software, the imported data file was used by double-clicking on the name of the model, then the data were moved to the lower left of the screen, and the name of the data file was green indicating readiness for drawing the theoretical path model in the modelling window. The icons at the top of the screen, select, latent variable, and connect, were used to insert latent variables into the modelling window (Hair et al., 2018).

Naming and connecting the latent variables in the SmartPLS3 software

To rename and connect latent variables, left-clicking and holding down were done on one variable, and the cursor was dragged over a second variable, then a left-click was done a second time to connect all latent variables in the theoretical model (Hair et al., 2018).

Aligning indicators and latent variables in the SmartPLS3 software

To change the position of the measured variables, the cursor (in select mode) was placed on top of the measured variables, and right-clicked, leading to the appearance of a dialogue box to align indicators. Indicators and constructs were aligned in their respective position based on the proposed conceptual model (Hair et al., 2018).

Assessment of measurement model

The assessment of the measurement model is one of the main procedures in PLS-SEM. By definition, the measurement model represents the relationships between each construct and its associated indicators either reflectively or formatively (Hair et al., 2018). After all constructs and indicators were positioned into their respective positions, as shown in the conceptual model, the PLS algorithm was executed by clicking on the calculate icon then the PLS algorithm. After running the PLS algorithm, the theoretical model appeared with the results on the coefficient of determination (R^2) of the endogenous latent variable, the relevance of path coefficients and indicator reliability (outer-loadings). The report icon on the left-hand side of the computer screen was then clicked to obtain other values, including loadings, internal consistent reliability of the constructs, convergent validity and discriminant validity of the constructs, effect size of path coefficients (f^2), and collinearity (VIF) (Hair et al., 2018).

After running the PLS algorithms, the results revealed that all indicators for personal factors had outer-loadings above the threshold value of.0. On the other hand, the outer-loadings for other construct's indicators had unsatisfactory loadings but were left in order to preserve their composite reliability. The internal consistency was checked using composite reliability, which was 0.598 for the intention to visit supermarkets, 0.705 for marketing factors, 0.811 for personal factors, and 0.723 for socio-economic factors. To a large extent, the results were in accordance with the widely accepted social science cut-off of 0.7–0.9 for each variable (Hair, Hult, Ringle, and Sarsted, 2017). Convergent validity, which is

Table 3.2 Heterotrait–monotrait ratio

	Marketing Factors	Personal Factors	Socio-economic Factors
Marketing factors			
Personal factors	0.647		
Socio-economic factors	1.005	0.763	
Visit	0.844	1.355	0.956

the extent to which a measure correlates positively with alternative measures of the same construct (Hair et al., 2017), was tested using Average Variance Extracted (AVE). An AVE value of 0.33 was obtained for the intention to visit supermarkets, which indicates that the construct explains about 33% of the variance of its indicators; an AVE of 0.269 for marketing factors means that the construct explains about 27% of the variance of its indicators; an AVE of 0.683 for personal factors implies that the construct explains about 68% of the variance of its indicators; an AVE of 0.479 for socio-economic factors indicates that the construct explains about 48% of the variance of its indicators. The AVE results are slightly contrary to the rules of thumbs, which require the AVE to be 0.5 or higher (Hair, Risher, Sarstedt, and Ringle, 2018). The discriminant validity, which is the extent to which a construct is empirically distinct from other constructs in the structural model, was measured using the heterotrait–monotrait ratio (HTMT). Ahrholdt, Gudergan, and Ringle (2017) suggest discriminant validity based on the report and analysis of the heterotrait–monotrait ratio (HTMT), which seems to be better than the Fornell–Larcker criterion results and/or cross-loadings that perform poorly, especially when indicator loadings of the constructs under consideration differ only slightly. The HTMT values are presented in Table 3.2, the revealing presence of discriminant validity while others revealing problems in discriminant validity among the constructs.

Assessment of the structural model

After the assessment of the measurement model, the next important steps in PLS-SEM involve the assessment of the structural model. The structural model represents the structural paths between the constructs (Hair et al., 2018). The assessment of the structural model included a number of activities, especially checking collinearity to make sure it does not bias the regression results, calculating the coefficient of determination (R Squared), blindfolding based cross-validated redundancy measure (Q Squared), as well as performing the statistical significance and relevance of the path coefficients.

The first task of the assessment of the structural model in this study was therefore to examine the collinearity problem, if any. The Variance Inflation Factor (VIF) scores revealed the absence of the problem where both indicators and constructs had a VIF of below 3. The R Square for the endogenous variable, intention to visit a supermarket, was 0.222. This is an indication of the weak explanatory power of the exogenous variables on these endogenous variables, but it also indicates the influence of the exogenous variables on the endogenous variables. The relationship between these variables can be seen in Figure 3.2.

To assess the statistical significance of the path coefficient of the structural model, bootstrapping analysis was performed. To determine the *p*-values of the hypothesised relationships, the bootstrapping process was executed by clicking on the calculate icon then on bootstrapping. PLS-SEM employs bootstrapping process with the help of SmartPLS3 to generate a sub-sample by randomly sampling with a replacement of the original sample to be used in the calculation of standard errors for hypotheses testing under the assumption that sub-sample distribution is a reasonable representation of the intended population distribution (Hair et al., 2014).

PLS-SEM does not assume that the data are normally distributed, which implies that parametric significance tests used in regression analyses cannot be applied to test whether coefficients such as outer weights and loadings are significant. Instead, PLS-SEM relies on a nonparametric bootstrap procedure to test coefficients for their significance (Hair et al., 2018). In bootstrapping, a large number of sub-samples (i.e. bootstrap samples) are drawn from the original sample with a replacement. Replacement means that each time an observation is drawn at random from the sampling population, it is returned to the sampling

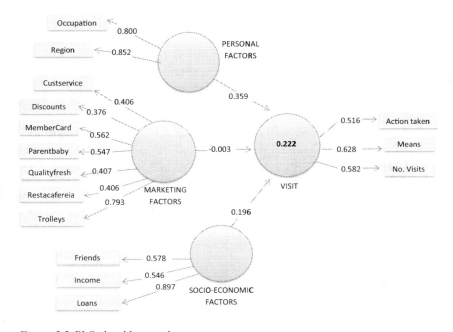

Figure 3.2 PLS algorithm results.

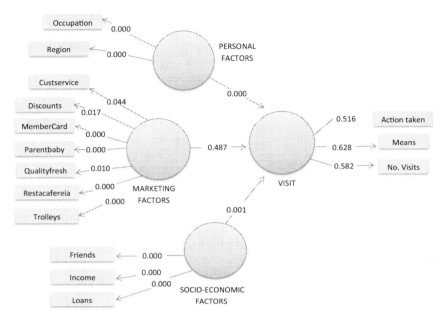

Figure 3.3 Bootstrapping results.

population before the next observation is drawn (i.e. the population from which the observations are drawn always contains all the same elements) (Hair et al., 2018). Therefore, the observation for a certain sub-sample can be selected more than once or may not be selected at all for another sub-sample. The number of bootstrap samples should be high but must be at least equal to the number of valid observations in the dataset. The recommended number of bootstrap samples is 5,000 (Hair et al., 2018).

In this study, the results of the bootstrapping analysis revealed that socio-economic factors positively influence decisions to visit a supermarket, and the relationship was significant (ß = 0.001, $p < 0.05$); hence, the first hypothesis was accepted. The results also revealed a positive but insignificant relationship between marketing factors and deciding to visit supermarkets (ß = 0.487, $p < 0.05$); hence, the second hypothesis was rejected. Finally, the results revealed that there was a positive and significant relationship between personal factors and decisions to visit a supermarket (β = 0.000, $p < 0.05$). All these relationships can be seen in Figure 3.3.

Discussion of findings, conclusion, and recommendations

This study was carried out with the intention of assessing factors influencing consumers' visits to the supermarket in the modern and large cities of Dar es Salaam and Arusha in Tanzania. As per the expectations of the researchers, all respondents surveyed were those who visited supermarkets at least twice in the last six months.

The majority (93%) of the respondents revealed that they visit supermarkets up to three times per month. These findings reveal that Tanzania's urban population has not lagged behind in adapting to such new habits of shopping in supermarkets. The findings, however, are in contrast with those in a study by Toiba (2015), who found that traditional food retailers are still used most frequently by the majority of consumers despite the existence of modern retail outlets.

The results of the Structural Equation Modelling revealed that personal factors, especially a person's occupation and area of residence, are important factors in explaining consumers' visits to a supermarket. These findings are in line with the findings in a study by Meng et al. (2014), who found that occupation had a statistically significant effect in determining the food shopping frequency in retail outlets. The current results add a new personal factor, the geographic area where the customer resides, something which was not examined before in attesting its influence on visits to supermarkets.

In addition, this study confirmed the positive relationship between socio-economic factors and the decision to visit a supermarket. The dominant socio-economic factors were accompanying friends, availability of loans, and higher incomes. These findings are supported by a number of authors, including Davies et al. (2001) and Meng et al. (2014), who also revealed a positive relationship between incomes and shopping behaviour.

A surprising relationship was found between marketing factors and the intention to visit supermarkets, where the relationship was positive but not significant. Such results contradict the results of previous studies such as Prince (1990), who found a positive role for advertising on consumer intention. The results also differ from those in a study by Toiba (2015), who found a positive role for marketing factors such as pricing and credit cards on shopping intention.

This study contributes to the worldwide discussion of consumer visits to supermarkets, which is a growing lifestyle in developing countries such as Tanzania. The study reveals that visits are made by people of different ages, occupations, and marital statuses, though some groups of people within these categories are dominant. The factors influencing consumers into visiting supermarkets in developing countries are, however, very complex and multiple. This study indicates that marketing factors, such as the availability of discounts, quality of fresh produce, availability of trolleys, availability of parent and baby facilities, customer services, assistance facilities, and membership card benefits, though insignificant, still influence consumer visits to supermarkets. These findings are in line with the findings in a study by Kumar et al. (2016), who found that most customers visit supermarkets for convenience shopping and for the advantage of sale offers and promotions. Socio-economic factors such as meeting friends, income levels, and the availability of loans, as well as personal factors such as occupation and geographical location significantly influence visits to supermarkets. These are some factors that need to be considered by supermarkets owners in the course of designing their marketing strategies in developing economies.

Despite the relevance of the findings discussed in the foregoing sections, the factors influencing consumer visits to supermarkets in developing countries cannot be generalised. Future studies need to be carried out in this area with an increased sample size, to include several regions, for intra-country studies. Inter-country studies in developing economies can also give a vivid picture of the factors influencing visits to supermarkets. Similarly, future studies can also be longitudinal in nature to allow for observing consumer actions over time.

References

Ahrholdt, D.C., Gudergan, S.P., & Ringle, C.M. (2017). Enhancing service loyalty: the roles of delight, satisfaction, and service quality. *Journal of Travel Research*, *56*(4), 436–450.

Ajzen, I. (1991). The theory of planned behaviour. *Organizational Behaviour and Human Decision Processes*, *50*, 179–211.

Dadzie, S.H., & Nandonde, F.A. (2019). Factors influencing consumers' supermarket visitation in developing economies: the case of Ghana. *Case Studies in Food Retailing and Distribution*. DOI: https://doi.org/10.1016/B978-0-08-102037-1.00005-0

Davies, F.M., Moutinho, L.A., Goode, M.M.H., & Ogbonna, E. (2001). Critical factors in consumer supermarket shopping behaviour: a neural network approach. *Journal of Consumer Behaviour*, *1*(1), 35–49.

Emongor, R., & Kirsten, J. (2009). The impact of South African supermarkets on agricultural development in the SADC: a case study in Zambia, Namibia and Botswana. *Agrekon*, *48*(1), 60–84.

Hair, J.F., Ringle, C.M., & Sarstedt, M. (2014). PLS-SEM: indeed a silver bullet. *The Journal of Marketing Theory and Practice*, *19*(2), 139–152.

Hair, Jr, J.F., Hult, G.T.M., Ringle, C.M., & Sarstedt, M. (2017). *A Primer on Partial Least Squares Structural Equation Modelling (PLS-SEM)* (2nd Ed.). New Delhi: SAGE Publications.

Hair, J.F., Risher, J.J.,Sarstedt, M., & Ringle, C.M. (2018). When to use and how to report the results of PLS-SEM. *European Business Review*, *31*, 5–14.

Khan, M.J., Chelliah, S., & Ahmed, S. (2017). Factors influencing destination image and visit intention among young women travellers: role of travel motivation, perceived risks, and travel constraints. *Asia Pacific Journal of Tourism Research*, *22*(11), 1139–1155.

Kotler, P., Keller, K., Brady, M., Goodman, M., & Hansen, T. (2016). *Marketing Management* (3rd Ed.). Pearson Prentice Hall, United Kingdom.

Kotler, P., Wong, V., Saunders, J., & Armstrong, G. (2005). *Principles of Marketing* (14th Ed.). Pearson Education Limited, Harlow, England.

Kumar, K., Kumar, R., & Naveen, C. (2016). Consumers' motivating factors in shopping at organized retail outlets. *Saudi Journal of Business and Management Studies*. DOI: https://doi.org/10.21276/sjbms.2016.1.3.11

Mai, L., & Zhao, H. (2004). The characteristics of supermarket shoppers in Beijing. *International Journal of Retail and Distribution Management*, *32*(1), 56–62.

Mandalu, M., Thakhathi, D.R., & Costa, H. (2018). Investigation on Tanzania's Economic History since Independence: the search for a development model. *World Journal of Social Sciences and Humanities*, *4*(1), 61–68.

McGuire, W.J. (1976). Some internal psychological factors influencing consumer choice. *Journal of Consumer Research*, *2*, 302–319.

Meng, T., Florkowski, W.J., Sarpong, D.B., Manjeet S. Chinnan, M.S., & Resurreccion, A.V.A. (2014). Consumer's food shopping choice in Ghana: Supermarket or

traditional outlets? *International Food and Agribusiness Management Review*, *17*, 116–121.
Market Research. Com. (2016). The grocery retail market in Tanzania. Accessed on 26 October 2020 at https://www.marketresearch.com/Trendtype-Ltd-v4027/Grocery-Retail-Tanzania-9834388/.
Martınez, S.C., Vadell, J.B.G., & Ruiz, M.P.P.M. (2010). Factors influencing repeat visits to destination: The influence of group composition. *Tourism Management*, *31*, 862–870.
Nandonde, F.A. (2016). Integrating of local food suppliers in modern food retail in Africa: The case of Tanzania. Unpublished Doctoral Thesis Submitted at Aalborg University, Denmark.
Nandonde, F.A. (2019). A PESTLE analysis of international retailing in the East African Community. *Global Business and Organizational Excellence*, *38*(4), 54–61.
Nandonde, F.A., Kuada, J. (2016). Modern food retailing buying behaviour in Africa: the case of Tanzania. *British Food Journal*, *118*(5).
Podsakoff, P.M., MacKenzie, S.B., Lee, J.Y., & Podsakoff, N.P. (2003). Common method biases in behavioural research: a critical review of the literature and recommended remedies. *Journal of Applied Psychology*, *88*(5), 879.
Prince, D. (1990). Factors influencing museum visits: an empirical evaluation of audience selection. *Museum Management and Curatorship*, 9,149–168.
Reardon, T., & Hopkins, R. (2006). The supermarket revolution in developing countries: policies to address emerging tensions among supermarkets, suppliers, and traditional retailers. *The European Journal of Development Research*, *18*(4), 522–545.
Salkind, N.J. (2012). *Exploring Research* (8th Ed.). Pearson, New Jersey.
Shand, N. (2017). Wholesale and retail of food in Tanzania. Accessed on 26 October 2020 at https://www.whoownswhom.co.za/store/info/4487?segment=Wholesale+and+Retail+of+Food+in+Tanzania).
Toiba, H. (2015). A study of the relationship between modern food retail penetration and urban Indonesian Consumers' Food Shopping Behaviour, consumption and dietary patterns. Thesis submitted to the University of Adelaide in fulfilment of the requirements for the degree of Doctor of Philosophy in Global Food Studies, Global Food Studies, Faculty of the Profession, The University of Adelaide.
The Daily Nation. (2016). Ukwala supermarket bought by Botswana retail chain. Accessed on 26 October 2020 at https://businesstoday.co.ke/ukwala-supermarket-bought-by-botswana-retail-chain/
The East African. (2020). Competition in Dar, Kenya sends Choppies out of East Africa. Accessed on 26 October 2020 at https://www.theeastafrican.co.ke/tea/business/competition-in-dar-kenya-sends-choppies-out-of-east-africa-1439708.
United Republic of Tanzania (URT). (2019). *Economic Survey 2018*. Ministry of Finance and Planning, Dodoma.
United Republic of Tanzania (URT). (2013a). 2012 Population and Housing Census: Population Distribution by Age and Sex. National Bureau of Statistics Ministry of Finance, Dar es Salaam and Office of Chief Government Statistician President's Office, Finance, Economy and Development Planning, Zanzibar.
United Republic of Tanzania (URT). (2013b). *2012 Population and Housing Census: Population Distribution by Administrative Areas*. National Bureau of Statistics Ministry of Finance, Dar es Salaam and Office of Chief Government Statistician President's Office, Finance, Economy and Development Planning, Zanzibar.
Wong, G.K.M., & Yu, L. (2003). Consumers' perception of store image of joint venture shopping centres: first tier versus second-tier cities in China. *Journal of Retailing and Consumers Services*, *10*, 61–70.

4 Understanding consumers' preference of purchasing items from supermarkets as opposed to traditional markets in Ghana

Emmanuel Kojo Sakyi

Introduction

Many developing countries have experienced a tremendous shift in the architecture and structure of shopping complexes due to the rapid introduction of supermarkets and malls (Meng, Florkowski, Sarpong, Chinnan, and Resurreccion, 2014; Minten and Reardon, 2008). The supermarket revolution in developing countries, which emerged in the early 1990s, has influenced customers choice of place for shopping (Meng, Florkowski, Sarpong, Chinnan, and Resurreccion, 2014; Reardon and Gulati, 2008; Reardon and Hopkins, 2006).

The rise of shopping malls/supermarkets has influenced both the traditional market system and consumers consumption and shopping preferences. The emergence of supermarkets and malls have rendered the traditional market less competitive in some selected household items such as processed foods, although local markets have still retained the competitive advantage of local fresh products (Minten and Reardon, 2008).

In Ghana, many supermarkets and malls, such as Melcom, Shoprite, and Game, have arisen due to the increase in the socio-economic status of consumers (Goldman and Hino, 2005; Meng, Florkowski, Sarpong, Chinnan, and Resurreccion, 2014). There are different views on the factors influencing the rise of supermarkets in developing economies. For example, previous studies indicate that customers' preference for malls and supermarkets results from their ability to make a one-stop shop rather than making multiple shopping trips to different traditional stores, which has a lower opportunity cost in terms of time (Goldman and Hino, 2005; Betancourt and Gautschi, 1990). Another group of scholars consider the structure of malls or supermarkets, quality check out services, conducive shopping environment, convenience, low price tags, and quality products as promoting customer satisfaction, making supermarkets or malls a place for shopping over the traditional market system (Minten and Reardon, 2008; Orel and Kara, 2014).

On the other hand, the establishments of malls and supermarkets have created a lot of problems, posing a major threat of driving traditional markets out of business and reducing the sales of traditional retailers. For example, previous studies indicate that the coming of shopping malls and supermarkets have affected

DOI: 10.4324/9780367854300-4

the patronage and sales of items by traditional market retailers (Matsa, 2011; Schipmann and Qaim, 2011; Suryadarma, Poesoro, Budiyati, and Rosfadhila, 2010; Taylor, 2007).

As a result, several strategies have been adopted by traditional market retailers to cope with the competition from supermarkets. In this respect, it is very important to understand consumers' preference when purchasing items from supermarkets as opposed to traditional markets in Ghana. The study therefore is intended to respond to the following critical questions:

(i) What are the effects of shopping malls on customers' choice of shopping location? ii) Which factors influence customers' choice of the traditional market over malls or vice versa? iii) How are traditional retailers coping with the competition exerted by the rapid growth of malls. Since their emergence at the beginning of this millennium, shopping malls have changed the architecture of shopping and consumer choice of where to shop.

Within a centralised shopping mall environment in the retailing sector, certain factors were observed to drive customer satisfaction, namely market location, the choice of goods, atmosphere, convenience, and availability of salespeople to assist when the need arises (Anselmsson, 2006). These factors are often lacking in the traditional retail market sector and have an implication on influencing customers' preference of a place to do their shopping. As a symbol of globalisation and the modernisation of the retailing system, malls have dramatically changed traditional retailing consumers' preferences and traditional retailing structure not only in Ghana but also in many other countries in the developing world. This chapter explores the influence of the shopping mall system on traditional retail markets and customer behaviour in Ho in the Volta region of Ghana.

The rest of the chapter is organised as follows: the next section reviews the literature on traditional markets and the advent of shopping malls, followed by a section that provides a brief background to Ho Municipal Assembly, the next section describes the data collection process; then the findings of the study are presented in the next section, and the final section discusses policy implications and concludes the chapter.

Overview of traditional markets in Ghana

The evolution of traditional markets dates back to the colonial period where the barter system of trade was in operation. The barter trade system was a means of exchange where an individual in a transaction directly exchanged goods or services for other goods or services without using money as a medium of exchange. The inefficiencies in the barter system led to its collapse, and this was attributable to a double coincidence of wants, lack of a standard unit of measure, the impossibility of subdivision of goods, asymmetry of information, the unfeasibility of production, and very costly goods.

The traditional market system operated daily in an open market without sheds or stalls. In addition to the daily market, there were weekly or monthly markets which were locally called market days where people from all over the country would come and trade and go back to their various destinations.

The traditional market consists of small-scale sellers or petty traders who sell food items. Traditionally, the markets mainly sold food items (Anku and Ahorbo, 2017; Minten, Reardon, and Sutradhar, 2010); however, a wave of globalisation and urbanisation has forced traditional market retailers to include electronics, hardware, clothes, and so on in their trade package to remain competitive. An increase in population has led to an upsurge of buyers and sellers in the traditional market system (Anku and Ahorbo, 2017), leading to a spill-over effect (Anku and Ahorbo, 2017; Lomotey, 2013; Ministry of Local Government and Rural Development, 2013; MOFA, 2013).

As Bednar (1989) reveals, the traditional market system could not satisfy the new demand for the enhanced distribution of goods and services, faster sales, and better promotion offered, brought about by shopping malls or supermarkets. This raised many unanswered questions on the influence of the emergence of supermarkets on the growth and development of the traditional market (Anku and Ahorbo, 2017; Readon and Hopkins, 2006; Suryadarma, 2011). In this regard, studies (i.e. Anku and Ahorbo, 2017; Suryadarma, 2011) consider traditional markets systems as surpassing the supermarkets in a competitive market environment.

Similarly, some studies have also shown that traditional markets have built a strong resilience to competition from supermarkets or shopping malls (Anku and Ahorbo, 2017; Hamilton, 2003). This is particularly because the industrial sector in the Ho municipality is less developed. There are currently no large industrial holdings in the municipality. The commercial sector is dominated by retail activity. There are limited wholesale activities in the agricultural and industry sectors (Ghana Statistical Service, 2014). Furthermore, the service sector is dominated by small-scale operators in activities such as telecommunication services, hairdressing and barbering, electronic repairs, vehicle repairs, and footwear repairs. The municipality has a number of small-scale industries. These include cassava flour processing, mushroom growing, beekeeping, gari production, soap making, batik tie and dye making, carpentry, and metalwork (Ghana Statistical Service, 2014).

On the other hand, the works of Anku and Ahorbo (2017) hold that despite building resilience against shopping malls and supermarkets, traditional markets are on the losing side of the competition.

The evolution of supermarkets in Ghana

The evolution of supermarkets in Ghana goes back to the mid-1990s (Anku and Ahorbo, 2017; Reardon et al., 2005), attributed to the rise of globalisation, which has had an impact on the political, socio-economic, and cultural sectors in Ghana. For example, the wave of globalisation, together with structural adjustment programme (deregulation, privatisation, market liberalisation), created a new macroeconomic policy which stimulated the coming of foreign direct investment (FDI) that injected retail business into Ghana (Rodríguez, Berges, Casellas, Paola, Lupín, Garrido, and Gentile, 2002).

Political factors in the global system influenced Ghana, as was the case with other countries, to embrace neoliberal policies such as trade liberalisation to ensure easy movement and access to goods and services all over the world without any barriers (Oteng-Ababio and Arthur, 2015). The implementation of neoliberal policies led to the transfer of economic resources or forces from the public to the private sector. The embracing of the free market and capitalism led to the emergence of multinational corporations and non-governmental organisations into the international system. These multinational corporations and non-governmental organisations produced western goods at large economies of scale and sold them at lower prices. As rational beings, consumers wanted to maximise value satisfaction at a relatively lower cost. Shopping malls and supermarkets became a place for economic entertainment because of the low cost of entry (Ahmed, Ghingold, and Dahari, 2007). This shifted the behaviour and preference of consumers from the traditional markets to the supermarkets, which were considered to offer quality products at lower costs.

Several opportunities and challenges emerged subsequent to the coming of shopping malls and supermarkets in different geographical jurisdictions where they operate. Studies by Ahmed, Ghingold, and Dahari (2007) and Kaufman (1996) show that customers prefer shopping malls and supermarkets because of the short time spent purchasing the required items. The adoption of market power and economies of scale by shopping malls and supermarkets have had a competitive advantage over traditional markets (Anku and Ahorbo, 2017; Reardon and Gulati, 2008). The traditional markets were rendered less competitive or driven out of business due to their inability to change production practices to the standards of supermarkets and of the required volume (Anku and Ahorbo, 2017; Faiguenbaum, Berdegué, and Reardon, 2002; Reardon et al., 2005; Rodríguez et al., 2002). A similar situation is reported in a study by Faiguenbaum et al. (2002), indicating that traditional retailers in Chile were driven out of business by the supermarket revolution. Also, Reardon and Gulati (2008a) reported that an increase in the sales of supermarkets by 15% in a year resulted in a 2% decline in sales of traditional retailers.

The fast rise of shopping malls and supermarkets is a double-edged sword as the low prices of food items have become a challenge for the traditional market system (Anku and Ahorbo, 2017; Reardon and Hopkins, 2006). In developing countries, the coming of supermarkets and shopping malls sparked a conflict between traditional market retailers and their counterpart shopping malls or supermarkets (Anku and Ahorbo, 2017). Pricing, quality, and convenience are indicated as the cause of the conflict between the traditional markets retailers and supermarkets or shopping malls (Anku and Ahorbo, 2017; Reardon and Hopkins, 2006). In addition, scholars (i.e. Anku and Ahorbo, 2017; Reardon and Gulati, 2008b; Reardon, Henson, and Gulati, 2010) are of the view that the utilisation of market power and economies of scale are the cause of the conflict between traditional market retailers and supermarkets in Ghana.

Despite the conflict, studies (i.e. Anku and Ahorbo, 2017; Coe and Wrigley, 2007; Humphrey, 2007) show that traditional market retailers have strongly resisted supermarkets in relation to the market of fresh food products. Furthermore, Anku and Ahorbo (2017) and Reardon and Gulati (2008) observe that the rise of supermarkets has become a 'double-edged sword' through lowering the prices of food for consumers, raising the income of farmers and processors, and helping farmers to gain access to a quality food market. However, the rise of supermarkets has posed a threat to the survival of traditional market retailers, farmers, and processors who are unequipped to meet the requirement and competition from the supermarkets (Anku and Ahorbo, 2017; Reardon and Gulati, 2008).

Over the past few decades, there has been tremendous diversification in the retailer sector in Ghana (Anku and Ahorbo, 2017). The 1990s is marked as the first evolution of the supermarkets in Ghana. Supermarkets such as Melcom started in 1989 as retail stores, and they were the only household name store in Ghana until the entrance of Shoprite in 2005 (Anku and Ahorbo, 2017; Melcom Group, 2010). Several factors are attributed to the evolution of the supermarkets, and these include urbanisation and an increase in income levels (Anku and Ahorbo, 2017). Other factors include liberalisation of FDI, intense competition, consolidation, multi-nationalisation and modernisation, which have all accelerated the spread of supermarkets in Ghana (Anku and Ahorbo, 2017; Reardon and Gulati, 2008).

Methodology

The qualitative approach was used to collect data for this study and to respond to the key research questions. Data were collected from purposive sampled respondents who frequent the Central Market as well as the selected shopping malls. The purposive sampling technique has the potential of helping the researcher to obtain information that relates to the study objectives (Saunders, Lewis, and Thornhill, 2009). The target sample population for the study comprised traditional retailers in Ho market and customers within the Ho municipality who patronise both the traditional market and the shopping malls for their shopping activities. The study participants included a) the market queen; b) market administrators; c) market toll collectors from the Municipal Assembly, retailers, and buyers. The selected customers for the study showed similarities in shopping behaviour regarding the regularity of shopping, location preference, sensitivity to price, customer rapport, and marketplace quality.

The data collection activities commenced in the second week of 2019 and terminated in December 2019, covering the Ho Central Market, Melcom Shopping Mall, and Stadium Gate Shopping Mall. The data collection process was delayed for one week due to interruptions in conducting interviews with selected consumers and vendors who initially did not understand the purpose of the research and assumed that this study would expose them to tax authorities and may have adverse effects on their business. The interview process was spread over three weeks with an average of between three to six respondents per week in the selected shopping centres. As shown in Table 4.1, 23 semi-structured interviews were conducted with willing and knowledgeable informants, comprising 13 interviews

Table 4.1 Biographical data on participants**

Biographical data	Number of interviewees	%
Age group		
20–30	8	36.36%
31–40	8	36.36%
41–50	2	9.09%
51–60	4	18.18%
Marital status		
Single	8	36.36%
Married	14	63.64%
Gender		
Male	6	27.27%
Female	16	72.73%
Work position		
Customers	10	45.45%
Retailers	12	54.55%
Number of working years		
1–5	9	40.9%
6–10	4	18.18%
11–15	2	9.09%
16–20	2	9.09%
21–25	2	9.09%
26–30	3	13.64%

Source: Field Data, 2019. **$N = 22$

from traditional retailers in the Ho market and ten (10) customers who patronise both traditional markets and the shopping malls or centres.

Essentially, 15 questions were asked during the interviews, and these focused on mall and traditional market usage, factors pushing shoppers to malls, buying preferences, shopping choices, coping strategies, and the perceived implications and effects of shopping malls. The data gathering was time-consuming because of the busy schedules of most of the traditional retailers and customers. Also, it was very difficult to access customers, so the researcher had no choice than to position himself at the shopping malls so as to scout and snowball for customers to interview.

The data, which were in the form of interviews notes, field notes, observations, and informal discussions with retailers, were analysed to gain an in-depth understanding of the choice between malls and traditional markets, the shifting of customers to malls, buying preferences, shopping choices, coping strategies, and the perceived implications and effects of shopping malls on traditional markets. Thematic analysis based on steps suggested by Braun and Clarke (2006) enabled systematic coding and the development of themes. Through exploratory, the study emphasised the choices and preferences of interviewees and encouraged them to provide answers that reflected their lived opinions. In analysing the qualitative data for this research, coding entailed reading all the 23 interview transcripts and isolating words and phrases that related to the main research question, namely buying preference, choice of shopping location, types of goods, coping strategy effects of the mall, and customer attraction. The data obtained from the interviews and secondary sources were organised and analysed thematically with themes generated deductively from the key research questions but inductively from the qualitative data. Broad analytical and thematic headings were derived from the research questions.

During the fieldwork, we obtained opinions on experiences of buying from the traditional market and the shopping malls, the ways retailers at the traditional market interact with customers whenever they go shopping, and their new experiences at the shopping malls. After reading and transcription of the data and field notes, codes such as 'shopping place', 'types of good', 'shopping environment, market-women attitude', 'distance and time spend at the market', and 'value customer regularity' emerged for further interrogation and analysis., these words and phrases were refined further and grouped into themes upon which this research chapter is based. All the interviewees who took part in the study gave their informed consent for the use of the data they provided. But the identity of the interviewees is kept anonymous and is not disclosed for confidentiality purposes.

In addition to the interviews, library, archival, and other secondary sources that provided information pertaining to shopping preferences and behaviour and the purchasing activities of customers were consulted and reviewed. These documents mostly included journal articles and books. This review of secondary data helped in the acquisition of information to respond to the research questions. What follows is a presentation of the findings based on the thematic analysis of the data.

The findings of the study

The effect of shopping malls on shopping place preference

The study sought to obtain views on the effects of the introduction of shopping malls on customer behaviour and retailers' responses. In this regard, respondents were asked for their views on whether regular customers have stopped buying from the traditional market system. Many key informants reported that they have stopped buying from the traditional market system, however, and a few participants disagreed with this statement. Customers change of behaviour in terms of stopping buying from the traditional markets was attributed to convenience, lower and discount prices of goods, packaging, late closure, and free delivery services by shopping malls. One of the interviewees said,

> I will agree. With the supermarket, everything is branded and packaged in an attractive way as compared to the local market. You go to the local market and the place becomes uncomfortable. There are some inconveniences, people pushing you. But if you go to the supermarket, you will skip all these inconveniences.
>
> (Game Shopping/customer 2)

> Everything has changed nowadays. Previously, a lot of customers used to come to buy but now they don't come as they used to. I know if there is no money in the system or it is as a result of the existence of the supermarkets. Sometimes, when I come to the market to sell, I only sell yam worth ghc 20.00 before I go home; yams are a perishable food item, they spoil if they are not bought on time. If you look around, you will see that hardly will a customer pass by. They are not coming. We in the market are encountering challenges.
>
> (Retailer 9)

Apart from the aforementioned, some of the interviewees, however, disagreed with the perception that malls and supermarkets have stopped customers from buying from the traditional market system. Their opinion was that customers could not get everything at the supermarkets. In the words of a retailer,

> No, I disagree. Some people prefer to buy their goods at the supermarket, for instance, Stadium Gate Shopping Centre. Some too prefer to buy theirs here in the market. Some people consider discount before going ahead to buy. The customers cannot get everything at the supermarket. For instance, they cannot get vegetables at the supermarket so they will definitely come here.
>
> (Retailer, 1)

Interviewees cited household items such as rice, drinks, plates, utensils, toiletries, shito, tin tomatoes, toys, electrical appliances, lipton, beverages, soap, milk, milo, toothpaste, and vegetables as the items customers mostly buy from the traditional market, but they are now available in the shopping malls and supermarkets. The reason behind the shift is that the items are well arranged for easy access, display of expiry dates and the general conditions under which the items are being sold. A customer at Melcom revealed,

> Normal plates that we used to buy at the market, now when you go Melcom or Stadium Gate Shopping Centre, you will find it there. Our toiletries too, you can get them at the supermarket. You can get the canned foods as well as shito, tin tomatoes, and even toys; you don't need to go the market to get them for your kids. One could also get electrical appliances.
>
> (Melcom/Customer 1)

> I sell varieties of tomato paste such as tasty tom, Gino, and the rest, but customers are now buying them from the supermarket because they prefer where they will get them at a cheaper price.
>
> (Retailer, 12)

The revolution of shopping malls and supermarkets have affected customer and consumer behaviour in terms of customer choice of where to buy goods and services in the Ho municipality. The general opinion was that customer preference for shopping malls and supermarkets was because they perceive that goods from the malls and supermarkets are of high quality, they have good customer service, and one can do one-stop shopping rather than multi-stop shopping, as found in the traditional market system. On convenience and quality of the goods, customers had this to say,

> Yes, because it is convenient and availability of product line whereby if you need something you get it at the same place. Unlike the traditional market where you have to buy in small quantities from different shops before you can exhaust your market list.
>
> (Melcom/Customer 5)

> Yes, they are, because from my perspective, I am very particular about the quality of the things I buy, especially when it comes to food products so like the example I gave if I go to the mall and find fish or meat stored in a zipped package and stored in ice then I know it is under the right conditions. So, the quality is definitely good; I will buy it. But if I go to the traditional market and find house flies all over the meat or fish, I know the meat or fish is contaminated. So, the food is already being contaminated even before buying it. So, definitely, it will influence my choice of place to buy such produce. So, I will prefer going to the mall than to the local market.
>
> (Melcom/Customer 1)

The introduction of shopping malls and consumer choices

Another issue explored in the study was the influence of shopping mall culture on consumer choice and preferences. Supermarkets are becoming a preferred place for shopping rather than the Ho traditional market due to convenience, quality customer service, proximity, suitability of the environment, and quality of the product. The general opinion from interviewees is that those who go to the shopping malls and supermarkets are salaried workers or middle-level income earners. This was reported by these interviewees,

> Yes, because I feel it is more conducive and the environment is okay as compared to the traditional market. The regular market is usually very congested. You have to move from one place to another to buy things and this becomes a bit stressful as compared to the supermarket.
>
> (Melcom/Customer 1)

> Yes, because when I tell them now a pack of indomie is ghc 1.10 and they get to a supermarket where it is sold at ghc 1.00, they go there instead. That is one of the challenges we are facing here in the market. The price differences! If we can all get the same distributors who will distribute to all of us at the same price, it will help solve the problem.
>
> (Retailer 12)

The majority of the respondents agreed that the coming of supermarkets had changed the entire system of retailing and buying, especially food items for household use in the Ho municipality. The general perception is that supermarkets have adopted several strategies such as price tag, discount sales, and facility expansion, which is not the practice of the traditional market system. Some of the interviewees observed,

> Yes, because when it comes to prices, if you pick Melcom, for instance, the prices are better than they are in the market. So, if I compare those prices, I think if I go to the supermarket to buy my things at discount prices, it is better.
>
> (Melcom/Customer 1)

> Yes, of course. Once there is the introduction of malls, shopping outlets, the change is significant when there is the expansion of the facility with other commodities coming on board. Previously, you could get only a few times at the mall and move to the traditional shopping areas to get the rest of the items. But now that more things are being sold in the malls, then it becomes an ideal choice of place.
>
> (Melcom/Customer 3)

The results indicate that some of the shopping malls and supermarkets pose a major threat to the traditional system in the Ho municipality. But this only depends on the kind of item to be purchased. An interviewee observed,

> Melcom, Stadium Gate Shopping Centre, Chances Mall, and the new one around barrack, LizzDee Shopping Mall.
>
> (Melcom/Customer 2)

There was price variation between items sold at the supermarkets/malls and those sold at traditional markets, and this affected the daily sales and profit of retailers in the traditional market in the Ho municipality. This means that the prices of goods sold at the supermarket are lower than those of the traditional market. One Melcom customer who was very critical about the price difference said,

> Some of the prices are the same; some are definitely different. Because not all the products have the same price, even within the mall, prices vary. They are all not the same. I know if I go to the market to buy a plate at ghc 10.00, if I go to Stadium Gate Shopping Centre I will have options; there will be ghc 5.00 and ghc 7.00. So rather than buying one for ghc 10.00 from the traditional markets, I would rather go to Stadium Gate Shopping Centre where I would get two for the same ghc 10.00. The price variation worries them seriously.
>
> (Melcom/Customer 1)

> Sometimes the price difference between us in the market and the supermarkets is ghc 1.00. I add only ghc 1.00 on some of the things I sell so I can make some profit at the end of the day. Perhaps, the prices on items at the supermarkets are cheaper than those in our markets. I sell some of the things depending on their size for ghc 32.00, while the supermarket may sell the same thing at ghc 31.00. Although the gap is not wide, customers will go and buy from there. The supermarkets can buy directly from the factories but we cannot because we don't have the same amount of money. The number of cartons of products they will buy will be more than ours so the manufacturers can lower their prices for them. But we don't enjoy the same privileges. You see, the tin of tomatoes I just sold? The profit I made on it was only 0.20 pesewas. Some people sell the same size for ghc 25.00, but I sell mine at ghc 22.00 because I want to sell at a faster rate. A carton of indomie contains 40 pieces; I sell each at ghc 1.10 while my other colleagues sell others at ghc 1.20. So the profit I make is just 0.10 pesewas on each.
>
> (Retailer, 12)

Product quality is one of the major reasons why customers frequently buy from the shopping malls and supermarkets rather than from the traditional market system in the Ho municipality. The general opinion is that products from the malls and supermarkets are of higher quality and safer than items sold at the local market. Interviewees who were critical about product quality said,

> Quality is very important because it affects the outcome of whatever services you are rendering. When you go to the mall, our fish, meat, and seafood are kept on ice, but if you go to the market, they put it in the open with flies all over it, which is not the right way of storing food. So definitely, I would rather go to the mall to buy such things because I know they are in the right condition.
>
> (Melcom/Customer 1)

> Besides, lack of money, quality becomes a factor, because the way in which we display what we sell here in the market is different from the manner in which they are displayed in the supermarkets/malls. You can see most of us display our tomatoes on a tray in the open, but at the supermarket, although they are displayed, they are kept in a conducive room. So some people feel we leave our goods in the sun for too long.
>
> (Retailer, 10)/(Ho traditional Market)

Copping with competition and other challenges

These findings demonstrate that the rise of supermarkets and shopping malls has brought competition into the retailing business in the Ho municipality. Generally, competition between supermarkets and the traditional market has emerged because supermarkets are now selling what were previously sold by traditional market retailers. In the words of interviewees:

I agree, there is a big competition; so it is up to both the malls and the traditional markets to satisfy their customers. Some of the prices at the mall are way better than that in the local market. So, people will prefer going to the malls than the local markets. And the malls do promotion sales which draw a lot of people to them.

(Melcom/Customer 1)

I will say I think so since they are now selling some of the food items we sell here in the market.

(Retailer, 2)

The general perception is that the traditional market is congested, items are kept under poor conditions, and there is also a lack of organisation and awareness that items are sold on a competitive basis. It was observed by customers,

Sometimes they (traditional markets) expose food items such as tomatoes and meats to the sun. They should cover them to make them hygienic. They also cover the fish, especially the smoked fish they sell.

(Melcom/Customer 4)

They should brand their goods or whatever they sell. For instance, Stadium Gate Shopping Mall (*letsa*) has branded its shop. The environment is a nice place people will wish to visit. But the market is crowded, so you will find it difficult to penetrate or go to wherever you are going. But for the supermarket, it is very easy to move about freely.

(Game Shopping/customer 1)

Traditional market retailers and their customers

Recently, retailers at the traditional market in the Ho municipality have not been pushed out of business by the coming of the supermarkets and shopping malls. The results indicate that no matter how big the mall/supermarkets become, people still go to the traditional markets to buy things. It was discovered that customers who are literate go to the supermarket, whereas illiterate people go to the local market. This was reflected in the words of a customer at Melcom,

I wouldn't say so because day in day out, new markets are emerging; so, I don't think they will completely be kicked out of the market. So the trend is that I am not trying to look down upon others, but it looks as if more of the literates are moving to the shopping malls, and the traditional market is still being patronised by people who are illiterate, although there are no studies to justify that. What I have observed is that the malls are reserved for the educated ones, so I am not sure whether the traditional market will be kicked out completely because the traditional market also keeps on growing.

(Melcom/Customer 5)

A retailer at the Ho traditional market also said,

> Not at all because, like what I said earlier, the customers cannot get everything at the supermarket, so they will definitely go to the market to buy such items.
>
> (Retailer 1)

The coming of supermarkets and shopping malls has led to many effects on the traditional market system, such as the reduction of the number of customers and the reduction of sales and profit margin. It was also found further that most enlightened individuals prefer to buy from the malls and supermarkets rather than from traditional markets. Results from both customers and retailers attested to this,

> Yes, it does because there are some people who rush to the supermarkets/malls rather than the local market to buy things, because the former is conducive and convenient. Everything has been segmented at the mall. You get there, you know this is toiletries and so on. But at the local market you have to roam to get these things. It is pushing them out of business because we can't guarantee the safety of their products.
>
> (Melcom/Customer 1)

> Yes, it has. Because people do not go there often.
>
> (Game Shopping/customer 3)

> It has affected us greatly because the amount of money I make on the sale of fish at the end of the day has come down. I don't sell much anymore. You can even see the fish I have displayed on the tray.
>
> (Retailer, 4)

Specific actions retailers and traditional market administrators should take to remain attractive

Several policy guidelines and recommendations have been made for traditional market retailers to stay competitive in the retailing business and to keep both old and new customers in the Ho municipality. Interviewees who were concerned about customer relations said,

> I think customer relations is very important. How they talk to customers is important because the person may not have the money at that moment to buy, but the person would like to know the price. Some people too will like to do window shopping before going back to do the actual shopping. So they should know how to talk to customers. They should find a better way of preserving their items to last longer, so that I don't buy something, get home and

realise it is not of good quality. Because they do that a lot, especially when you tell them, please rub it for me I am going to buy something by the time you come back they have given you something which has nothing to write home about. It is deception, so they need to be careful. They should also do promotions as the malls do. They could come together, do something to win the customers over because that is what the malls are doing, and they are getting people. Because when it is time to go to school, they do school promotions, Christmas promotions, Easter promotions, so you see everyone would like to participate and do something.

(Melcom/Customer 1)

Some of our colleagues who sell their meat in the open should begin to think of the safety of their customers and cover the meat. They should also take customer service seriously because, I told you, customers will keep coming back to you based on how they are treated.

(Retailer, 6)

Discussions

The study reveals that shopping malls are now an indisputable part of our retail trade in Ghana. Shopping culture is being influenced by many factors, including place, ambience, physical structure, and the type and style of displaying goods. It is further observed that shoppers are shifting from the traditional retail market to the malls. Customers appear to be more comfortable spending more money in the large shopping malls due to the planned shopping programme without higher perceived risk as compared to traditional retail markets. The preference of buying familiar brands in large shopping malls also pushes customers into purchasing goods of higher value as compared to other categories of shopping malls.

The study findings revealed further that malls have introduced considerable competition into the retail trade sector within the municipality. But the traditional market retailers have devised their own coping strategies to mitigate the adverse effects on their profit and retailing activities. However, the results reveal that the ambience of malls and their related variables such as physical amenities, time to reach, packaging, and price tag system are positively affecting customers' choice of shopping place.

Also, the results revealed that shopping at malls is also influenced by consumers' level of education and vocation. Further, traditional retailers are adopting and copying some new styles and strategies from the malls as a way of improving sales.

Administrative and managerial implications

The growing retail business and urbanisation have prompted the development of shopping malls in the Ho Municipal Assembly. However, the traditional retailing market system also coexists along with shopping malls though the latter poses a threat to the survival of the former. The coexistence of street markets and shopping malls in urban areas has been accepted by the consumers based on the sociocultural beliefs even though it is generating many operational problems.

The level of competition and perceived conflicts between shopping malls and the central markets include accessibility of shoppers, perceptions of consumers on the quality of goods, modern mall amenities and security, price of goods, cost of shopping, customer services, and overall shopping experience of consumers. The malls pose a continuous threat to traditional markets and are playing a major role in influencing customer preferences.

The management of the Ho Municipal Assembly would have to initiate strategic policies of ensuring balanced growth between the traditional market and the malls since both are a major source of internally generated revenue (IGR) for the assembly. A re-location policy of the traditional market to a relatively good and safe distance from the central business area and from shopping malls needs to be considered to help avoid potential conflict and enhance the sustainable growth of the traditional markets in the municipal marketplace. The Ho Municipal Assembly should allocate more resources and land in particular to traditional markets, and develop tenancy regulations to support prospecting and existing retail traders. The security of public places and conveniences should also be planned and incorporated in the traditional retail market system.

Conclusion

Shopping malls have become a common feature of the retail trade in Ghana's cities. Mall activities in the retail business sector have had a strong influence on the growth of traditional market retailers and a change of behaviour of customers. This study discusses the impact of the shopping mall on the welfare of traditional market retailers and the behaviour of customers with regards to the choice of shopping place and the goods to buy in the Ho municipality. The study results are mixed and indicate complex consumer decision-making styles towards shopping from these two types of business retailers. Even though the establishment of malls has changed the retail business, the traditional markets are still popular and preferred by many shoppers. Some middle-class customers express great support for shopping malls because of the ambience in the shopping mall environment. The discussions in the study emphasised that shopping malls brought about competition and challenges, forcing a good number of traditional market retailers to start changing their customer relations and general mode of operations.

Limitations of the study

Like many other empirical qualitative studies, this research had limitations regarding the number of respondents, data collection procedures, and processes and generalisation of the findings. The samples drawn for the study may not be enough to generalise the study results. However, the study results may be useful in understanding how malls are influencing the retail business sector and the shopping behaviour of urban consumers in Ghanaian urban retail markets.

Future research studies

The objective of the study was to examine the effects of shopping malls on the traditional retail market and shopping behaviour of customers. This study reviewed extent scholarly works and contributions on the subject and generated some interesting research findings in reference to the influence of shopping malls in retailing marketing. The study revealed retailers' concern about competition and conflict and the effects of mall culture on consumer choices of place and of goods to buy. There are few studies on traditional retail markets and shopping malls that have addressed these questions. Researchers exploring the area of traditional markets and shopping malls are encouraged to carry comparative studies on the effects of shopping malls on traditional retailers and consumer behaviour regarding place and preference for particular items to buy or not buy from malls and traditional market. Also, future studies may consider a quantitative approach and the use of very powerful statistical analysis to interrogate the relationship between shopping mall preference and traditional market retailing.

References

Ahmed, Z. U., Ghingold, M., & Dahari, Z. (2007). Malaysian shopping mall behaviour: an exploratory study. *Asia Pacific Journal of Marketing and Logistics*, 19(4), 331–348.

Anku, E. K., & Ahorbo, G. K. (2017). Conflict between supermarkets and wet-markets in ghana: early warning signals and preventive policy recommendations. *International Journal of Business and Social Research*, 7(10), 01–17.

Anselmsson, J. (2006). Customer perceived service quality in the supermarket and the discount store-examination of a service quality measurement scale in a Swedish context (No. 1).

Arku, F. S., Filson, G. C., & Shute, J. (2008). An empirical approach to the study of well-being among rural men and women in Ghana. *Social Indicators Research*, 88(2), 365–387.

Bednar, M. J. (1989). *Interior Pedestrian Places*. Whitney Library of Design, New York:

Betancourt, R., & Gautschi, D. (1990). Demand complementarities, household production, and retail assortments. *Marketing Science*, 9(2), 146–161.

Braun, V., & Clarke, V. (2006). Using thematic analysis in psychology. *Qualitative Research in Psychology*, 3(2), 77–101.

Coe, N. M., & Wrigley, N. (2007). Host economy impacts of transnational retail: the research agenda. *Journal of Economic Geography*, 7(4), 341–371.

Faiguenbaum, S., Berdegué, J. A., & Reardon, T. (2002). The rapid rise of supermarkets in Chile: effects on dairy, vegetable, and beef chains. *Development Policy Review*, 20(4), 459–471.

Felker Kaufman, C. (1996). A new look at one-stop shopping: a TIMES model approach to matching store hours and shopper schedules. *Journal of Consumer Marketing*, 13(1), 4–25.

Ghana Statistical Service. (2014). *2010 Population and Housing Census, District Analytical Report, Ho Municipal Assembly*. Accra: Ghana Publishing Corp. Retrieved

23 August 2019 http://www2.statsghana.gov.gh/docfiles/2010_District_Report/Volta/HO%20MUNICIPAL.pdf

Goldman, A., & Hino, H. (2005). Supermarkets vs. traditional retail stores: diagnosing the barriers to supermarkets' market share growth in an ethnic minority community. *Journal of Retailing and Consumer Services*, 12(4), 273–284.

Hamilton, S. (2003). The economies and conveniences of modern-day living: frozen foods and mass marketing, 1945–1965. *Business History Review*, 77(1), 33–60.

Lomotey, D. (2013). Madina market women defiant about moving from road side. Accessed 14 January 2020.

Mabogunje, A. L. (1964). The evolution and analysis of the retail structure of Lagos, Nigeria. *Economic Geography*, 40(4), 304–323.

Matsa, D. A. (2011). Competition and product quality in the supermarket industry. *The Quarterly Journal of Economics*, 126(3), 1539–1591.

Meng, T., Florkowski, W. J., Sarpong, D. B., Chinnan, M. S., & Resurreccion, A. V. (2014). Consumer's food shopping choice in Ghana: Supermarket or traditional outlets? *International Food and Agribusiness Management Review*, 17(2): 107–130.

Ministry of Local Government & Rural Development. (2013). Metropolitan, Municipal and District Assemblies in Ghana. *MMDA's Chart*. Homepage: Ministry of Local Government & Rural Development (MLGRD). http://www.mlgrdghanagov.com/default/index.php/mmda-s-chart. Retrieved 29 November 2019.

Minten, B., & Reardon, T. (2008). Food prices, quality, and quality's pricing in supermarkets versus traditional markets in developing countries. *Review of Agricultural Economics*, 30(3), 480–490.

Minten, B., Reardon, T., & Sutradhar, R. (2010). Food prices and modern retail: the case of Delhi. *World Development*, 38(12), 1775–1787.

MOFA. (2013). Ga east municipal. Ministry of Food & Agriculture (MOFA), Republic of Ghana. http://mofa.gov.gh/site/?page_id=1571. Retrieved 29 November 2019.

Orel, F. D., & Kara, A. (2014). Supermarket self-checkout service quality, customer satisfaction, and loyalty: empirical evidence from an emerging market. *Journal of Retailing and Consumer Services*, 21(2), 118–129.

Oteng-Ababio, M., & Arthur, I. K. (2015). (Dis) continuities in scale, scope and complexities of the space economy: the shopping mall experience in Ghana. *Urban Forum* 26(2), 151–169

Patton, M. Q. (2002). Two decades of developments in qualitative inquiry: a personal, experiential perspective. *Qualitative Social Work*, 1(3), 261–283.

Rajagopal. (2010). Street markets influencing urban consumer behaviour in Mexico. *Latin American Business Review*, 11(2), 77–110.

Reardon, T., & Gulati, A. (2008). The rise of supermarkets and their development implications: international experience relevant for India (No. 589-2016-39798).

Reardon, T., & Hopkins, R. (2006). The supermarket revolution in developing countries: policies to address emerging tensions among supermarkets, suppliers and traditional retailers. *The European Journal of Development Research*, 18(4), 522–545.

Reardon, T., Henson, S., & Gulati, A. (2010). Links between supermarkets and food prices, diet diversity and food safety in developing countries. Trade, food, diet and health: perspectives and policy options, Vol(Issue No), 111–130.

Reardon, T., Timmer, C. P., &Berdegué, J. A. (2005). Supermarket expansion in Latin America and Asia. *New Directions in Global Food Markets*, 47–61.

Rodríguez, E., Berges, M., Casellas, K., Paola, R. D., Lupín, B., Garrido, L., & Gentile, N. (2002). Consumer behaviour and supermarkets in Argentina. *Development Policy Review*, 20(4), 429–439.

Saunders, M., Lewis, P., & Thornhill, A. (2009). *Research Methods for Business Students*. Essex. Financial Times/Prentice Hall.

Schipmann, C., & Qaim, M. (2011). Modern food retailers and traditional markets in developing countries: comparing quality, prices, and competition strategies in Thailand. *Applied Economic Perspectives and Policy*, 33(3), 345–362.

Suryadarma, D. (2011). Competition between traditional food traders and supermarkets in Indonesia.

Suryadarma, D., Poesoro, A., Budiyati, S., Rosfadhila, M., & Suryahadi, A. (2010). Traditional food traders in developing countries and competition from supermarkets: evidence from Indonesia. *Food Policy*, 35(1), 79–86.

Taylor, J. W. (2007). Forecasting daily supermarket sales using exponentially weighted quantile regression. *European Journal of Operational Research*, 178(1), 154–167.

Urbany, J. E., Dickson, P. R., & Kalapurakal, R. (1996). Price search in the retail grocery market. *Journal of Marketing*, 60(2), 91–104.

5 ICT usage in supermarkets in East Africa

Benefits, challenges, and way forward

M. Kagoya Sumaya and A. R. Mushi

Introduction

Information and communication technology (ICT) has recently altered the way transactions are performed for businesses such as supermarkets in Africa and the world over (UN, 2018). Indeed, customers view the world as one village and one shopping centre where they can view and compare different products and prices from different continents, make a preferred choice, order, and get goods delivered just by clicking a button at any time (Kagoya, Maiga, and Jani, 2019).

In developed countries, most supermarkets utilise ICTs and reap the rewards in their day to day business operations. For example, they use ICT to sell merchandise to their customers, manipulate payments at the checkouts, monitor and control stock via automated orders for additional merchandise when stock is limited. In addition, ICTs can be used in stock management, hence meeting customer demands and satisfaction and also providing sales maximisation and hence maximisation of profit.

However, according to a UN report, 60% of African supermarkets, especially those in East Africa, are still using manual systems to conduct their business. Various reasons for this have been reported, including the cost of the ICT infrastructure, which is prohibitive with ever-changing technology (UN, 2018). It is expected that the cost component may not be an inhibiting factor when compared to the business benefits emanating from improved ICT technology to customers borrowing it from successful systems in the developed countries. Despite its importance, little has been done to investigate the extent of ICT use in supermarkets in East Africa and the challenges and recommendations for the way forward.

The region has witnessed the failure of some supermarket chains and a slow pace of expansion for others in recent years. It is important to find the contribution of ICT to the survival of these businesses and the mannerin which technology could be used to improve supermarkets' performance in the region. This chapter reviews the literature addressing ICT usage in supermarkets and the associated benefits and contributions of the same to the sustainability of supermarkets in the East African region, the challenges of implement ingICT technologies in the supermarkets in the region, and recommendations for helping businesses improve their performances using ICT tools.

DOI: 10.4324/9780367854300-5

ICT usage in supermarkets in East Africa 71

The next sections are organised as follows: first, the literature on ICT usage models and challenges in supermarkets is reviewed, followed in the second section by the methodology used in the study. The third section presents a discussion of the findings, and finally a conclusion with recommendations for the way forward.

Conceptual framework

The study employed a framework adopted from Giotopoulos et al. (2017) as applied to SMEs. In this framework, the determinants of adoption of ICT are technological competencies, the firm's human capital, internal organisation, and environmental and firm characteristics. The indicators of ICT adoption include the intentions of the firm, infrastructure, the extent of internet connectivity, and e-sales and e-procurement, as presented in Figure 5.1.

This framework fits well with supermarket activities as part of SMEs. Technological competencies are essential for supermarkets to be aware of the available technologies and the best ways of exploiting ICT for improving

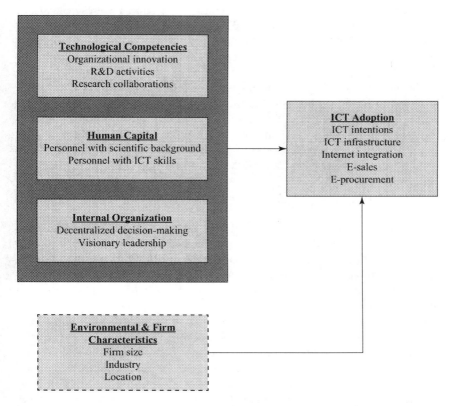

Figure 5.1 ICT adoption framework. (Source: Giotopoulos et al. 2017.)

performance. A supermarket business is expected to engage in R&D activities within ICT in collaboration with ICT research firms and specifically universities through corporate social responsibility measures. This will ensure that the business is always on top of technological advancements in regard to ICT.

Technological competencies are also linked to business human capital with scientific background or personnel with ICT skills. It is important to conduct training of the personnel from time to time to enable them to get abreast of the changing technology, and adopt and exploit new knowledge. Furthermore, the internal organisation structure contributes immensely to ICT adoption and use in the organisation. Specifically, decentralised structures allow for the involvement of all levels of employees in the decision making and therefore create a sense of ownership and willingness to use the technology in their daily activities. Visionary leadership is required if the supermarket is to adopt and use ICT to improve performance.

According to the Giotopoulos model in Figure 5.1, environmental characteristics and business features are also essential determinants of ICT adoption and use in any SME firm. These characteristics include business size and location, as supermarket size may determine the levels of technology adoption. The fact that the supermarket is located in the region implies that there are features that must be considered if ICT use is to be successful. For instance, one must invest in standby generators, consider customer background knowledge in creating user-friendly interfaces, and many other factors, which may vary from region to region around the world.

The indicators of ICT adoption and use include ICT intentions, in other words, the extent to which the business has implemented or intends to implement specific actions related to ICT, the level of ICT infrastructure in place, the number or percentage of business functions that the internet integrates, the supermarket e-sales activities, and supermarkets e-procurement activities. The framework was therefore used to guide the methodology and presentation of the findings.

Empirical literature review

A number of authors (i.e.Reese, 2018; Kagoya and Mkwizu, 2019a; Masele and Kagoya, 2018; Foster, Graham, Mann, Waema, and Friederici, 2018; Duncombe and Heeks, 2002; Perisa, Perakovic, and Vaculik, 2017; Kagoya and Mkwizu, 2019b) have researched ICT usage in general. Despite the plethora of studies, little has been done on ICT usage in African supermarkets, specifically in the East African region.

ICT applications in the supermarket business can be viewed in two forms, namely physical and online systems. Physical shopping involves direct customer visits to the supermarket while online shopping is done through the internet, followed by the delivery of the goods to customers using various transport facilities. This review is categorised in terms of the workflows of the supermarket business from the input–process–output model. Input processes reviewed in this work include inbound logistics, store operations, and human resource management. The process activities include customer servicing, pricing, product promotions, delivery, and marketing research data collection. The output is basically the assessment of business performance with respect to profit, customer satisfaction, market share, and competitive advantage for future business expansion. The traditional and online system workflows mainly differ in order processing and vehicle routing plans, as shown in Figure 5.2.

Inbound logistics

Transportation systems need information in order to manage logistical processes effectively. These processes normally require integration of activities such as inbound transport, warehousing, and fleet planning in order to save on cost and other objectives, including the environment and time. ICT is very important because, through these technologies, companies can make the right information available at the right place and at the right time (Introna, 1991). Hidalgo and Albors (2010) applied the Structure–Conduct–Performance (SCP) conceptual framework to investigate the drivers of ICT adoption in transport and logistics systems in the European Union and concluded that growth of the transport and logistics sector through innovations had a positive impact on the overall economy in the European Union. The current application of ICT is supported by a number of technologies that are growing over time. These include local and wide area networks and recently the development of web technologies, which have brought new concepts such as cloud computing (Weber, 2010). There is an ever-increasing use of wireless technologies such as mobile phones, QR codes, radio frequency identification (RFID), and telematics tracking (Harris et al., 2015). Eckhardt and Rantala (2012) discuss the use of intelligent logistics centres in transport systems, focusing on business logistics models for area-level automatic identification (AutoID) services based on RFID technology, which was applied successfully in a case study in Finland.

Western African researchers analysed the impact of the use of ICT in logistics activities in the region. For example, a study by Adebambo and Toyin (2011) in

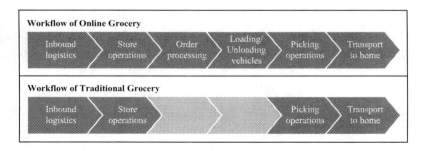

Figure 5.2 Comparison of traditional and online grocery shopping activities. (Source: Tadei et al. 2016.)

western Nigeria revealed that there is a strong relationship between ICT usage and the performance of logistics activities, although managers concentrated more on taking advantage of ICT facilities to reduce costs than improving service levels. Ekene (2014) studied the usage of ICT in logistics systems in south-eastern Nigeria. The results indicated that ICT adoption by then was 37% in the region for logistic operations and revealed that the impact of ICT use was very high for companies that adopted the technology. However, 37%adoption of ICT is rather low, and the author recommends that more efforts be made to improve the situation through training and building intelligent systems.

One of few papers on East Africa that relates to supermarkets is by Mlimbila and Mbamba (2018), who investigated the role of ICT usage in the performance of port logistics operations from the Dar es Salaam port in Tanzania. This port is the main gate for the import of products, which also feeds the supermarket business. Their findings indicate the existence of a relationship between the level of ICT usage and a decrease in shipping and trucking costs leading to a timely delivery of goods and services, an increase in trade volume, and an improved organisational logistic capability. Apart from cost saving, the transportation of groceries and other products must be conducted in a way that considers environmental factors such as the reduction of emissions. A study conducted by Wang et al. (2013) on UK grocery stores revealed a significant contribution of ICT usage in the reduction of CO_2 emissions. These were achieved through various processes, which were ICT enhanced, including centralised manufacturing, reducing order frequency through the consolidation of orders, creating new distribution channels for delivery convenience, promotion, and shelf availability to reduce fleets. A thorough review of the literature on ICT for logistics and transportation is presented by Perego et al.(2010),who classify them into public and private transportation systems. Their research revealed, among other things, that most of the literatureis conceptual or empirical-based with little simulation and modelling.

Despite the prevalence of research work on ICT usage in transportation and logistics systems in the developed world, there is very little research on supermarkets in East Africa. Most of the studies in the region focused on general applications of ICT to development and were not specific to the use of ICT in supermarket transportation systems (see Matambalya and Suzanna, 2001; Yonazi et al.,2012;Esselaar and Adam, 2013). Thus, there is a research gap in these studies as they do not specifically address ICTs in supermarkets despite their importance on the success of the business and protection of the environment. Given the economic growth in the region and business expansion opportunities, it is important to establish the extent to which ICT can be applied in transportation and logistics and learn from best practices around the world.

Storage, order, and delivery processing

From a processing point of view, supermarket activities are associated with product processing (inventory control), improved customer services through state-of-the-art ICT facilities such as Electronic Point of Sale (EPOS), Electronic Funds

Transfer Point of Sale (EFTPOS), product item locations, issuing and processing loyalty cards, data collection tools for business market research, and delivery mechanisms tools.

Dube and Gumbo (2016) investigated the use of ICT in supermarkets in Zimbabwe and found that most of the supermarkets use ICT technology, including point of sales (POS) and mobile money, although the majority of customers still preferred transactions using cash. Despite challenges associated with network connection problems and poor adoption by customers, the study revealed major benefits of the use of ICT in supermarket processes for those who apply the technology and therefore recommended measures to improve the situation.

Awuah-Gyawu et al. (2015) studied the application of warehouse and inventory management systems at Unilever Ghana Limited. They found that the major ICT tools used in the company are the WMS and CCTV cameras. Despite the challenges associated with training, costs, and power outage, they found a positive relationship between ICT usage and performance of warehouse and inventory systems.

Interestingly, a few studies in ICT applications in supermarkets in East Africa are associated with Kenyan markets. Nyakango and Rotich (2016), for instance, studied the influence of ICT tools in inventory management using the case of Uchumi supermarkets in Kenya. The study concentrated on the application of vendor managed inventory and distribution resource planning systems and revealed that ICT usage was essential for the efficiency of inventory systems. Another study was conducted by Achieng et al. (2018) about the influence of inventory management practices in retail outlets in the city of Nairobi.

However, they noted that inventory process automation was given the least priority and therefore calls for supermarkets to improve automation, which indicates the necessity of improving ICT usage in inventory management. Similarly, a study by Kitheka and Ondiek (2014)in western Kenya revealed a good application of inventory management practices with the exception of automation systems. Project investments of large supermarkets were investigated by Waweru and Ngugi (2015) in relation to the role of ICT in Nairobi supermarkets in Kenya. Their results indicated a significant positive contribution of ICT to investment costs, employee competence, ICT policy, and government regulations. A similar study was conducted in Indonesia by Surahman and Gunadi (2018) on the agility of a supermarket's supply chain using inventory control and ICT systems. The study also concluded that ICT is highly important for inventory management in order to meet the challenges of quick response requirements in supermarkets. In a nutshell, all the studies are in agreement that ICT tools are very important in the supermarket business in terms of logistics and inventory management. However, studies in the region indicate a low application of automation processes, which implies low ICT usage in supermarkets.

ICT's role in supermarket performance in general

ICT's role in supermarket performance refers to assessing the performance of the system in terms of profits, customer satisfaction, market share/expansion, competitive advantage, and others. According to Hjort and Poulsen (2018), ICT usage, specifically the internet, resulted in 23%of business firms' net entry into business in South Africa. They also report that ICT usage resulted in higher value-adding sectors and a substantial rise in productivity levels among Ethiopian Manufacturing firms. In addition, they maintain that ICT usage increased firms' exports and imports, increased communications by 13% when coupled with more on-job training among employees. However, they did not specifically address the case of supermarkets, but rather the aspect was implied through the general discussion.

Foster et al. (2018) undertook a qualitative study examining Kenyan and Rwandan firms in the tea, tourism, and business process outsourcing sectors from a global-value-chains perspective. The study concluded that increased connectivity (that is, internet connection) results in an increase in sales and hence larger profits.

A study conducted by Duncombe and Heeks (2002) in Botswana examined information needs and sharing techniques among rural micro-entrepreneurs. Their findings revealed that *mobile telephony* could be beneficial to informal businesses, contrary to other ICTs, which made it difficult for single persons to cope with text, the internet, and fax. Therefore, to circumvent such challenges, they recommended that these technologies be routed via well-informed intermediate companies.

From the literature above, it is clear that ICT infrastructure, especially internet connectivity in a country, is of paramount importance to its usage in business, including supermarkets. According to Internet World Statistics (Internet World Stats, 2020), internet penetration in the region is growing very fast. Tanzania, for example, has a penetration of 38.77% of the population while Uganda has above 40%, and Kenya is leading with over 87% of the population. The rate of internet growth in the region for the past ten years, according to the Internet World Stats, is above 20%, which is very promising for business growth. Given this internet status, it is expected that businesses in the region will take advantage of the situation to improve services through ICT usage, especially through internet facilities.

The adoption of information systems simplifies business processes and removes unnecessary activities. Information systems add control to employee processes, ensuring that only users with the applicable rights can perform certain tasks (Foster et al., 2018). ICT usage provides rich current information that aids businesses (supermarkets inclusive) and other cluster firms to become creative and execute more innovative tasks as they develop very strong linkages and networks within themselves (Grant, 2015; Foster and Heeks, 2013).

Through ICT, Supermarkets can utilise special tools such as *artificial intelligence techniques* to study and track their customers' patterns and increase their online capabilities. It should be remembered that the obtained intelligent data can raise sales and chatbots can aid potential and actual customers to get information and purchase anytime anywhere while online; hence, locking them in as they get maximum utility or total satisfaction (Murphy and Carmodys, 2015).

In this information technology era, with the presence, adoption, and implementation of ICTs and information systems in various businesses, such as supermarkets, managers do not bother to manually manage their data and information via hard copies and registers. This can be done by utilising data mining tools to extract all the comprehendible pieces of historical data required at that moment of their business from comprehensive and sophisticated databases.

Information systems store, update, and analyse information, which the company can use to access solutions for current or future problems. Furthermore, these systems can integrate data from various sources, inside and outside of the company, and keep the company up to date with internal performance and external opportunities and threats.

Similarly, with the stiff competitive business environment in the 21stcentury, ICT should be viewed and implemented as a strategic means of decreasing the workload and complying with obligatory rules and regulations in line with quality standards using analytic data techniques (Ojanpera et al.,2017).

It is also worth noting that ICT usage in businesses such as supermarkets can enable an upsurge of accuracy, effectiveness, and efficiency via jettisoning (discarding) redundant routines. More so, ICTs can be used to make sale analyses so as to determine which products are frequently sold to which kind of customers and vice versa. This enables the trackingof purchasing habits of loyal customers, who may be rewarded, managing inventory, and improving business process re-engineering (Paunov and Rollo, 2015).

The usage of ICT deletes repetitive tasks and increases accuracy, hence permitting employees to concentrate on more high-level functions. Additionally, in supermarkets, as with any other businesses in Africa, IS can also lead to better business planning and implementation through effective monitoring and comparison against established criteria, which results in high productivity (Haller and Lyons, 2015). More so, ICT usage can help people in Africa to get jobs in supermarkets and elsewhere, hence to achieve one of the sustainable development goals of employment for all (UN, 2015, SGD 8).

The study carried out by Ojanpera et al. (2017) to examine the relationship between broadband internet connectivity and the African knowledge economy indicates a positive relationship between internet connectivity (ICT usage) in business, academic work, and productivity.

From the literature above, it is apparent that only a little has been done in the region on the extent of the use and impact of ICT specifically to the supermarket business. As the business is facing challenges that have forced some of the big chains to close, it is important to understand the extent of exploitation of ICT in supermarkets and find out whether technology can be used to improve performance.

Methodology

This study aimed at examining the benefits, challenges, and prospects of ICT usage in supermarket businesses in East Africa. Using a qualitative method, data were gathered using an interview guide, and analysed using a thematic analysis technique and supplemented with secondary data. Samples were collected from five supermarkets around Dar es Salaam, specifically Mlimani City Mall and individual supermarkets within the mall. The supermarkets studied requested we not mention their trade names for confidentiality reasons.

The selected supermarkets served as a good representation of East African supermarkets. This is supported by the fact that the major supermarkets have their stores across the region and have therefore similar features. ICT usage was investigated in accordance with the conceptual framework by Giotopoulos et al. (2017), as described in the literature review section, which was categorised into four factors, namely technological competencies, human capital, internal organisation, and environmental characteristics. The investigated indicators included business intentions, infrastructure, internet integration, e-sales, and e-procurement activities to guide the data collection tool and findings.

Findings and discussions

The study investigated the major benefits of ICT usage in supermarkets through the conceptual framework. These are discussed with respect to responses from the questionnaire guide as follows:

Technological competencies

The study intended to find out the involvement of supermarket businesses in research on ICT. None of the interviewed supermarkets had participated in ICT research. They were users of ICT but had no involvement in research.

Supermarkets need to be creative and work with local universities through corporate social responsibility strategies to come up with training programmes that can create a pool of competent personnel. It is ironic that there are thousands of graduates annually from East African universities who have no job, while the supermarkets are poaching the few available employees from each other.

Human capital

Only a few staff in the ICT department had competencies in technology and were responsible for recommending the acquisition and maintenance of new technologies. As a consequence, staff had been complaining about complicated systems that they could not handle, resolving to go back to manual systems due to difficulties in understanding and using the new technologies.

One of the respondents had this to say,

> ... we have the challenge of untrained staff, so we have to keep on training them all the time on how to use the tools we have in place. This is time-wasting, and no sooner have we finished training them, they leave for greener

pastures in other places hence wasting business resources for training and recruiting new staff to fill in the vacancies.

Internal organisation

As pointed out earlier, the internal organisational structure is an important aspect in the successful acquisition and usage of ICT. Decentralisation is considered in the framework as an important managerial decision in order to provide opportunities for staff to participate fully in the development of the institution. In general, visionary leadership is a quality that is crucial for a successful business.

As presented in the recommendation section, staff are complaining about a lack of proper training, unfair work shifts, imposed technologies that are difficult to understand, poaching of competent staff by other supermarkets, and long queues due to scheduling of a few staff in POS. This is a clear indication that supermarket business managers need to involve staff in solving problems associated with business performance, rather than using a top-down approach which demoralises staff and reduces business performance.

Environmental characteristics

According to the framework, the adoption of ICT is dependent on the business environment, including type, size, and location. The supermarkets investigated included large chains with branches across East Africa and that intended to expand into other urban locations. Business growth must be guided by proper information and business plans, which are based on data analysis and well-calculated demand forecasting. In this respect, one of the respondents had this to say,

> We have managed to open new branches in different locations via internet-based market research and advertising through our websites; this has resulted in business growth, hence increased sales and profits.

The supermarket chains are therefore aware of the environmental factors; as a result, they are located in areas where decisions are based on market surveys, some of which are facilitated by the internet and other ICT tools.

It was also found prudent to investigate the use of ICT through the input–process–output model; specifically, looking at logistics and supply chain management, inventory control, staff scheduling, waiting for lines management in the POS, promotion, and demand forecasting. These are important components in the supermarket business as they can exploit the available ICTs for business performance, as discussed in the next sections.

Logistics and supply chain management

ICT usage was found to enable supermarkets in managing their logistics and supply chain as stated below,

The use of ICT helps us in the management of our supply chain from input, process, output and distribution of our products to our branches and to some loyal customers who purchase in bulk and require transport to their destinations.

Through ICT, managers can plan effectively for the supply chain, including inventory management, supply of timely products, forecast demand, and many others through automatic data capture and data generation strategies.

Inventory control

Although all supermarkets (100%) are using ICT equipment for POS, about 60% have revealed that they are using software for inventory control and product pricing. However, the respondents claimed that some of this software was complex and not user-friendly to the extent that they resorted back to manual systems. A respondent had this to say, on the matter,

> The ICT tool used in our business is so complex, and most of the staff do not understand it, and that explains why we opt to use the manual methods most of the time, which we know better although they are tiresome, but we can manage since we are used to them.

There is a clear link between better inventory management and profitability (Ashok, 2013). Through reliable and well-planned ICT systems, EPOS data can be captured directly from the source and used to update the central database, which in turn performs inventory control decisions depending on the performance of each product. A complete system that collects data from EPOS to inventory database, distributers, and planners is essential for the effective use of ICT technology. Collecting data through EPOS and then controlling the inventory manually is a missed ICT opportunity. Supermarket managers should consider taking advantage of their investment in ICT to the fullest.

Staff scheduling

Staff turnover has been noted as another challenge to supermarket operations. It has been noted that there is an insufficient number of qualified local staff to work in the supermarket stores. Managers train staff, and before becoming experts they are poached by other supermarkets. We wanted to know whether supermarkets had any software systems to assist managers in staff shift scheduling. It was revealed that managers rely on experience. This resulted in complaints from staff who are forced to work long days and during days off. The software systems could help managers create better staff rosters and manage emergency situations better.

Some respondents echoed the following,

> Among the challenges in our business is that we do not keep our staff for long, they are stolen by our competitors who come in disguise to buy goods

and end up snatching our good, hardworking staff. This in turn increases the workload on the remaining workers who get exhausted at the end of each day. It takes time to get a replacement and therefore results in delays in finishing work on time.

Each worker here has one day off, but the biggest challenge, which is highly annoying, is that anytime you may be called to work on the day you were meant to be off due to peak days and months, or a staff member is sick who was meant to be on that day or has left and may not come back. For me personally, I hate this and at times I switch off my phone, and my boss will be mad at me the next day.

Despite many efforts to improve customer experience with self-service checkout facilities and online shopping, employees are the backbone of any successful retail business. Jake (2018) presented an online staff scheduling system called findmyshift. The system is web-based and allows scheduling in advance in order to meet future busy periods. Many such systems exist and, if well exploited, can help improve staff scheduling to meet needs. For instance, Daniel (2019) describes a mobile system for staff shift management. In this case, staff and managers can use their mobile devices to create and access their shift schedules and take advantage of real-time alerts, better communication, budgeting, and instant access to schedules.

Waiting line management

As far as queuing systems are concerned, all supermarkets use point of sale systems, mostly bar-coded to tender services from cashiers. However, the number of cashiers has been a problem since managers want to save on costs by reducing the number of servers or allocating other duties to the same cashiers, leaving some counters closed at times when they are highly needed.

One respondent stated,

> Our managers want to minimise operations costs by having one serving point, but this has led to long queues during peak hours and customers get disgusted, and some opt to go away without taking the goods for fear of staying longer to get the service. Madam, I tell you, to me this strategy is not good at all as it reduces sale maximisation and hence profits for the business.

Another challenge leading to long queues is the use of ICT equipment which is not reliable and hence breaks down frequently. It is claimed that some of the ICT equipment in use is obsolete and cannot cope with the current needs of customers in the supermarkets. This is evidenced by a respondent who had this to say,

> The biggest challenge we have with our current ICT system is that it breaks down many times and it seems to be obsolete. I wish our bosses could move

with the current ICTs such that our business can increase and double in terms of productivity and achieve a competitive edge over other supermarkets.

Many articles have been written on the importance of ICT in the supermarket business. State-of-the-art technology is used to provide real-time data about arrivals distribution and special services that are required to reduce queue length. Balaji (2017)reported on the efficiency of the control system in supermarkets using a simulation in the Matlab/Simulink software. Balaji concluded that modern technology gives a better service to customers with less expenditure. A lot of technologies are available for helping to reduce queues through ICT; among them are electronic counting technologies. Hami (2016) identifies a number of counting technologies, including photoelectric sensors, radar and laser, infrared, and video-based 2D and 3D systems, which have been very successful. The East African supermarkets must embrace state-of-the-art technology by setting a sufficient budget to invest in the latest and competitive technology, especially aimed at reducing queues, which can be achieved using many of the available electronic devices.

Promotion and demand forecasting tools

It was revealed that the majority (60%) of the respondents were not using any software systems for promotion planning or demand forecasting. They relied on manual systems and the experience of managers when planning these important activities for the efficient and productive performance of the supermarket business. In general, the findings indicate some degree of ICT facilities being applied (40%). However, there are challenges associated with their usage which must be addressed if the supermarkets are to take full advantage of ICT in their business. Furthermore, the software is only used for data processing but not so much for professional business planning.

Demand forecasting is a challenging and very complex task in any business, as it defines all the planning activities of the business. Promotion strategies depend mostly on successive demand forecasting models. A white paper by Joanna (2019) briefly describes better promotion management in four steps, namely separating sales promotion data from normal demand, tracking the impact of promotion on demand, utilising quantitative models for promotion forecasting, and analysing factors bearing on demand and using them for planning promotions. All four steps involve the use of ICT tools in their implementation. Furthermore, promotion and demand forecasting depend on time series data in addition to other factors, such as cultural, location and the attractiveness of the stores. EPOS data, customer loyalty cards, and online transactions are among the main sources of reliable data for the forecasting exercise. A complete ICT system is therefore essential for the effective running of the supermarkets business.

Benefits to supermarkets when using ICT in their daily operations

Some respondents from the supermarkets who were using ICTs in their routine business operations were asked to state the merits they derived from ICT. The following were identified as merits: customers get served very quickly hence reducing long queues, efficiency and effectiveness in service delivery (customer care), customers enjoy the convenience of service delivery, and access to a vast amount of information about the available products. Supermarket staff mentioned the merits of ICT usage to include better management of inventory through software systems, the ability to forecast demand, and the ability to allocate staff well via staff scheduling systems, hence reducing staff turnover.

Competitive advantage

Proper ICT usage is definitely expected to provide a competitive advantage over non-ICT dependent business systems. This was echoed by one of the respondents, who stated that,

> The inventory management we are using helps us to keep a competitive edge over our competitors who are not using this system. We are able to forecast demand by stocking enough such that we can meet the customers' needs. This has also helped us to increase efficiency and effectiveness in our daily business operations.

Clearly, those using ICT properly have a competitive advantage over those who are not.

Quick and faster service delivery

Quick and fast service delivery is one of the advantages that draws customers from competitors since it is one of the desired features of the business. One respondent commented on the system as being beneficial since

> it aids customers to get quick and fast services and hence become locked into our business as they are satisfied with both the products we offer and the mode of service delivery all the time, including busy hours and days like weekends, where the number of customers triples. This helps us to reduce the waiting times for both the system and customers in the queue.

Vast information access

Information access is crucial to business success since customers need to make up their minds after they have obtained sufficient information about the products. A respondent had this to say:

> Managers, staff, suppliers, and customers can access a different and vast amount of information about the available products at their convenience. This helps managers to make strategic management decisions and to manage

employees, suppliers, and customer relationships, which in the long run results in sales maximisation and hence profits.

Easy and fast communication with internal and external stakeholders

Through ICT, supermarkets are expected to take advantage of the available technologies to simplify communications with stakeholders, collect feedback, and work upon raised queries in a fast and reliable mechanism. Social media is a relatively new set of tools that can be productively used to improve business performance. One respondent stated:

> ICT usage has helped us to communicate just in time with our customers, suppliers, top bosses and get feedback about our business operations which has helped us to plan well and survive the highly competitive business environment. We use social media, email, WhatsApp, Instagram, Skype, Twitter, websites, telephone systems to communicate to all our stakeholders as the need arises and update them about new products or reductions in price for some products, among others.

Easy payment transfers and staff development

Financial transactions have for a long time been a stumbling block for business effectiveness due to complicated procedures such as queuing in banks for services or taking risks associated with carrying a huge amount of cash in bags. With the current technology, one can perform many transactions directly from a mobile phone, saving a lot of time. Any forward-looking retail business must embrace this technology for a business' competitive edge. One of the respondents stated:

> ICT usage enables our human resource manager and accountant to send money to our banks through EFTS just in time. This motivates our staff to work and be productive at work since they are rewarded instantly towards the end of the month. Also, HRM uses the human resources management system in place to train, recruit, reward, compensate, promote, give leave, etc., the staff who qualify according to the system.

Why are some supermarkets not using ICT?

When some respondents were asked why they were not using up-to-date ICT technologies in their supermarket business operations, they cited a number of hindrances which entailed, among others, cost factors, lack of technological skills, ever-changing technologies, the complexity of the new technologies, ICT technophobia by some staffs and customers (fear of using technology), and privacy and trust issues.

On the issue pertaining to the costs and complexity of ICT systems, one respondent had this to say:

> The current technology is too costly to buy and maintain. We try as much as possible to minimise costs, and this explains why we use manual methods which are cheaper and not complicated like the ICT systems.

These results are supplemented by Billon et al. (2017), who argue that poor technological savvy, insufficient management, and low financial resources explain the low adoption and application of ICTs. On the whole, financial constraints appear to be the main barrier to firms' adoption and effective usage of ICTs for business processes in East Africa. The financial constraints problem could be solved by hiring local programmers who can develop local systems at an affordable price and also provide maintenance.

Lack of technical IT skills

On the above challenge, one interviewee held that it was a big challenge that discourages business owners from adopting and implementing ICTs in the supermarket as paraphrased below:

> ICT system usage requires IT skills yet most of our staff not only lack the skills but fear to use them. This, I think, discourages our bosses buying and implementing those systems in our supermarket business.

These results are in agreement with Franco and Garcia (2017), who found out that availability of ICT experts plus networking are vital determinants of ICTs usage, although their influence has been reported not to be significant enough. As a way forward, we recommend in-service training for staff so as to attain the ICT skills necessary to work competitively.

Incompatible systems

It was noted that the new systems that were procured and installed didn't work as they were incompatible with the old systems. As a result, the management decided to leave it, although they had a lot of hope that it would have solved some operational activities and would speed productivity and efficiency at work. The solution for this, we suggest, is that customised/bespoke systems should be developed by local programmers and tailored to business and customer needs. These systems should enable future upgrades to avoid problems of incompatibility.

ICT ethical issues (privacy issues, security and lack of trust in some ICTs)

ICT comes with the associated risks of information breaches through hacking or other means, which can be detrimental to business management. The investment must be made to secure data through state-of-the-art technology, which also requires constant updates and monitoring. One of the respondents maintained:

Some of our bosses feel that the systems which could be installed would deprive them of privacy for their business matters, as information may get to their competitors. Similarly, in our recent survey, we noted some of our older customers prefer to deal directly with staff than the systems to query aspects concerning products they are buying than dealing directly with the systems.

The way forward (solutions)

There is a need to build trust amongst staff and customers through sensitisation, seminars, workshops, and conferences on issues regarding privacy. Assuring customers that their credit card information will be secured and information on them will be kept private. Invest in state-of-the-art information security technology and constantly update it to ensure data security.

Additionally, there is also a need for training bosses and staff to raise awareness of the many benefits of the utilisation of ICTs in their business activities, coupled with benchmarking from successful big supermarkets and other businesses that have adopted and implemented ICTs in their routine business activities as revealed in the literature review.

Conclusion and limitations

This chapter examined ICT usage in supermarkets in East Africa; specifically, it looked at the benefits, challenges, and the ways forward in the East African region. The study findings divulged some use of ICT in supermarkets in the region, although some important processes were still done manually, and in some cases ICT systems were no longer working (obsolete). This study suggests that in order to survive in the ICT era driven by customers' demands, supermarket stakeholders, especially top managers and owners, must embrace ICT usage in their daily business activities. Supermarket owners and managers should support their business development and growth using ICT to help improve customer convenience, build a richer, more dynamic, and more fulfilling African customer needs. The use of ICT must follow systems analysis and design principles in order to ensure a complete and effective system.

Implications and recommendations

The findings imply that supermarket stakeholders such as managers and owners have to incorporate the latest ICTs fully into their businesses. This will help to address the challenges they face, which might have contributed to the sudden closure of some of the big supermarkets such as Uchumi and Nakumatt in Uganda and Tanzania and Choopies in Kenya. Supermarket stakeholders should also adopt Human Resource Information Systems to address the staff/employee related challenges. The systems will help the firms in the retention of employees, among other merits, leading to a reduction of high staff turnover and other Management Decision Support Systems. Supermarkets have the obligation through corporate social responsibility to work with local universities by providing scholarships and developing training programmes to create a pool of qualified young graduates who are ready to accept the jobs and thus minimise competition for the limited available staff.

The supermarket management team and proprietors should first studythe business environment and know the product tastes and preferences of potential customers of a given region and carry out risk assessment plans before starting a business. ICTs have a lot to contribute to this process. In addition, policymakers should ensure the provision of conducive environments for the proprietors of such huge businesses, which employ their nationals, so as to achieve the United Nations' Sustainable Development Goals of 2030, particularly the eighth goal.

References

Achieng, J. B. O., Paul, S. N., & Mbura, L. K. (2018). Influence of inventory management practices on performance of retail outlets in Nairobi City County. *International Academic Journal of Procurement and Supply Chain Management*, 3(1), 18–43.

Adebambo, S., & Toyin, A. (2011). Analysis of information and communication technologies (ICT) usage on logistics activities of manufacturing companies in Southwestern Nigeria. *Journal of Emerging Trends in Economics and Management Sciences*, 2(1), 68–74.

Ashok, P. (2013). Relationship between inventory management and profitability: an empirical analysis of Indian cement companies. *Asia Pacific Journal of Marketing & Management Review*, 2(7), 107–120.

Awuah-Gyawu, M., Adzimah, E. D., & Brako, S. (2015). Assessing the effects of Information Technology (ICT) on the performance of warehouse and inventory operations (The case of Unilever Ghana Limited). *International Journal of Innovative Research and Studies*, 4(9), 28–50.

Balaji, N. (2017). Efficiency of controlled queue system in a supermarket using Matlab/Simulink. *International Journal of Pure and Applied Mathematics*, 114(6), 283–288.

Billon, M., Marco, R., & Lera-Lopez, F. (2017). Innovation and ICT use by firms and households in the EU: a multivariate analysis of regional disparities. *Information Technology and People*, 30(2), 424–448.

Daniel, W. (2019). How mobile technology improves shift scheduling management. https://advancesystems.ie/how-mobile-technology-improves-shift-scheduling-management/.

Dube, C., & Gumbo, V. (2016). Adoption and use of information communication technologies in Zimbabwean supermarkets. *Applied Economics and Finance*, 4(1), 84–92.

Duncombe, R. A., & Heeks, R. B. (2002). Enterprise across the digital divide: information systems and rural micro-enterprise in Botswana. *Journal of International Development*, 14(1), 61–74.

Eckhardt, J., & Rantala, J. (2012). The role of intelligent logistics centres in a multimodal and cost-effective transport system. *Procedia – Social and Behavioural Sciences*, 48, 612–621.

Ekene, E. A. (2014). ICT adoption in logistics operations; an emerging trend for sustainable development and human capacity building in South-Eastern Nigeria. *Journal of Emerging Trends in Engineering and Applied Sciences (JETEAS)*, 5(7), 24–28.

Esselaar, S., & Adam, L. (2013). Understanding what is happening in ICT in Tanzania, a supply- and demand side analysis of the ICT sector. *Evidence for ICT Policy Action Policy Paper11*, 2013, Research ICT Africa (RIA).

Foster, C., Graham, M., Mann, L., Waema, T., & Friederici, N. (2018). Digital control in value chains: challenges of connectivity for East African Firms. *Economic Geography*, 94(1), 68–86. DOI: 10.1080/00130095.2017.1350104.

Foster, C. G., & Heeks, R. B. (2013). Conceptualising inclusive innovation: modifying systems of innovation frameworks to understand diffusion of new technology to low-income consumers. *European Journal of Development Research*, 25(3), 333–355. DOI:10.1057/ejdr.2013.7.

Franco, M., & Garcia, M. (2017). Drivers of ICT acceptance and implementation in micro-firms in the estate agent sector: influence on organizational performance. *Information Technology for Development*, 24(4), 658–680.

Giotopoulos, I., Kontolaimou, A., Korra, E., & Tsakanikas, A. (2017). What drives ICT adoption by SMEs? Evidence from a large-scale survey in Greece. *Journal of Business Research*, 81, 60–69.

Grant, R. (2015). *Africa: Geographies of Change*. Oxford: Oxford University Press.

Haller, S. A., & Lyons, S. (2015). Broadband adoption and firm productivity: evidence from Irish manufacturing firms. *Telecommunications Policy*, 39(1), 1–13.

Hami, A. (2016). Dwell time forecast and checkout optimization in supermarkets. Doctoral thesis, Charles Sturt University.

Harris, I., Wang, Y., & Wang, H. (2015). ICT in multimodal transport and technological trends: unleashing the potential for the future. *International Journal of Production Economics*, 159, 88–103.

Hidalgo, A., & Albors, J. (2010). The drivers of ICT adoption in transport and logistics services: an approach from the SCP model. 4th International Conference on Industrial Engineering and Industrial Management. XIV Congreso de Ingeniería de Organización Donostia-San Sebastián, 8–10September 2010.

Hjort, J., & Poulsen, J. (2018). The arrival of fast internet and employment in Africa. National Bureau of Economic Research (NBER) Working Paper 23582. Cambridge, MA.

Internet World Stats (2020). Internet Users Statistics for Africa. www.internetworldstats.com/stats1.htm

Introna, L. D. (1991). The impact of information technology on logistics. *International Journal of Physical Distribution & Logistics Management*, 21(5), 32–37.

Jake, W. (2018). Online employee scheduling for retail stores, shops and supermarkets. https://www.findmyshift.com/blog/online-employee-scheduling-for-retail-stores-shops-and-supermarkets.

Joanna, S. (2019). Better Promotion Management in 4 Steps. White Paper, RELEX https://s9783.pcdn.co/wp-content/uploads/2017/05/whitepaper_better-promotion-management.pdf.

Kagoya, M. S., Maiga, G., & Jani, D. (2019). An E-government readiness assessment tool in Uganda: a study of Ugandan Ministries. 14th ORSEA Conference Proceedings, Tanzania.

Kagoya, M. S., & Mkwizu, K. (2019a). ICT usage in panellist sessions to enhance completion of PhD studies in Public Universities: study of Uganda and Tanzania. ATLAS Africa Conference Proceedings, 2019-Kampala-Uganda.

Kagoya, M. S., & Mkwizu, K. (2019b). ICT usage in procurement practices for successful health care supply chain management: a study of Uganda and Tanzania. Proceeding of the 19th International Conference on African Entrepreneurship & Small Business (ICAESB, 2019), 33–42.

Kitheka, S. S., & Ondiek, G. O. (2014). Inventory management automation and the performance of supermarkets in Western Kenya. *International Journal of Research in Management & Business Studies*, 1(4), 9–18.

Masele, J., & Kagoya, S. (2018). Academic Safety and Health (ASH) requirements for ICT usage by PhD students in developing countries: a case of University of Dar es Salaam (Tanzania) and Makerere University (Uganda). *International Journal of Education and Development using ICT*, 14(3), 27-42.

Matambalya, F., & Suzanna, W. (2001). The role of ICT for the performance of SMEs in East Africa: Empirical evidence from Kenya and Tanzania. ZEF Discussion Papers on Development Policy, No. 42, University of Bonn, Center for Development, Research (ZEF), Bonn. http://hdl.handle.net/10419/84717.

Mlimbila, J., & Mbamba, U. O. L. (2018). The role of information systems usage in enhancing port logistics performance: evidence from the Dar Es Salaam port, Tanzania. *Journal of Shipping and Trade*, 3, 10.

Murphy, J. T., & Carmody, P. R. (2015). *Africa's information revolution: Technical regimes and production networks in South Africa and Tanzania*. Chichester, UK: Wiley.

Nyakango, J. N., & Rotic, G. (2016). Influence of information and communication technology tools on inventory management: a case of Uchumi supermarkets limited. *The Strategic Journal of Business and Change Management*, 3(4), 1–22.

Ojanperä, S., Graham, M., Straumann, R. K., De Sabbata, S., & Zook, M. (2017). Engagement in the knowledge economy: regional patterns of content creation with a focus on sub-Saharan Africa. *Information Technologies & International Development*, 13(2), 33–51.

Paunov, C., & Rollo, V. (2015). Overcoming obstacles: the internet's contribution to firm development. *The World Bank Economic Review*, 29(Supplement): S192–S204.

Perego, A., Perotti, S., & Mangiaracina, R. (2010). ICT for logistics and freight transportation: a literature review and research agenda. *International Journal of Physical Distribution & Logistics Management*, 41(5), 457–483.

Perisa, M., Perakovic, D., Vaculik, J. (2017). Challenges of Information and Communication Technologies in E-Business Systems.

Reese, B. (2018). *The Fourth Age: Smart Robots, Conscious Computers, and the Future of Humanity*. New York, NY: Atria Books.

Surahman, S., & Gunadi, S. (2018). Managing the agility of supermarkets supply chain using inventory management and ICT systems approach. *International Journal of Scientific & Technology Research*, 7(8), 125–129.

Tadei, R., Fadda, E., Gobbato, L., Perboli, G., and Rosano, M. (2016). An ICT-based reference model for E-grocery in smart cities. In Alba et al. (Eds.), In *International Conference on Smart Cities* (pp. 22–31). Springer, Cham. Publishing.

UN (2018). UN E-government Survey 2018: E-government in Support of Sustainable Development. New York: UN - Department of Economic and Social Affairs.

UN (United Nations) (2015). Sustainable development goal 8. Sustainable Development Goals Knowledge Platform. Retrieved from https://sustainabledevelopment.un.org/sdg8

Wang, Y., Rodrigues, V. S., & Leighton Evans, L. (2013). The use of ICT in road freight transport for CO_2 reduction – an exploratory study of UK's grocery retail industry. *The International Journal of Logistics Management*, 26(1), 2–29.

Waweru, E. W., & Ngugi, K. (2015). Role of information and communication technology investment on project performance of large supermarkets in Kenya; a case of Nairobi county. *International Journal of Innovative Social Sciences & Humanities Research*, 3(1), 102–118.

Weber, T. (2010). Cloud computing for business goes mainstream. Available at: http://www.bbc.co.uk/news/10097450.

Yonazi, E., Kelly, T., Halewood, N., & Blackman, C. (2012). The transformational use of information and communication technologies in Africa. The World Bank and the African Development Bank, with the support of the African Union, eTransform AFRICA project.

6 Assessing the technological relevance of South African supermarkets in the face of changing consumer behaviour

Tendai Chiguware

Introduction

Globally, the retail space has been undergoing a major transformation, driven partly by evolving technology and by changing consumer expectations and preferences. For example, retailers have introduced the use of self-checkout tills and loyalty programmes that not only benefit the consumers but also promote sales for the supermarkets. In some cases, the rapid emergence of strong supermarket chains in the retail sector and the proliferation of shopping malls and their preference as shopping spaces mean that the supermarket industry is forever changing. This growth not only responds to consumer demand but also in some cases to research on consumer behaviour. Consequently, there have been wholesale changes, developments, and trends globally.

This study therefore seeks to determine the extent to which the South African supermarket industry has managed to keep up with these changes and the possible reasons as to why some of the changes have not been adopted. A preliminary overview of the South African retail industry shows that South Africa has adopted most of the emerging trends in supermarkets (Makhitha, Van Scheers, and Mogashoa, 2019). This is especially so in the case of technology such as online shopping and loyalty programmes, which are increasingly preferred by consumers. This is probably because consumers are increasingly becoming tech-savvy and expect some level of tech-inspired convenience during their shopping (Rathore, 2016). While technology has made significant inroads in the South African supermarket retail industry, there are still some bottlenecks, which limit wholesale adoption of the innovations. For example, shops such as Woolworths and Pick n Pay that offer innovations including loyalty programmes and online shopping are not the preference for the majority of low-income South Africans. Additionally, there is a minimum threshold for one to fully access some of the facilities through technological innovations such as smartphones with the right shopping apps and the right debit and credit cards.

The two research questions defining the current study include the following: To what extent have South African supermarkets adopted contemporary retail technology in their daily operations? And to what extent has the technology adopted by South African supermarkets been responsive to consumer demands

DOI: 10.4324/9780367854300-6

and expectations? To answer these research questions, a desktop review was used. This technique involved using secondary material already published by other authors.

Evolution of the supermarkets in Africa

Before looking at the extent to which the trends in South Africa are consistent with, and reflect, global trends, it is important to look at the emergence and growth of the supermarket revolution in Africa in general. Global trends are immediately reflected in some African countries such as South Africa. As Reardon, Timmer, and Minten (2012) observe, the drivers of the supermarket industry are the same all over the world. These include the growth of disposable incomes and the need for diversifying from agriculture based industry. Other drivers of the supermarket retail industry include foreign direct investment from retail concerns and corporations and urbanisation. It is also important to note the significance of the rapid independence of African countries, which was immediately followed by the growth of black middle-class families whose numbers necessitated the presence of supermarkets. Reardon, Timmer, and Minten (2012) particularly note that although in all instances the supermarkets started in urban areas and slowly moved to the rural areas in Asia, that pace was deliberated accelerated. In China and Vietnam, for example, the need to move to the rural areas was not driven by profit, but it was facilitated by state investments in the sector.

Some authors believe that the supermarket industry take-off in Africa can be attributed to twin variables, namely rapid urbanisation and an increase in the black middle-class population size (Dakora, 2012). Touting it as the 'fourth wave' of the global supermarket evolution, Dakora (2012) acknowledges that the end of colonialism also gave an impetus to the supermarket industry in terms of both new potential customers as well as flows of investments. The author refers to the first wave like the one that occurred in East Asia and South America in the early to mid-1990s, the second wave occurred in South East Asia and Mexico in the mid to late 1990s, and the third wave occurred in southern and eastern Africa and in other countries such as Russia, India, China, and Vietnam. According to the author, the end of colonialism in many parts of the world released capital that was either limited or withheld because of apartheid policies, as was the case in South Africa, which was under international sanctions during the apartheid regime. Dakora (2012) observes further that the supermarket industry in South Africa evolved and developed to the point where it does not have to follow global trends, including relying on retail chains such as Spar, but it is capable of offering custom innovations, including formal support for Stokvels. Rather, the country has homegrown chains such as Shoprite that are expanding into regional markets, and setting regional trends of their own. In other words, the supermarket industry in South Africa no longer has to follow global trends like conventional supermarket layouts and focus on grocery retail as the primary business model (Juel-Jacobsen, 2015). Now, decisions are made based on the needs of local regions as well as an intimate knowledge of the local customer that dictates some of the sub-brands within the local chains.

The most recent venue for supermarket take-off is Africa, especially in eastern and southern Africa (Weatherspoon and Reardon, 2003). South Africa was chosen as a case study because of the size and significance of the retail industry in the country. According to the United States Department of Agriculture (2017), South African retail sales reached US$38 billion in 2017. To put this into proper perspective, the whole of the SADC region has a GDP of $737.33 billion. In other words, the South African food retail sector is roughly worth the same as the GDPs of Namibia and Zimbabwe combined (World Bank, 2019).

Technologies introduced by South African supermarkets

In line with international trends where the supermarket acts as a hub around which several other services are offered, the African supermarket has embraced the same trend. For instance, in several Shoprite supermarkets, consumers can purchase travel (bus and flights) tickets and send money at reduced rates at the Money Market counter (Janse van Rensburg, 2016). Additionally, Pick n Pay and Boxer Superstores have also entered into a partnership with Tyme Bank, where several of the banks ATMs are located in the store. As of 2019, Tyme Bank, through its partnership with the two supermarket chains, has established around 730 physical points and around 10,000 till points (Vanek, 2019). Considering that Tyme Bank itself does not have physical branches where clients can interact with the bank consultants, Pick n Pay serves as the *de facto* banking hall. It is also important to point out that that the relationship between Tyme Bank and Pick n Pay goes beyond providing access to Tyme Bank ATM infrastructure. Rather, the supermarket also has an extended partnership with the bank in connection to its Smart Shopper loyalty programme. Clients of the bank who opt for the Pick n Pay loyalty programme receive extra points when they swipe their cards; they receive an incentive for shopping at Pick n Pay as the points represent a significant saving over time.

The other feature, which is increasingly finding its way in the supermarkets, is the presence of pharmacies in-store. Both Shoprite and Checkers brands now have dedicated pharmacies in selected stores. This indicates a growing trend where a number of tasks and errands that would normally require a visit to several shops and outlets can now be accomplished at one point within the modern-day supermarket.

Still looking at the financial services offered within the supermarkets, there is a need to indicate the significance of the cashback programme in Africa, which allows shoppers to make withdrawals directly from the tellers (Venter and Dhurup, 2005). Considering the specific conditions prevailing in Africa, this arrangement has two practical advantages to the consumers. First, because the banks are not always located in all towns, with some only offering ATMs in small towns, this partnership makes it convenient for the shoppers to access limited banking services provided by the supermarkets, which have significant convenience to customers. Second, in many instances, the cashback at the tills does not attract any banking charges, unlike withdrawing the same amount of money from the banks either from the bank teller or from an ATM. The banking services within the supermarkets attract low-income earners whose incomes are severely eroded by bank charges. The cashback programme is widely available in South Africa with retailers own specific conditions on how the programme can be used, including the maximum limit of cash to be dispensed or customers' preference of whether they purchase the products first. The innovation represents a huge step for supermarkets in extending their services beyond the purchase of household items. Other important services South African supermarkets provide include collection points for the government's payments of social grants. This is significant because the first place that the recipients of social grants spend the money is the groceries in the supermarket itself.

Other emerging trends in southern African supermarkets include having technology-driven distribution centres that have streamlined operations and have significantly improved the supply chain capabilities. This is a departure from the conventional store-to-store procurement model. The new distribution centres employ sophisticated technology such as radio-frequency identification (RFID) scanning, warehouse management software, advanced transportation due to improved scheduling, and routing and telemetric software. According to Bone (2019), some of the benefits of these large distribution centres include a reduction in running costs, which can be passed on to consumers, low carbon emissions, and a better distribution of perishables. In the case of Spar, the distribution centres account for up to 85% of store needs, with the rest being made up by local suppliers. This is confirmed by Probyn (2017), who notes that the significance of the distribution centres is their efficient inventory management. While most of the benefits are not directly faced by the consumers because they are not customer-based, there are other benefits such as low price, fresh produce, and assurance of constant stock to customers. It is important to note, however, that while there are obvious advantages to the efficient and potential cost-cutting benefits accrued from large distribution centres, these same benefits become an entry barrier for small chains and family-owned businesses (Nair, 2017). As a result, there is a likelihood that the retail sector will become increasingly oligopolistic where large chains such as Shoprite, Spar, and a few others become dominant.

In line with new emerging consumer trends globally, one of the emerging trends in South African supermarkets includes the presence of food courts inside the supermarket. This makes the shopping experience holistic, family-oriented, and designed to provide an end-to-end experience so that consumers do not need to go to another outlet to eat after their shopping experience. One notable example is that of Woolworths, which has a restaurant section within its retail space. The other example is Shoprite, which provides an eating experience through its association with the Hungry Lion franchise, which is either inside or next to most Shoprite outlets. This follows an international trend of global chains such as IKEA, which, besides its core business, provides an eating experience as part of retaining its customers and providing them with an improved customer experience. Kinsey and Senauer (1996) provide two possible explanations for the rise of an eating experience inside supermarkets. First, according to the authors, the rise of major supercentres such as Wal-Mart, K-mart, Fred Meyer, and Meijer Stores with cheaper and generally price-conscious 'home meal replacement' options compels supermarkets to follow suit, so that they do not lose out to these supercentres who may provide even more options than those provided by the supermarkets. Second, the authors suggest that an increase in the number of two working adults in the homes means more disposable incomes, which makes eating at a supermarket while shopping more 'convenient'.

Another shopping experience that has been proving popular among the South African supermarkets is a 'pop-up' experience (Benn, Webb, Chang, and Reidy, 2015). A good example is supermarket employees having a hot dog stand outside the shop or a stand offerings free sample of various merchandise. This is an experience where various stakeholders, either independent or from the store family, pitch up a tent and offer extra services that are not normally offered in the store. This is usually in the form of selling hot dogs or a barbecue experience outside the shop where consumers can purchase a meal after their shopping experience. This can also be in the form of a booth offering samples of new products or banking partners registering new clients. As Baird (2018) notes, these are usually found over the weekend and come Mondays the tents are folded, and the pop-up vanishes to come back the next weekend, sometimes offering a new experience or product. Baird (2018) notes further that, when it comes to food, the pop-up experience with its informal set up occupies a niche area between the triangle providing a full restaurant experience, a meal on the go, experience of buying food from the supermarket deli section, and the semi-informal experience of eating from the open air of a mall food court. The author observes further that the pop-up experience brings the same experience to the supermarket, which a food truck would bring to occasions such as shopping events where the opportunity of consuming food in a semi-informal setting adds to the whole consumer preference of purchasing 'an experience' not just food.

One other trend that has attracted customer interest in the South African supermarket industry is online shopping. While this still represents a negligible fraction of total purchasing trends, it is still growing (Hung-Joubert, 2017). Almost all the supermarket chains, including Pick n Pay, Checkers, and Woolworths, offer online services. The most noticeable exceptions are the Spar and Shoprite brands, which happen to be among the largest, who still do not have online purchasing services. Such services are unavailable to Shoprite, probably because the brand targets lower-income consumers who are unlikely to be make use of the online shopping facility. However, while the online shopping experience might not have been common among all South African retail chains, one trend linked to online shopping and which is available across all the brands is smartphone apps. All the leading brands have mobile apps, which can be used by users for a number of things. In some shops like Pick n Pay, the apps offer a shopping portal, collect, and track loyalty points. As for Shoprite and Spar, the applications mostly serve to tell the customer of local specialities and the newest shops. As of 2020, Spar's application offers an additional functionality to register for the Spar discount programme, but this can be done outside the application. The experience varies from the sophisticated and machine learning-driven Pick n Pay application, which recommends products to the consumer based on their previous purchases, to the Shoprite app, whose features can be readily accessed with a simple search engine query. Thus, the South African retail market has embraced the growing trend of smartphone apps to make their services more accessible.

The trend towards online shopping has been steadily increasing and, in many instances, is now becoming common, as much as shopping in-store. One online trend, which has been exploited by some supermarkets, is the application of machine learning technology not only to offer customised marketing to the consumer but also to improve the whole purchasing experience. In a typical scenario, the shop keeps track of what each customer buys. This information is captured when customers swipe their loyalty cards. Over time, the machine learning algorithms start to discern and pick up patterns, like usual purchases, frequency of purchases, the usual times and day of the month the purchases are made, and most importantly the purchases that are usually made/paired together. With this kind of information, the shop is able to learn not only what the customer prefers but also to anticipate the needs of the consumer before they know it themselves. While there are several supermarkets with loyalty programmes, the Pick n Pay option seems to make the optimum use of machine learning. This is based on the customised recommendations that the shop pushes the customer to consume the product often at the exact time the consumer is considering buying the items. Currently, only a limited number of supermarkets are employing the technology, probably because the skills needed to deploy the technology are limited and conventional marketing still results in decent customer turnouts; it is possible that this is one of the options that will become a mainstream marketing experience, as more supermarkets start to offer loyalty programmes to their customers. It is important to note that although there is still the limited application of machine learning and artificial intelligence in general within the South African supermarkets, this is now common in other retailers such as Makro and Takealot, who over the years have developed a more robust way of collecting customer data instead of just relying on loyalty programmes. While there are debates and concerns about consumers' privacy when it comes to collecting user data, it is important to note that in the case of the two retailers cited above, expression of permission is sought from the consumers to track their online habits using cookies. In addition, at any point, consumers can revoke this permission by deleting the cookies from their devices. It needs to be acknowledged that the debate on consumer privacy on the one hand and consumer convenience on the other hand is more extensive and complex than the simplification provided above and has been significantly examined in the relevant literature.

In line with the current trend of making online purchases, home delivery, which is directly tied to online shopping, is also a new trend (Galante, López, and Monroe, 2013). What is interesting to note about the South African supermarkets is the extent to which they have tailored the delivery system to suit individual clients over and above the standard shopping options. For example, in Woolworths, there is an option to have fresh produce sent early and expeditiously with the rest of the basket following later. There is also the option of choosing a specific time window when they are sure to be home when the groceries are delivered. Some of the retailers also offer the option of shopping online and then picking up the groceries later at the store. All the supermarkets that offer online shopping also offer some kind of home delivery system, which in itself is standard and highly innovative in today's tech-inclined shopping climate. What is interesting therefore is that home delivery systems seem undeveloped when compared to other online retailers in South Africa who are not necessarily supermarkets. For example, Takealot, which is the largest online shop in South Africa, offers an overnight delivery system driven by its own logistics company. The organisation also offers personal collections, and these are technology-driven to make them as efficient and as time conscious as possible while delivering a pleasant experience to the consumer. Makro also offers an option for online purchases to be delivered to a locker from which the consumers can retrieve the purchases at their own convenience. As a result, while some of the South African supermarkets now offer a home delivery system, the experience, just like that of the mobile apps, is still fragmented, ranging from innovative to just mere presence with a lot of variable experiences within that spectrum.

Product placement is one of the strategies that, at first, was the preserve of supermarket chains in developed countries, but is now widespread even in South Africa (Cohen, Bogart, Castro, Rossi, Williamson, and Han, 2018). This strategy, which has been adopted by the South African supermarkets, is based on the study and understanding of consumer behaviour. Product placement puts the most expensive products, which the supermarket wants to sell, at eye level on the shelves, while cheaper options are placed at the bottom where customers either have to bend or kneel to look at or access (Cameron, Charlton, Ngan, and Sacks, 2016). As supermarkets understand their client communities better and the psyche that drives them to buy, more often more than what they need, some of the marketing strategies have become global. Considering the number of products competing for consumers' attention, product placement has become one of the primary marketing strategies in the supermarket industry. Most supermarkets have realised that besides increasing their profits through product visibility, they can also reduce costs by making optimum use of shelf space allocation and product display. As shown in a study by van Zyl (2016), product placement has become common in South Africa, with most supermarkets having more or less the same layouts. This is found especially at the entrance to the supermarkets as well as the checkout counter where items 'on sale' and a number of products such as magazines are prominently placed. To show the relative importance of product placement, not only in the developed countries but also globally, authors such as Aloysius and Buni (2013) suggest the adoption of the PrefixSpan algorithm, which determines the products to be prominently displayed based on previous purchasing patterns. The adoption of product placement by South African supermarkets shows that consumer behaviour is more or less the same globally (Gillespie, Muehling, and

Kareklas, 2018). The South African supermarkets' adoption of product placement as a marketing tool is an indication that these supermarkets are in line with the overall trends of other supermarkets.

Globally, supermarkets have come to realise that most customers have a unique set of expectations and preferences; supermarkets have been trying to match these with the services they provide (Jhamb and Kiran, 2012). Some of these trends, which include advanced security, a safe and family-friendly shopping environment, trained sales personnel, ample and safe parking, and a large assortment of merchandise and different brands, explain why there is a proliferation of malls and why most supermarkets now prefer to be located in the malls. Most importantly, supermarkets now seek to provide more than just a location where consumers can purchase groceries but also where they can get a complete (and enjoyable) shopping experience. According to Jhamb and Kiran (2012), there is a significant relationship between modern retail formats, their attributes, the changing preferences of consumers across these retail formats, and the marketing strategies followed by retailers for effectiveness and enhancing the sales of the retail outlet.

In view of what supermarkets do, one of the emerging trends is the gradual disappearance of local grocery stores because of the pressures from the big corporations (Borraz, Dubra, Ferrés, and Zipitría, 2014). Using the example of the Paraguay retail environment, the authors note that the rise of supermarkets in the past 30 years has seen a corresponding decrease in the number of small shops, as they largely fail to compete with supermarkets, especially the large chains. The disappearance may take the form of either a corporate takeover or going out of business when operating next to a large supermarket chain. Using the example of the slow disappearance of street corner chemists and pharmacies, Dixon (2007) argues that this disappearance is in line with the new global trend where supermarkets have evolved into a monolithic system, which is no longer limited to groceries, posing a threat to local bookstores, DVD stores, chemists, butcheries, cafes, liquor stores, bakeries, and pharmacies. This is because all these business models are now within the contemporary supermarket structure. As for the growth and expansion of supermarkets, Dixon (2007) notes further that the current supermarket is trying to grow not only by absorbing some smaller stores within the supermarket structure but in some cases by trying to control the whole value chain from end to end. Consequently, supermarket chains now own and manage farms and logistics centres, manage food laboratories, and serve as quality assurance agencies. They also produce food items either in their own kitchens or under contract from outside suppliers. Supermarket chains are emerging as major players in the distribution of petrol and the supply of entertainment needs, including books, films, music, and computers. Additionally, they offer dry-cleaning and photographic services, pet care products, gardening and homewares, beauty products, clothing, footwear items, and office supplies. Even some traditional business models such as boutiques and hardware shops, which seemed to coexist with supermarkets, are now under threat. This is similar to mobile phones, which have absorbed the functions of several standalone gadgets such as music players, cameras, and alarm clocks into a single device; the supermarket system has achieved the same. Most of the leading supermarket chains in South Africa have all these different functions, meaning customers see no need to visit individual bakers, butcheries, and drug stores as all purchases can be done under the same roof. In South Africa, all the chains have diversified their formats to include a variety of services. This has also been the strategy for targeting different income groups.

There has been a shift in buying patterns, especially in the townships where the penetration of big brands has put out of business the local 'spaza' or tuck-shops, on which township consumers used to rely (Competition Commission, 2019). According to the Competition Commission (2019 in Kroll et al., 2017), this is exacerbated by the fact that sometimes social grants are disbursed through these retail outlets making them the first option for confers when it comes to purchases. Designed to provide easy access to household consumables such as bread and milk, these shops provide a source of livelihood to many families. However, after noticing the trend, some supermarkets chains have also introduced customised shops to compete directly with the spaza shops. For example, the Shoprite USave brand is designed to target these low-income consumers that typically make their purchases from 'spaza' shops. Because they stock almost all the products the 'spaza' shops have, albeit at cheaper prices, it forces the consumers to access the goods from the supermarket rather than from the shop. According to Monnakgotla (2019), big retail chains are a much bigger threat to 'spaza' shops than the Somalis who have penetrated and dominated the 'spaza' economy. Even though they try to supplement their incomes with other additional services such as DSTV payments and running Lotto and soccer betting, the threat from the big supermarket chains is still significant. To compound the problem, 'spaza' shops rarely accept debit cards, which are currently used by most township users as most social funds require a bank card, making it cheaper to swipe the card at a supermarket than withdraw money at a cost for making purchases later.

Areas in which South African supermarkets are trailing

While South African supermarkets can broadly be described as advanced and forward-looking and in some cases innovative in view of the bold moves they have made to include consumer preferences in their operations, they can hardly be described as a leading class in supermarket brands. This is because there are some global consumers and shopping trends that are yet to become mainstream in the South African supermarket brands. For example, while self-checkouts are quite common in supermarket chains such as Aldi and Tesco, these are, by 2020, yet to be introduced to mainstream supermarkets like Checkers, Spar, and Shoprite.

Given the socio-economic conditions prevailing in South Africa, characterised by high unemployment and crime rates, it is unlikely that such innovations will hit the mainstream supermarket chains because of the risks involved. Even after the elimination of the crime variable, replacing cashiers with self-checkout counters will likely have some significant pushbacks from the labour unions. *The Economist* (2019) describes a futuristic supermarket at the Alibaba Campus in China whereby shoppers do not pay via phones or cards, but rather through facial recognition software. The groceries are then taken to couriers who deliver them on behalf of the shoppers who do not have to push a trolley or carry a shopping bag inside the store. Similar findings are reported by Stone and Day (2019), who looked at the use of technology by Amazon in their Go Stores that operate in selected cities where the company identifies customers with their mobile phones and charges them as they exit the store without the customers having to take out their phones. Although it is possible that such high tech will eventually make its way to South Africa, it is not likely to happen soon. This is not because of a dearth of technology to support such a sophisticated e-commerce platform but simply because such shipping trends are just not compatible with the average South African shoppers.

The other category where South African supermarkets are trailing in international trends is in the provision of local experiences and healthy options, which are increasingly resonating with millennials (Sevelius, 2019). First, the contemporary consumer is more discerning, opting for healthier, organic, and sustainable options. In some extreme cases, the consumer would prefer to know how their food was grown as well as the welfare of the farmer and the extent to which they were treated and the eventual journey of the product from the farmer to their plate. This forms the basis of the Fair-trade brand. However, considering the logistical and practical challenges of bringing this information to the consumer and the likely impact this is going to have on marketing campaigns, this information is not easily available. However, according to current trends, this is the information that consumers are already beginning to demand, and in some limited cases getting. Second, the new trend is to make the supermarket experience local, as reflected not just in buying the products but in the whole customer experience. In some instances, this means each shop will have its individual theme, which reflects its clientele. Consequently, a Pick n Pay outlet in a mall in Cape Town needs to look very different from the same Pick n Pay near the University Campus in Limpopo. An individual shop experience contributes to the customer experience, and this is the trend that consumers around the globe are starting to expect and get. This is unlikely going to happen to the South African industry in the near future.

First, the branding experience of many shops requires a certain consistency across the shops, which are in conflict with the customised experience. Second, central purchasing and the general and well-documented failure of the South African smallholders to penetrate into the mainstream food retail industry means that it is unlikely that shops will offer a localised experience as this is inconsistent with the current management trends.

Unlike most countries, especially in the developed world, where the trend is for farmers, especially smallholders, to become involved with supermarkets to ensure that the produce is local, this is hardly the case in South Africa. This is especially because the supermarket industry in South Africa is designed such that the focus is on centralised purchasing to minimise costs. This excludes smallholder farmers from the value chain, as they do not have the capacity of making regular supplies to supermarkets, who need to ensure that they have regular stock. In fact, some of the literature suggests that the relative limited success of the smallholder industry in South Africa result from their apparent failure of penetrating the local supermarket industry due to high entry costs (Sender, 2016). It is safe to assume that as long as supermarkets are owned by big chains, with purchasing decisions being made at a central level and with branding given more priority than the individualism of the shop, smallholder farmers believe that what they bring will forever be excluded from the supermarket industry.

It is important to note that while there has been some level of technology penetration in the South African supermarket industry, there are still some bottlenecks, which are holding the technology back. As alluded to earlier in this chapter, some of the technologies, such as online shopping, are based on supporting technologies, including access to the right banking cards, smartphones, and a stable internet connection. Second, one needs to have a bank account to access these technologies. Most importantly, consumers need to be in a position of understanding some of the benefits, which can be accrued from various technologies that the supermarkets offer. In other words, one of the challenges against rolling out the technologies and innovations by the South African supermarkets is that they unwittingly target the middle class who do not constitute the largest consumer population in South Africa (Burger, Louw, Pegado, and van der Berg, 2015). While some progress has been made on making some of the cards, such as debit cards, available to the public, there is a technology divide that limits consumers' access to South African supermarkets.

Conclusion

While the South African supermarket might be on a par with other supermarkets globally regarding online shopping experience, there is still a world of difference when it comes to the manner in which the goods are delivered. With on-demand delivery, especially for fresh food, becoming the norm in developed countries, the South African trend still presents a fragmented delivery experience characterised by each retailer in isolation trying to adopt a solution they think is either more innovative or convenient to the customers. While South African supermarkets are advanced and innovative in other areas, there remain areas of improvement.

In conclusion, it is important to point out that despite all the technology that has been employed in the supermarket industry and all the latest trends that have been adopted to date, the industry still experiences disruption as has been happening in other industries. While Netflix, Uber, Blockchain, and Airbnb have been disrupting the broadcasting, transport, finance, and hotel industry, respectively, the same cannot be said of the supermarket industry where no single developer has managed to disrupt the industry. While this is likely to change in the future, for now it is hardly conceivable to have a situation where technology replaces the traditional supermarket and grocery store as we know it.

References

Aloysius, G. and Binu, D. (2013). An approach to products placement in supermarkets using PrefixSpan algorithm. *Journal of King Saud University-Computer and Information Sciences*, 25(1), 77–87.

Baird, N. (2018). Six trends from the frontier of grocery consumer experiences. https://www.forbes.com/sites/nikkibaird/2018/05/30/six-trends-from-the-frontier-of-grocery-consumer-experiences/#ce064f711b4d. Accessed 13 February 2020.

Benn, Y., Webb, T.L., Chang, B.P. and Reidy, J. (2015). What information do consumers consider, and how do they look for it, when shopping for groceries online? *Appetite*, 89, 265–273.

Bone, M. (2019). The beating heart of spar. https://www.africaoutlookmag.com/company-profiles/303-spar-distribution. Accessed 03 May 2020.

Borraz, F., Dubra, J., Ferrés, D. and Zipitría, L. (2014). Supermarket entry and the survival of small stores. *Review of Industrial Organization*, 44(1), 73–93.

Burger, R., Louw, M., Pegado, B.B.I.D.O. and van der Berg, S. (2015). Understanding consumption patterns of the established and emerging South African black middle class. *Development Southern Africa*, 32(1), 41–56.

Cameron, A.J., Charlton, E., Ngan, W.W. and Sacks, G. (2016). A systematic review of the effectiveness of supermarket-based interventions involving product, promotion, or place on the healthiness of consumer purchases. *Current Nutrition Reports*, 5(3), 129–138.

Cohen, D.A., Bogart, L., Castro, G., Rossi, A.D., Williamson, S. and Han, B. (2018). Beverage marketing in retail outlets and the balance calories initiative. *Preventive Medicine*, 115, 1–7.

Competition Commission South Africa (2019). *The Grocery Retail Market Inquiry Final Report*. Non-confidential.

Dakora, E. (2012). Exploring the fourth wave of supermarket evolution: concepts of value and complexity in Africa. *International Journal of Managing Value and Supply Chains*, 3(3), 25–37.

Dixon, J. (2007). Supermarkets as new food authorities. In *Supermarkets and Agri-Food Supply Chains: Transformations in the Production and Consumption of Foods*. Edward Elgar Publishing, Cheltenham, UK.

Galante, N., López, E.G. and Monroe, S. (2013). *The Future of Online Grocery in Europe*. McKinsey & Company, 22–31.

Gillespie, B., Muehling, D.D. and Kareklas, I. (2018). Fitting product placements: affective fit and cognitive fit as determinants of consumer evaluations of placed brands. *Journal of Business Research*, 82, 90–102.

Hung-Joubert, Y.T. (2017). Investigating the construct validity of quality measures influencing online shopping in a South African context. *Management & Marketing*, 12(3), 376–401.

Janse van Rensburg, M. (2016). *Efficiency Through Design: Interior Design Components for South African Shoprite Interior Which Minimize Resources and Maximizes the User Experience*. Unpublished PhD Thesis, Submitted at the University of Pretoria.

Jhamb, D. and Kiran, R. (2012). Emerging trends of organized retailing in India: a shared vision of consumers and retailers' perspective. *Middle-East Journal of Scientific Research*, 11(4), 481–490.

Juel-Jacobsen, L.G. (2015). 'The World for a Crooked Street': towards a supermarket morphology of shopping aisles and retail layout. *Interiors*, 6(1), 59–89.

Kinsey, J. and Senauer, B. (1996). Consumer trends and changing food retailing formats. *American Journal of Agricultural Economics*, 78(5), 1187–1191.

Makhitha, K.M., Van Scheers, L. and Mogashoa, C. (2019). Which consumer attributes influence South African consumers to shop online. *Journal of Business and Retail Management Research*, 13(4), 312–325.

Monnakgotla, M. (2019). They still take all the credit. *Forbes Africa*, May 2019.
Probyn, J. (2017). In pictures: Shoprite's massive new distribution Centre one of Africa's most advanced, https://www.howwemadeitinafrica.com/pictures-shoprites-massive-new-distribution-centre-one-africas-advanced/59533/. Accessed 4 May 2020.
Rathore, H.S. (2016). Adoption of digital wallet by consumers. *BVIMSR's Journal of Management Research*, 8(1), 69.
Reardon, T., Timmer, C.P. and Minten, B. (2012). Supermarket revolution in Asia and emerging development strategies to include small farmers. *Proceedings of the National Academy of Sciences*, 109(31), 12332–12337.
Sender, J. (2016). Backward capitalism in rural South Africa: prospects for accelerating accumulation in the Eastern Cape. *Journal of Agrarian Change*, 16(1), 3–31.
Sevelius, A. (2019). Grocery retail trends 2019. https://www.relexsolutions.com/resources/grocery-retail-trends-2019/. Accessed 13 February 2020.
Stone, B. and Day, M. (2019). The Zillion Dollar Convenience Store, Bloomberg. *Business Week*, 22 July 2019.
The Economist (2019). Special report: global supply chains. *The Economist*, 13 July 2019.
Van Zyl, J. (2016). *The Impact of Product Placement on Consumer Involvement in the South African Automotive Industry*. Unpublished PhD Thesis. Submitted at Doctoral the University of the Free State.
Vanek, M. (2019). The big bank theory. *Forbes Africa*, June 2019.
Venter, P.F. and Dhurup, M. (2005). Consumer perceptions of supermarket service quality: scale development and validation: management. *South African Journal of Economic and Management Sciences*, 8(4), 424–436.
Weatherspoon, D.D. and Reardon, T. (2003). The rise of supermarkets in Africa: implications for agrifood systems and the rural poor. *Development Policy Review*, 21(3), 333–355.
World Bank (2019). GDP per capita (current US$) – Sub-Saharan Africa. https://data.worldbank.org/indicator/NY.GDP.PCAP.CD?locations=ZG. Accessed 4 May 2020.

7 Operations research contribution to the performance of supermarkets in East Africa

A. R. Mushi and Sumaya M. Kagoya

Introduction

Operations research (OR) is a discipline that deals with the development and application of analytical tools in order to make better decisions. Due to its major applications in management decision-making systems, it is sometimes referred to as management science. OR is a relatively new field, which started in the 1930s for decision-making in military operations. It later spread to other application areas, including engineering and business problems involving complex decision-making situations. Operations research problems have three main characteristics:

1. Determining systems for optimal/better situations (Optimisation) – This aims at deriving optimal or better solutions to maximise various attributes such as sales or profits and/or minimise attributes such as costs, losses, or risks.
2. Analysing systems for behaviours (Simulation) – This is useful when the real situation cannot be manipulated, and therefore an analytical model is designed and used to simulate behaviours. The aim is to use the simulated environment to get insight into actual system performance and therefore provide tools for better decision-making.
3. Predict future behaviour (Probability and Statistics) – Most real-life systems are associated with uncertainties and therefore stochastic in nature. For instance, a business environment is mostly dependent on the predictions of customer demands, which are always stochastic. Operations research involves the development of mathematical models and algorithms that can be applied to the data in order to uncover helpful insights and risks in making scientifically informed forecasts and allowing for the testing of possible solutions.

Therefore, OR is a cross-cutting field that draws applications from many disciplines, including mathematics, business, economics, engineering, psychology, and other physical and social sciences disciplines. The purpose of OR is to provide a rational basis for decision-making when complex situations are involved, such as finding the best business decision when resources are scarce and making the best use of resources when required, among many possible solutions. Business problems often require one to find an optimal or better decision strategy

DOI: 10.4324/9780367854300-7

that would maximise profit or minimise the cost of sales subject to a number of restrictions, including resource-based, which are always scarce.

Specifically, the supermarket business is highly competitive and thereby OR has been extensively used to provide decisions in helping businesses make profits by cutting costs and maximising profits throughout the supply chain. Various research projects into OR have been reported on supermarket operations globally. These include supermarket customer behaviours (Kubera et al., 2010), productivity modelling (King and Park, 2004), store simulations (Miwa and Tatakuwa,2008), promotion planning (Cohen et al., 2017a), and many other similar types. However, not much is known about the use of specific features that inform the optimality requirements of supermarkets in East Africa.

The objective of the current study therefore is to determine the extent of applications of OR in supermarkets in the region and to identify gaps for further research. The findings are envisaged to be useful for improving efficiency and business sustainability to supermarkets in the region.

The next section presents a review of the literature on applications of OR in supermarkets in the region as well as around the world, followed by a specific literature review on the features of the East African retail market. The section is devoted to surveying the extent of applications of OR tools in the region and proposing possible improvement measures to address the identified gaps. The last section is the conclusion.

Literature review

In this chapter, applications of OR in supermarkets are categorised into groups depending on the stage in the supply chain, starting from facility location, transportation problems, shelf space design, demand forecasting, inventory control, promotion strategies, staff scheduling to quality of service through to queuing systems monitoring. Various OR tools are used in all these supermarket problems to assist in better decision-making. A review of some articles related to each of the above-stated groups is hereby provided to highlight the current state of research and applications around the world.

Facility location

The determination of facility location is a critical business strategic decision and may lead to business success or failure. When starting a new retail store or chain of stores, it is important to consider factors that will lead to choosing the best location for business success. These factors are market share, the purchasing power of the customers, distance from customers, and attractiveness of the retail facility. The last three are independent variables, while the first is the dependent variable (Drezner and Drezner, 2002). In many cases, a supermarket chain would be introducing a new store into a competitive environment; in other words, competitors have already established themselves, and the task is therefore to maximise the market share of customers who are expected to patronise the newly established store. The store will have to consider the purchasing power of the customers in the communities that are expected to use the facility and the proximity of the facility to the targeted customers. Furthermore, the store has to introduce attractive features that would draw customers into the store. These factors are normally formulated into utility functions with the output of market share, which in turn influences business profit. The objective is therefore to maximise market share (maximise profit) by deciding on the type and quality of the input factors mentioned above. There is much literature discussing the ways of formulating market share models in relation to input factors. For example, Drezner (2014) reviewed competitive facility location models for estimating market share. These models are proximity, deterministic utility, random utility, cover-based, and gravity-based approaches.

Proximity approach: market share is assumed to depend on the distance between the facility and the customer's community. These ideas are based on the principles by Hotelling (1929), who developed a model by considering the location of two facilities. Purchasing power between the communities is assumed to be constant, and there is no price differential between facilities. In this case then, consumers are expected to patronise the closest facility to their community. When a new facility is introduced, it is assumed that consumers will be divided among the facilities by patronising the closest facility. However, these assumptions have been shown to be unrealistic since customers patronise a facility depending on other factors as well including price sensitivity and attractiveness of the facility.

Deterministic utility approach: when the attractiveness of facilities is not uniform (which is more realistic), the proximity model is no longer applicable. Therefore, Drezner (1994) and Hodgson (1978) suggest the inclusion of attractiveness into the competitive location model by introducing the deterministic utility function. It is assumed that all consumers residing in one location apply the same utility.

Gravity-based approach: this is the most common approach used by marketers and is based on the following rule: two cities attract retail trade from an intermediate town in direct proportion to the populations of the two cities and in inverse proportion to the square of the distances from them to the intermediate town (Reilly, 1931). Furthermore, as Huff (1966) proposes, the probability that a consumer patronises a retail facility is proportional to its size and inversely proportional to the power of the distance to it. Suppose that there are k existing facilities and n demand points, let the attractiveness of facility j be A_j for $j = 1,\ldots,k$, and the distance between demand points i and j be d_{ij}. The purchasing power at the demand point i is b_i. Given the proposed relations above, the market share attracted by facility j is $M_j = \sum_{i=1}^{n} b_i \dfrac{A_j/d_{ij}^\lambda}{\sum_{m=1}^{k}\left(A_m/d_{im}^\lambda\right)}$ where λ is the power to which the distances are raised. More details on the gravity model are found in Anas (1982).

Most facility location models attempt to find the maximum share of facility location within the current market conditions. However, market conditions may change in the future while the business is in operation. Drezner and Drezner (2002) propose a model that takes into consideration the possible changes in the future market conditions since they have an impact on the choice of an optimal location. They propose models that are based on the criteria of minimax regret, Stackelberg equilibrium, and threshold models and consider the possible changes in purchasing power and the changing retail facilities (Drezner, 2014).

Recent works include a bi-level model developed by Shan et al. (2017) for optimisation of competitive facility location on chain stores. The model optimises location based on the principle of the Nash equilibrium. The results were obtained through a heuristic algorithm, which showed the feasibility of the model. A recent state of the art review on competitive facility locations problems is provided by Ashtiani (2016) based on seven components, namely variables, competition type, solution space, customer behaviour, demand type, the number of new facilities, and relocation and redesign possibility. The work provides a good taxonomy of research in the field. Some facility location problems require optimisation of more than one objective, leading to Multi-Criteria Decision Analysis Methods (MCDM). Apart from maximising market share, the company may seek to optimise other criteria simultaneously. These may include minimising setup costs, minimising the longest distance from the facility, minimising fixed costs, minimising operating costs, maximising service, minimising responsiveness, and many others. Literature on the same include the work by Awasthia et al. (2011) for location planning on urban distribution centres, Amin and Zhang (2013) on location models for a closed-loop supply chain network under uncertain demand and return. A survey of MCDM on facility location problems is provided by Farahani et al.(2010).

In general, facility location is an important OR problem, applying the tools worldwide in deciding the location of facilities since it is a very important management decision. The failure of making a better decision may be a source of future failures of the business.

Transportation problem

The aim of any supermarket business is to maximise profit while meeting other requirements such as customer satisfaction and loyalty for future business sustainability and to maintain competitive advantage. Profit maximisation is achieved by minimising the costs of sales, including transportation costs of the products from vendors or warehouses to the stores in different locations. This is the transportation problem, which is mostly modelled as linear programming. The aim is to find the least cost routes and vehicles to ship items from vendors or warehouses while satisfying the demands from stores and without exceeding the capacity of warehouses or vendors. The distribution channel is normally modelled as a network of supply and demand centres. Similarly, there is a network of delivery channels to customers, referred to as the business to customer (B2C) channel. This is likewise an important optimisation process of attracting customers and improving product pricing. A study by Shilpa et al. (2014)presents a thorough discussion on various components of supermarkets logistics channels in the B2C network and the impact of cost reduction on the efficiency and effectiveness of the business. Jingya et al. (2017) present an optimisation model for transport in supermarkets chains of the Isle of Wight in the United Kingdom. The task was modelled as a vehicle routing problem with time windows and solved by a genetic algorithm with good success. Transportation planning for food retailing in Japan is discussed by Masatochi et al. (2013), who developed a linear programming model and examined the optimal solution that performed well in reducing transportation costs. Further studies on transportation logistics in supermarkets, including frameworks for better performance, are discussed by other scholars (i.e.Sternbeck andKuhn, 2014; Jian and Gao, 2012; Corinne et al.,2014;Kumar, 2008). Last-mile logistics is a new concept in transportation, and it concerns the last stretch of distribution from a store to the recipient destination. This is of paramount importance because it is estimated that the last-mile accounts for 13–75%of the supply chain transportation cost. After all, it involves distribution in the highly congested routes of the cities with great cost in terms of time, fuel, and environmental pollution. John et al. (2019) reviewed a research work on the concept of last-mile logistics and identified major research gaps.

Transportation optimisation in supermarkets has therefore been extensively studied in the developed world and is important for the supermarket business, which cannot be ignored in the competitive environment.

Shelf space design and utilisation

In a competitive environment, retailers strive to improve their market share and profitability through various strategies. Among them is customer satisfaction through improving the efficiency of shelf space. During shopping, customers are influenced by in-store factors, especially when doing unplanned purchases and when searching for alternative products after missing what they have been looking for. A clever product arrangement on the shelves is crucial for visibility, consumer awareness, and demand for the products. This has been shown to improve product sales and therefore market share and financial performance. Retailers work to get the right goods to the right places at the right time (Aguiar,2015). The process is even more complicated because there are increasingly more products to display than the available shelf space. It is therefore necessary to find the right products to display to maximise profit by selecting the most profitable products to display in the right positions.

The shelf space allocation problem (SSAP) refers to the distribution of the shelf space of a retail store among a set of products in a category. The objective is to obtain the maximum profit from the available space by considering consumer demand in the function of the space allocated to the products. The problem can be modelled with objective functions and constraints and solved by OR tools such as linear programming, dynamic programming, and heuristics, to name but a few. One of the approaches is to model SSAP as a knapsack problem (Aguiar, 2015). The knapsack problem relates to finding items to place in a knapsack (out of many) that will give the maximum weight without exceeding the capacity of the knapsack. Since there are many products to be placed on the fixed scarce shelf space, SSAP is a variation of the multi-commodity knapsack problem. The problem has been extensively studied over the years, with different models developed depending on the business environment.

One interesting general model is given by Zufryden (1986), who applied dynamic programming techniques in finding the solution of shelf space allocation. The model is formulated as follows.

Suppose we have a general product demand function on an arbitrary specification, where the demand for product $j(j = 1,...,J)$ is a function of a vector $x_j = (s_j, x_{1j}, x_{2j}..., x_{Ij})$. This vector includes space allocated to product j, s_j, plus other variables x_{ij} $(i = 1,...I, j = 1,...,J)$, which may affect product demand. These may include item prices, advertising, promotions, store characteristics, and many others. The unit demand for product j is defined as,

$$Q_j(x_j) = Q_j(s_j, x_{1j}, x_{2j},...x_{Ij}).$$

The total gross margin function over all the products can be specified in terms of the space allocated to each product as $M_j = m_j Q_j(x_j)$, where m_j is the gross margin rate for product j.

The cost C_j of product j is a function of demand vector x_j and the total cost over all products is therefore given by $TC = \sum_j C_j[Q_j(x_j)]$.

The objective function is to maximise profit margins by the choice of s_j for each product j; $\underset{(s_j)}{Max} \sum_j \{m_j Q_j(s_j) - C_j[Q_j(s_j)]\}$

Subject to: $\sum_j s_j \leq T$ (Restriction on available space T),

$L_j \leq s_j \leq U_j, j = 1,...J$ (Restrictions on the lower bound L_j and upper bound U_j on slot allocations of each product j),

$Q_j(s_j) \leq A_j, j = 1,...,J$ (Upper bound A_j for the availability of each product j),

$s_j = 0, d_j, 2d_j,..., j = 1,...,J$ (Incremental allocation rules), and $d_j \geq 1$ and integer, $j = 1,...,J$.

Realistic formulations of this model will involve non-linear functions, and therefore non-linear programming methods are applied. In this case, Zufryden (1986) applied a forward dynamic programming technique and successfully tested the sample problems from the simulated data.

The problem has been studied extensively, including in early work by Corstjens and Doyle (1981), who developed a geometric programming mathematical model for maximising profit due to space allocation effects. The model was solved through the branch and bound method and tested on a real problem of a retailer with 140 shops, and the results compared well with other previously presented models. The optimisation of product shelf space using data mining techniques was presented by Surjandari et al. (2012). The authors studied the relationship between product categories and product prices using a data mining method known as multilevel association rules, then developed a zero-one integer programming model. The authors tested their model on real data from minimarkets in Jakarta, Indonesia, and arrived at successful outputs. In another study, Abouali et al. (2014) presented a Non-Linear Integer Programming model that combined inventory replenishment and shelf space management to maximise retail store profit. The model was applied to real cases of retail stores in Alexandria in Egypt and showed an improvement over the practiced system. Tsai and Huang (2015) considered customer purchase and moving behaviours and applied data mining techniques to optimise shelf space allocation. Association rules were applied to generate categories of items as major and minor and reassigned to the best shelf locations using the Hungarian method.

These are just a few among many studies that applied OR in shelf space planning for maximising profit. Many of these studies are problem-specific and may not be applicable in all business situations. Therefore, the supermarket business is expected to employ specific mathematical models and algorithms in finding the best shelf space organisation to add value to their profit margin in their highly competitive business.

Inventory control

Inventory control is another very important process in the supermarket business and has an impact on the performance of a business. The main objective is to balance the amounts to be kept in the inventory for each item and the necessity of meeting customer demand. Over-storage will incur unnecessary storage costs, while under-stocking may lead to lost demand from customers. Two questions need answers: how much to order? And when to order? The most desirable approach is when the store will not need to keep any inventory but make sure that customer demand is met in time whenever an order is placed. This is called the Just-In-Time (JIT) system. However, in the supermarket business, JIT cannot be attained due to the nature of the business requirements, and therefore storage is necessary. The optimal order amount is called Economic Order Quantity (EOQ) and is found through mathematical modelling and optimisation techniques of OR.

There are many types of inventory models depending on the business features, but they can be grouped into deterministic and stochastic. Deterministic models are easier to formulate but may not reflect reality in many business situations. Stochastic (probabilistic) models are more realistic but also more complex to formulate and solve. In cases where parameters are possible to estimate within the acceptable range, deterministic models are common. The basic inventory cost function is presented by Taha (2007) as follows;

$$\text{Total cost} = \text{Purchasing cost}(p) + \text{Setup cost}(k)$$
$$+ \text{Holding cost}(h) + \text{Shortage cost}(s)$$

The inventory may be based on periodic review or continuous review modes of replenishment. In a periodic review, the stock is placed after every fixed period, while in a continuous review, an order is placed after the stock has reached a level called re-order point. The main difference in inventory systems is associated with the nature of demand; the deterministic demand, which can either be constant or vary with time and stochastic demand, which may be stationary or non-stationary over time. In a classic EOQ model, the simplest formulation for a single item model is as follows;

Suppose y= order quantity, D= demand rate (quantity per unit time), and t= ordercycle length (time units). Assuming there is no shortage cost, then the EOQ is given by $y^* = \sqrt{\frac{2kD}{h}}$ items, to be ordered after every $t = \frac{y^*}{D}$ period. Other variations of deterministic models presented by Taha (2007) include cases where there are price breaks, the existence or non-existence of setup costs, shortages, and many others. Of interest to supermarkets are models which represent multiple items with deterministic demand; and the case where there is limited storage space is presented as follows.

Suppose there are n items and D_i= demand rate of item i, k_i= setup cost of item i, h_i=holding cost of item i, y_i= order quantity of item i, a_i=storage area required per item i, and A= maximum available storage space, then the problem is:

$$\text{Minimize } Cost(y_1,\ldots y_n) = \sum_{i=1}^{n}\left(\frac{k_i D_i}{y_i} + \frac{h_i y_i}{2}\right),$$

$$\text{Subject to } \sum_{i=1}^{n} a_i y_i \leq A, \ y_i > 0, \ i = 1,\ldots,n.$$

One solution to this formulation uses the Lagrangian algorithm by changing the problem to an unconstrained form by integrating the constraints into the objective function. However, more realistic problems are probabilistic in nature and require stochastic approaches. Several variations have been studied, but they all involve the introduction of a probability distribution function on demand and finding out expectations of the outcomes. Simchi-Levi and Zhao (2012) provide a review of stochastic multi-echelon inventory systems. They compare and contrast three generic methods: queuing inventory, the lead-time demand, and flow-unit methods in the supply chain. They thoroughly review the many methods and mathematical formulations of various classifications of inventory models. More studies on realistic inventory control problems variations include Jiang et al. (2015), Fergany (2016), Oberoi (2017), and Lesmono and Limansyah (2017). Supermarkets are expected to apply OR tools in deciding on their inventories in order to maximise profit.

Product promotions

Promotion is an important component of the supermarket business in order to attract customers and increase sales. Promotions aim to improve product profit due to increased sales, create awareness, especially on new products, clear unsold products, enhance customer loyalty, increase market competition, and act as a tool for pricing. Mathematical models have been developed over the years to assist in decision-making. The promotion optimisation problem (POP), which involves decisions on which product to promote, the depth of price discounts, and the schedule of promotions to maximise profit, is subject to satisfying a number of business rules.

The problem has been studied over the years with variations in promotion strategies and mathematical formulations. The early work by Rao and Thomas (1973) presents a dynamic programming model for the so-called 'promotion mix' problem that involved making decisions on a combination of advertising, sales promotion, and individual selling programmes.

Cohen and Perakis (2018) present models for optimal promotion planning of multiple items in the retail business using mass pricing promotions for Fast Moving Consumer Goods (FMCG). They formulated a non-linear mixed linear programming problem (NMIP) and solved itwith approximation approaches due to the complexity of the problem. Simulated results were very promising and recommended that supermarkets should use the available massive amount of data to decide simultaneously on the promotion prices of multiple items through optimisation approaches rather than relying on experience and trial and error methods. More details on promotion models are found in Cohen et al. (2017b). In another study, Li (2013) applied the Euler-Lagrange equation in the Calculus of Variations to develop a dynamic model for an optimal price promotion strategy. The author applied time and promotion expenses variables to the linear demand equation and investigated the effects of marketing parameters on decision-making, and concluded that the developed tool is a valuable contribution topricing promotion. Beltov et al. (2006) also applied a dynamic optimisation model for retailers' promotion of two brands. The authors investigated the impact of promotion on consumer behaviours, namely immediate positive impact, brand substitution, and consumer stockpiling of the promoted brand. Optimal policies for a forward-looking retailer wereidentified. The cited literature in this section is only but a few of the many pieces of literature on promotion optimisation, and the extent of its application in the region is of great interest.

Staff scheduling

Staff scheduling is a very common problem in the business industry and has been widely studied. Staff costs have a major contribution to general business costs. Therefore, proper planning to ensure the optimal use of staff is very important for business profitability. The challenge is to find a staff schedule to meet the needs of the business without overstaffing. Ernst et al. (2004) provide a review of studies on staff scheduling and rostering, including application areas and solution methods. An extensive review is provided by Jorne et al. (2012) on personnel scheduling systems, who reviewed 306 articles and developed a classification of the problem with respect to various problem characteristics. However, only a few papers have addressed the supermarkets staff-scheduling problem, as stated in Chapados et al. (2014). The papers cited proposed a model that starts with sales forecasting and then generates weekly schedules by applying Mixed Integer Programming formulations (MIP) and Constraint Programming approaches. Models were solved through both exact and heuristic algorithms depending on the complexity of the problems and managed to get optimal weekly schedules for retail store staff. A specific study of cashier staff scheduling in a supermarket was presented by Melachrinoudis (1995), who observed that customer service is an important issue in supermarket sales since it may negatively affect performance and discourage customers if they (customers) have to wait for a long time in long queues during purchase. A linear programming model is proposed for the solution that determines the number of cashier staff on an hourly basis and shifts the lengths without violating staff restrictions and minimising staff requirements. It is therefore expected that supermarkets will use OR tools in determining staff requirements, shifts, and schedules.

Demand forecasting

Demand forecasting is one of the most important factors for business success or failure because it is the backbone of all business planning. It is through demand forecasting that a company can plan for inventory, queuing systems, future expansions such as facility locations, staff scheduling, and many others. Retail systems demand forecasting is a very complex process because of the nature of consumers who come from different cultural backgrounds, have different preferences, and have varied purchasing powers. The demand also depends on other factors such as the influence of promotions, product quality, and brand loyalty, to name but a few. Demand is generally influenced by social, cultural, psychological, and personality factors (Pataket al.,2015).

The quality of the forecasting process is reflected in the accuracy of forecasts produced from previous forecasts. There are two types of forecasts, namely, qualitative and quantitative. Qualitative forecasting depends on retailers' opinions, expert estimations, or marketing studies. Due to the time required, the most common forecasting tools are quantitative. The common methods in this kind of forecasting are based on time series analysis, which uses a series of past sales to forecast the future. These are also grouped into linear and non-linear time series models. The linear models include moving averages, exponential smoothing, and Auto-regressive Integrated Moving Average (ARIMA). Non-linear models include the Artificial Neural Networks (ANN); there is also a combination or hybrid of methods in various applications of demand forecasting in the retail business (Shetty et al., 2018).

The basic Moving Average (MA) model is very simple and uses previous n sales values to predict the future sales figures (Shetty et al., 2018). Suppose that past n actual sales figures are $A_t, A_{t-1},\ldots, A_{t-n}$, where the last known sale is at period t; then the predicted sales figure for the period $t+1$ is

$$F_{t+1} = \frac{A_t + A_{t-1} + \ldots + A_{t-n}}{n}.$$

An improvement over the Moving Average is the weighted Moving Average method, where each of the actual sales is weighted depending on the significance placed on each timeframe. Therefore, if the weight given to timeframe t is W_t, then;

$$F_{t+1} = W_t A_t + W_{t-1} A_{t-1} + \ldots + W_{t-n} A_{t-n}, \text{ where } W_t + W_{t-1} + \ldots + W_{t-n} = 1.$$

Future projections can learn from the comparison between past projections and the actual figures that appeared afterwards. A smoothing consistent factor α is used to show the significance of the past error in the forecast. This gives an exponential smoothing model, which is defined as follows;

$$F_{t+1} = F_t + \alpha \left(A_t - F_t \right)$$

The ARIMA model extends the previous models by combining previous data and previous forecasting errors to inform the future forecast. It is a combination of both the MA of previous errors and Auto-Regressive (AR) models. In general, the AR model is one where F_t depends only on its own past values, that is,

$F_t = \sigma + \beta_1 F_{t-1} \ldots + \beta_p F_{t-p} + \epsilon_1$, where β is the coefficient of lag that the model estimates σσ is the intercept term, and ϵ is the error term. Likewise, the general MA of previous errors can be modelled where the current value only depends on the previous forecast errors in the form:

$F_t = \sigma + \epsilon_t + \varnothing_1 \epsilon_{t-1} + \ldots + \varnothing_q \epsilon_{t-q}$ where the error terms are the errors of the AR models of the respective differences. The ARIMA model is therefore a combination of AR and MA to form

$$F_t = \sigma + \beta_1 F_{t-1} \ldots + \beta_p F_{t-p} \epsilon_1 + \varnothing_1 \epsilon_{t-1} + \ldots + \varnothing_q \epsilon_{t-q}$$

In simple words, predicted F_t = constant + linear combination of actual sales of F (up to p sales) + linear combination of previous sales errors (up to q sales). For more details, see Selva (2019),who provides a simple description of the ARIMA model and example implementations in Python. A version that considers seasons in the forecast is an extension of ARIMA and is known as SARIMA. This model is popular in retail sales forecasting; however, other studies combine several models into one forecasting process. ARAS et al. (2017) provide a comparative study between a single model and a combination of models for retail forecasting. They conclude that a combination of forecasting models can give statistically better accuracy than single models using empirical data obtained from Turkey's retail business.

Intelligent Artificial Neural Network systems are also common in forecasting models. This is a net of many units linked by connections, and each unit receives and gives numerical data through the connections. These are artificial intelligence training rules where the connection weights are adjusted according to the data received and can be generalised beyond the data seen during training (Thiesing and Vornberber, 1997). Aburto and Weber (2003)studied the ARIMA and ANN models and proposed a hybrid system that combines the two, which performed better than each separate system in forecasting demand in supermarkets. Kilimci et al. (2019) reporteda demand forecasting model in the supply chain using a deep learning approach. This is a subset of machine learning and is capable of learning from unstructured or unlabelled data, also known as deep neural learning. After a long range of testing, the results revealed that the model performed better. From these studies, it is clear that demand forecasting in the retail business is a complex problem where variables vary with the environment, and therefore careful considerations must be taken when using the existing models. Efforts must also be made to developmodelsthatfit well with the business environment in the African region and specifically in the East African region.

Queuing systems

Cashiers are the service windows in a supermarket; they determine one of the most important service attributes in the business. Often in supermarkets, customers have to wait in long queues for service, which is an unacceptable situation. Given the similar quality and prices of products, customers prefer supermarkets with shorter queues or no queues at all. However, employing staff to serve on counters is expensive and negatively affects the profitability of the business. Balancing the two with the aim of satisfying customers with minimum cost in order to maximise profit is a challenge.

Fortunately, queuing theory has been used widely to design models that can assist in determining various queue measures of performance. Supermarket queues fall into the M/M/c queuing model, which is a multi-server queuing system (see Taha, 2007). This notation is called Kendall notation, where the first M stands for poison arrival distribution, the second M stands for exponential service distribution and c stands for number of servers in the system. Given a system with c number of servers in a situation where there are n customers, a queue situation will only happen when there are more customers than there are servers, that is, $n > c$. Given that there are customers in a queue (i.e. $n > c$) and suppose the arrival rate is λ and service rate is μ, the probability of having n customers in the system is given by

$P_n = \dfrac{\rho^n}{c! c^{n-c}} P_0$, where $\rho = \dfrac{\lambda}{\mu}$ with $\dfrac{\rho}{c} < 1$ and P_0 is the probability of having no customers in the system and is given by,

$$P_0 = \left[\sum_{n=0}^{c-1} \dfrac{\rho^c}{n!} + \dfrac{\rho^c}{c!} \left(\dfrac{1}{1 - \rho/c} \right) \right]^{-1}.$$

The system performance measures of the M/M/c system include the average length of the queue, which is given by,

$$L_q = \left[\dfrac{(c\rho)^c}{c!(1-\rho)^2} \right] \rho P_0$$ and the average waiting time in the queue, which is given by

$$W_q = \frac{L_q}{\lambda}.$$

Valverde and Succar (2010) developed a model for managerial decision-making in the supermarket business that analyses the queuing system and suggests opening or closing checkout stands optimisation. Their work involved queuing theory model simulation by Factored Markov Decision Process (FMDP) (Boutilier et al.,1999). They concluded that the simulated results, which assisted checkout controller decision-making, worked according to the optimal policy. An interesting case study in Makurdi town in Nigeria was presented by Igwe et al. (2014),who studied cases of the M/M/I queuing model in businesses in the town. Their analysis revealed that, on aggregate, queuing management in the town was grossly inadequate, inefficient, and ineffective and therefore called for an improvement in system performance. A specific case was also presented by Burkul et al. (2015) on the analysis of the queuing system at a local grocery store in Texas, USA. They considered various layout designs, including single-queue-single-server, multiple-servers-multiple-queues, single-queue-multiple-servers, and checkout systems. The presented analysis is very useful in understanding queuing system performances when various changes are incorporated to reduce waiting times. Queuing theory is used normally in collaboration with simulation methods, and the most common tool is Discrete Event Simulation (DES), such as in work by Mohamad and Saharin (2019) on hypermarkets in Malaysia. Hypermarkets are special types of supermarkets, which deal with only Fast Moving Consumer Goods. They combined queuing theory models with DES tools using ARENA software to analyse queuing situations for the selected type of supermarkets, which managed to reduce consumer-waiting times by up to 26%. Other articles in supermarket queuing systems with simulations include Xian et al. (2016), Jiao S (2010), and Zhou (2017). Queuing system analysis is therefore very important for successful supermarket businesses in determining the criteria for decision-making in order to improve the quality of service with respect to waiting times in the queues.

Product pricing

Finding the right price for products in any business is a complex process that involves more factors than the costs of sales. Pricing considers many factors, including market demand and competition, customers' willingness to pay, promotion strategies, branding, seasonality factors, types of products and many others. OR provides various optimisation tools that can be used to propose optimal pricing strategies for particular products for profit maximisation. Ellickson and Misra (2008) discuss everyday low prices (EDLP) against temporary price reduction (promotion) pricing strategies. They applied game theory approaches to compare the pricing methods of various stores and concluded that demographic and store characteristic features have a significant impact on successful pricing. Tekin and Erol (2017) presented a dynamic pricing model for perishable products in supermarkets. Their objectives were to minimise the cost of waste, maximise profit, maximise product utilisation rates, and ensure product sustainability. They presented a mathematical programming model that was utilised successfully and achieved the objectives. A dynamic model for optimal price promotion strategies was introduced by Bo-Jian (2013) using the Euler-Lagrange equation in the Calculus of Variations. The author concluded that the developed model is a good decision-making aid in relation to product pricing in promotions. Dynamic pricing and learning is an area of research that has received much attention in recent years.For example, Den Boer (2013) provided a survey of research work in the area to identify the various methodologies used. Other works include Candogan et al. (2012) on approximation algorithms for optimal pricing in networks, who managed to show that some variants of the optimal pricing problem are NP–Hard combinatorial optimisation problems. These are onlya few research works on supermarket product pricing that applied OR tools to determine optimal strategies. Table 7.1 presents a summary of

Table 7.1 Summary of OR applications in supermarkets around the world

OR area	OR supermarket problem	OR Tools used
Facility location	Optimal supermarket store location	Integer programming, Stochastic programming, heuristics, multi-criteria decision methods
Transportation problem	Vendor to stores transport optimisation, vehicle routing	Linear programming, mathematical programming, genetic algorithms
Shelf space optimisation	Shelf space design and allocation optimisation	Linear programming, integer programming, dynamic programming, heuristics, Simulation, non-linear programming, geometric programming, data mining, Hungarian method
Inventory control	Inventory optimisation	Non-linear optimisation – Lagrangian methods, stochastic approaches – multi-echelon
Promotion planning	Promotion plans optimisation	Dynamic programming, non-linear programming, simulations
Staff scheduling	Staff schedules optimisation	Linear/Integer programming, Constraint Programming, heuristic methods
Forecasting	Demand forecasting	Time series analysis, ARIMA, Artificial Neural Networks, hybrid methods, deep learning-machine learning,
Queuing systems	Customer queues optimisation	Queuing theory models, simulations – Discrete Event Simulation, Markov decision process
Product pricing	Optimal product pricing	Game theory, dynamic programming, Euler-Lagrange equations, Calculus of Variations, approximation algorithms

the OR tools used in the reviewed literature with respect to the nine areas of OR in the supermarkets business.

Methodology

A review involved 74 articles from various international journals and books as listed in the references section. The articles were selected based on the theme of OR applications in the supermarkets business. A paper by Steeneken and Ackley (2012) provides a description of a complete model for a supermarket business. The author looked at a supermarket as a complex structure of suppliers, transporters, warehouses, retail stores, and customers. In this study, the researchers' academic experience in the use of OR tools in other applications helped identify important areas applicable in each of the supermarket structures. These are facility location problems (warehouses and retail stores), transportation problems (suppliers, transporters, and warehouses), and inventory control (warehouses and retail stores). Other OR tools, applicable in retail stores and service provision to customers, include shelf space design, promotion planning, staff scheduling, demand forecasting, queuing systems, and product pricing. The initial literature review helped the current researchers to identify the search terms, specific OR tools, and action terms to be used in the research. During the literature review, more terms were identified and added to the list, which were grouped as shown in Table 7.2. The search was conducted using Google Scholar, Research Gate, JSTOR, Wiley Online Library, semantic scholar, and others that the researchers had access to through the Google search engine.

The search results are presented next by grouping them into the nine stated categories of supermarket activity in the input, process, and output arrangement.

Features of the African retail market

In this section, the specific features of the African retail marketare studied. A report by Signe and Johnson (2018) shows that Africa is one of the fastest-growing

Table 7.2 Search terms categorisation

OR area	Supermarket terms	OR tools	Action terms
Facility location Transportation problems Inventory control Shelf space design Promotion planning Staff scheduling Demand forecasting Queuing systems Product pricing	Supermarket, retail business, point of sales, supply chain, grocery stores, department stores, consumer market, logistics, Africa, East Africa, sub-Saharan Africa.	Operations research, management science, mathematical programming, heuristics.	Optimisation, simulation, modelling, analysis, performance evaluation, decision analysis.

consumer markets in the world, and by 2030 the largest consumer markets will include Ethiopia, Kenya, and Tanzania. However, analysis of the literature identified the following main specific features of consumers in Africa.

Traditional markets influence: Supermarkets are a relatively new business model in Africa, especially in the food supply chain. According to the estimates of the International Livestock Research Institute (ILRI), informal markets still supply between 85 and 95% of all the food consumed in sub-Saharan Africa (Johnson et al., 2015). They observe further that the supremacy of informal markets is unlikely to be dented by the continent's spreading supermarket chains. ILRI estimates that by 2040, informal markets will still supply up to 70% of consumer demand for food. Small traditional markets therefore have a necessary place in the economy, and supermarkets must consider this fact when planning for food product sales. It is argued further that supermarkets have been branding their food products on the safety card. They have been claiming that their food products are safer and more hygienic than is the case in the traditional markets. However, the ILRI report has shown that the argument is contestable, and research findings revealed that traditional markets are also safe. Supermarkets must look for better competitive advantage over traditional markets and take a critical look into the traditions of the people in forecasting their market shares.

According to Nielsen (2015), Africa has six out of the ten fastest-growing economies in the world with a growing population consisting of the greatest proportion of young people. However, modern trade is quite new and in the early stages of growth. The most common shopping channel is the table top business, which is set up at the side of the road or in marketplaces. As Nielsen (ibid.) states,' Traditional and informal retail remains the most prevalent form of shopping in both urban and rural areas as it meets consumers' needs in terms of convenience, local proximity and flexibility in packaging, pricing and trading hours'. The Nielsen report also found that more than 80% of consumer shops are on tabletops in sub-Saharan Africa. The report revealed further that consumers in the region have shown a powerful preference for products that they have tried before or have been recommended to them. Shopping preferences and the types of products purchased also vary significantly from country to country. Another characteristic of the market is that a small proportion of retail outlets can have a dominant portion of sales. These features pose a huge and complex problems for introducing new products into the region. Promotion strategies must be carefully planned and well thought out to attract consumers. OR tools are highly necessary for this situation.

Of concern is also the fact that there is protest across Africa against the introduction of supermarkets into the African food supply chain. GRAIN (2018) asserts that the African food market, dominated by traditional small vendors, provides natural and healthy foods andgivesa source of livelihood for millions of smallholder vendors and local farmers. Consequently, local vendors and farmers are protesting against the introduction of big supermarket chains into their countries. Cases are cited for French supermarket chains such as Auchan in Senegal. This is a dimension that cannot be ignored when planning for the introduction or expansion of the supermarkets business, especially in the food sector in Africa.

Facility Location and Demand Forecasting troubles: Fraym (2017)provides reasons for the failure of a well-networked supermarket chain in East Africa, Nakumatt, which was a Kenyan retailer. According to Fraym (2017), Nakumatt forecasted a fast-growing economy with a fast-growing middle class in East Africa and therefore opened many stores, which did not live to their expectations. They located their stores in areas that were forecasted to have high demand and high purchasing power, but they did not work out as planned. For instance, in Uganda, the Oasis area was over-located with stores leading to their own cannibalisation, which means competing against themselves. Fraym's (2017) study revealed that Nakumatt had five stores in the Oasis area of Kampala, and one of them was just in front of the other. In addition, there were other competitors in the area, which caused them to fail to realise the projected numbers. Stores must use experts with knowledge and experience in demand forecasting so as to consider as many parameters as possible. Current tools include the use of geospatial data about African consumers, as suggested by Fraym (2017). Through geospatial data tools, one can track consumer information such as how they purchase, where they purchase, and how they are able to pay for the products. Detailed data mapping and the application of valid demand forecasting tools are essential for a supermarket's success.

OR in the supermarkets of East Africa

In addition to the characteristics of the retail market in the region, it is necessary to know the status of applications of OR in various areas of the supermarkets in East Africa. Data were collected from the selected supermarkets in Dar-es-Salaam city of Tanzania to access the situation. Specifically, the questionnaire was designed to assess the application of OR tools in nine areas, as discussed in the literature review section. An instrument was prepared to seek data from stores around Dar-es-Salaam. The team managed to collect data from five supermarkets out of the 30 current major supermarkets in Dar-es-Salaam (Ahmed, 2019), which is about 17%of the supermarkets. About 88 questionnaires were distributed through the central management of shopping centres to collect data from various staff, and 66 were responded to (75%) as shown in Table 7.3. Dar-es-Salaam is the major business city in Tanzania and therefore provides a significant representative sample of supermarkets around the country.

The collected qualitative data from five supermarkets in Dar-es-Salaam indicate that all the surveyed supermarkets have common features associated with the use or failure of using OR tools, as shown in Table 7.4.

Table 7.3 Summary of data collection

No. of Supermarkets	Branches in TZ	Responses	% Response
5	21	66	75%

Table 7.4 Summary of responses about OR applications in supermarkets in Dar-es-Salaam

Sno	OR problem type	Most common practice	% response
1	Facility location	Spreadsheets models	76%
2	Transportation – vendors	Vendor side	85%
3	Shelf Space allocation	Consultant	73%
4	Inventory Control	Special software	91%
5	Promotion Planning	Consultant	88%
6	Staff scheduling	Experience	94%
7	Demand forecasting	Special software	85%
8	Queuing models	Experience	97%
9	Product pricing	Experience	88%

In terms of facility location, most (76%) of the supermarkets indicated that they only used experience, including the popularity of the location, purchasing power of the residents in the surrounding environment, and rental charges. Data analysis through a spreadsheet was also indicated as one of the bases for decision-making. However, no optimisation models wereapplied;the final decisions were made by the management based on the results of the analysed parameters and general experience.

The cost of transportation of the products from vendors to the stores was included in the cost of sales, and this was mostly (85%) covered by vendors in the case of local products. On the shipping of products from foreign sources, the shipping costs depended on the requirements of the country of origin and the available shipping routes. There was no evidence of applications of OR tools in this case, and it largely depended on the vendor's experiences.

Shelf space optimisation was also done from the experience of managers with the help of supermarket shelf designers (73%) who were engaged from time to time to change the look and arrangement of the shelves. Interestingly, more stores (91%) indicated the use of software systems for inventory management, which was an indication of the application of OR tools in inventory matters. However, on the issue of promotion optimisation, most (88%) of the interviewed store managers indicated that they engaged promotion companies for planning. It was not clear how these companies decided on promotion strategies. Almost all the respondents (94%) indicated that they did not use any scientific tools for staff scheduling, and they depended on the experience of various situations in the daily running of the business. Pertaining to demand forecasting, more respondents (85%) revealed that they wereusing special software systems in forecasting various forms of future demand. Specifically, a software called footfall or foot trafficking is commonly used to track customer entrants to the supermarkets by connecting the software to the CCTV cameras. About 97%of the respondents revealed that they were not using any software tools for the management of queues in the stores. Managers' experience was employed to determine the number of POS servers to be working at particular times of the day in order to reduce queues. More respondents (88%)

revealed the use of experience and past data for product pricing. They indicated that prices were dependent on the cost of sales, customer demand, competition, the nature of product brands, and managerial experiences to determine prices from time to time.

These data were complemented with secondary data that provided insight from other research work about East African supermarkets. A report by Wagner et al.(2016) presented data that were collected from nine other supermarkets in Dar-es-Salaam. All nine supermarkets in the report indicated challenges, some of which were related to the absence of the use of OR tools. For instance, they revealed that there was an insufficient number of qualified staff in the local market to run their businesses, and as a consequence they resorted to poaching staff from each other. Staff-scheduling optimisation might have helped to reduce the magnitude of the problem by ensuring optimal scheduling of staff. Furthermore, the challenge of long queues is mentioned and claimed to appear in all supermarkets, where customers are unwilling to wait in long queues for services. This requires the application of queuing systems theory to determine the right resource requirements.

The application of OR was found in specific supermarkets in Kenya, through student dissertations, mostly from the University of Nairobi, who surveyed supermarkets in Nairobi for various tools utilisation. Kithinji (2015) investigated the impact of information technology on inventory management in supermarkets in the city of Nairobi. The study concluded that supermarkets in Nairobi, Kenya implemented vendor-managed inventory systems and warehouse management systems. Makori (2013) investigated real-time information processing in optimising the supply chain among supermarkets in Nairobi. Real-time information processing is very important in supermarkets business because it enables the real-time capture of data that can be used for future decision-making. The study revealed that all supermarkets in Nairobi use real-time information processing technology with the following technologies in place, barcodes, mobile phones, internet, Radio Frequency Identification (RFID), and Global Positioning System (GPS). This has led to improved inventory management, increased supply chain visibility, and a reduction in labour costs. Njoike (2015) surveyed the application of data mining in predicting customer purchase behaviour in Kenyan supermarkets. The report found that Excel is the most widely used software at 92%usage,mainly for measuring the frequency of sales and customer purchase. However, it emerged that various variables were not captured due to the use of manual systems. Many recommendations were drawn, including the need to invest in advanced data mining systems.

Observation: Some supermarkets apply software systems, which are fitted with OR tools, especially in inventory control. However, it is not clear as to what extent this software has been customised to fit the East African market. Save for the few software applications, it is clear that many processes that could have benefited from OR tools are manually operated.

As presented in the Kenyan case, large and medium scale supermarkets apply software systems for decision-making in their businesses. Some of the systems have OR tools that can be used to improve decision-making situations. For instance, Excel is a widely available system used in many applications that require a spreadsheet environment in data analysis. Within Excel, there are decision-making OR tools such as solver, goal seek, scenario evaluations, and several statistical analysis tools as add-ins. These can be very useful in data analysis and optimisation. In the Kenyan situation, it was noted that supermarkets are collecting vast amounts of data through electronic means, including barcodes, RFID and GPS, but techniques such as data mining are not common. These could be used to better forecast future demands, inventory control, queuing systems, and facility location decisions.

Conclusion

This chapter explored the applications of OR tools in supermarkets around East Africa. It was observed that OR tools are highly applicable and have been very useful in aiding managerial level decision-making situations through optimisation, simulation, and demand forecasting. It was also intended to establish specific features of the East African supermarket consumers. The reviewed articles revealed that African consumers have a specific shopping culture in local tabletop markets rather than going to supermarkets. In addition, more than 80% of consumers spend their money in tabletop markets. Furthermore, it was established that the environment is unlikely to change in the near future since millions of small vendors and farmers depend on traditional systems for their livelihoods. The African market is also noted to be dependent on a country and not uniform around the continent since shopping preferences vary across countries. Moreover, a small proportion of retail outlets can have a dominant portion of sales because of the culture of people; people tend to shop more on what they are used to or have been recommended to by trusted colleagues and tend to shy away from new products.

Research revealed that the application of OR tools in the supermarket business in the region is minimal. Managers rely more on experience and manual systems. The OR tools are essential in business growth, as presented in the literature. However, OR models must be customised by introducing variables of features specific to the region if the businesses have to succeed through better decision-making.

Limitations of the study

This study included as many articles as was possible within the set search criteria; however, the researchers could not access articles directly from some restricted databases due to financial constraints. Furthermore, data collection was limited to Dar-es-Salaam supermarkets as a representative sample of supermarkets in the region. The period of data collection and writing of the article was limited.

Further research directions

This study was able to reveal gaps in OR applications in supermarkets in the region. This calls for exploration of OR related research. Literature on OR problems in the supermarkets in the region such as inventory control, transportation optimisation, demand forecasting, queuing systems and others that include features of the regional market is scant. Further studies should include more databases so as to shed light on new areas that need OR tools in the supermarket business within the region.

References

Abouali, A., Harraz, N., &Fors, M. (2014). Optimizing inventory replenishment and shelf space management in retail stores. Proceedings of the Second International Conference on Advances In Social Science, Economics and Management Study-SEM 2014, Institute of Research Engineers and Doctors, USA.

Aburto, L., &Weber, R. (2003). Design and application of hybrid intelligent systems. The Third International Conference on Hybrid Intelligent Systems (HIS03), Melbourne, Australia, 14–17December 2003.

Aguiar, M. (2015). *The Retail Shelf Space Allocation Problem: New Optimization Method Applied to a Supermarket Chain.* Unpublished PhD Dissertation, submitted at the University of Porto, Portugal.

Ahmed, A. M. (2019). *Determinants of Supermarket Performance in Dar-es-Salaam, Tanzania.* Unpublished Masters dissertation, submitted at College of Business Education, Dar es Salaam.

Amin, S., &Zhang, G. (2013). A multi-objective facility location model for closed-loop supply chain network under uncertain demand and return. *Applied Mathematical Modelling*, 37(6), 4165–4176.

Anas, A. (1982). *Residential Location Markets and Urban Transportation Economic Theory Econometrics and Policy Analysis with Discrete Choice Models.* Academic Press, Waltham.

Aras, S., Kocakoç, I., &Polat, C. (2017). Comparative study on retail sales forecasting between single and combination methods. *Journal of Business Economics and Management*, 18(5), 803–832.

Awasthia, A., Chauhan, S., &Goyal, S. (2011). A multi-criteria decision making approach for location planning for urban distribution centres under uncertainty. *Mathematical and Computer Modelling*, 53(1–2), 98–109.

Ashtiani, M. G. (2016). Competitive location: a state-of-art review. *International Journal of Industrial Engineering Computations*, 7, 1–18.

Beltov, T., Jorgensen, S., &Zaccour, G. (2006). Optimal retail price promotions. *Anales de Estudios Economicos y Empresariales*, XVI, 9–36.

Bo-Jian, L. (2013). A dynamic model for an optimal price promotion strategy of new products for retailers. *The Journal of Global Business Management*, 9(2), 42–52.

Boutilier, C., Dean, T., &Hanks, S. (1999). Decision-theoretic planning: structural assumptions and computational leverage. *Journal of Artificial Intelligence Research*, 11, 1–11.

Burkul, V., Oh, J., Peel, L., &Yang, H. (2015). Reducing customer waiting time with new layout design. *International Journal of Engineering and Industries (IJEI)*, 6(2), 8–16.

Candogan, O., Pimpikis, K., &Ozdaglar, A. (2012). Optimal pricing in networks with externalities. *Operations Research*, 60(4), 883–905.

Chapados, N., Joliveau, M., L'Ecuyer, P., &Rousseau, L. (2014). Retail store scheduling for profit. *European Journal of Operational Research*, 239(3), 609–624.

Cohen, M. C., Kalas, J. and Perakis, G. (2017b). Optimizing promotions for multiple items in supermarkets. *SSRN Electronic Journal*. Retrieved from https://ssrn.com/abstract=3061451, http://dx.doi.org/10.2139/ssrn.3061451. Accessed on 29 October 2019.

Cohen, M. C., Leung, N. Z., Panchamgam, K., Perakis, G., &Smith, A. (2017a). The impact of linear optimization on promotion planning. *Operations Research*, 65(2), 446–468.

Cohen, M. C., &Perakis, G. (2018). Promotion optimization in retail. *SSRN Electronic Journal*, Retrieved from https://ssrn.com/abstract=3194640; http://dx.doi.org/10.2139/ssrn.3194640. Accessed on 1 December 2019.

Corinne, B., Saskia, S., &Barbara, L. (2014). A conceptual framework to understand retailers' logistics and transport organization-illustrated for groceries' goods movements in France and Germany. 93rd Annual Meeting Transportation Research Board – TRB, France, Jan 2014.

Corstjens, M. & Doyle, P. (1981). A Model for Optimizing Retail Space Allocations. *Management Science*, 27(7), 822–883.

den Boer, A. (2013). Dynamic pricing and learning: historical origins, current research, and new directions. *Surveys in Operations Research and Management Science*, 20(1), 1–18.

Drezner, T. (1994). Locating a single new facility among existing unequally attractive facilities. *Journal of Regional Science, Wiley Online*, 34, 237–252.

Drezner, T. (2014). A review of competitive facility location in the plane. *Logistics Research*, 7(114), 1–12.

Drezner, T., &Drezner, Z. (2002). Retail facility location under changing market conditions. *IMA Journal of Management Mathematics*, 13(4), 283–302.

Ellickson, P., &Misra, S. (2008). Supermarket pricing strategies. *Marketing Science*, 27(5), 811–828.

Ernst, A., Jiang, H., Krishnamoorthy, M., &Siear, D. (2004). Staff scheduling and rostering: a review of applications, methods and models. *European Journal of Operational Research*, 153(1), 3–27.

Farahani, R., Seifi, M.&Asgari, N. (2010). Multiple criteria facility location problems: a survey. *Applied Mathematical Modelling*, 34(7), 1689–1709.

Fergany, H. (2016). Probabilistic multi-item inventory model with varying mixture shortage cost under restrictions. *SpringerPlus*, 5(1), 1–13.

Fraym (2017). Getting store support ratios right – why nakumatt went down in East Africa?. Retrieved from https://fraym.io/getting-store-support-ratios-right-nakumatt-east-africa/. Accessed on 21 November 2019.

GRAIN (2018). Supermarkets out of Africa! Food systems across the continent are doing just fine without them. *GRAIN Reports*. Retrieved from https://www.grain.org/media/W1siZiIsIjIwMTgvMTEvMDgvMDdfMDBfMThfMjMxX1N1cGVybWFya2V0c19vdXRfb2ZfQWZyaWNhX0VOXzAzLnBkZiJdXQ. Accessed on 8 November 2019.

Hodgson, M. J. (1978). Toward more realistic allocation in location allocation models: an interaction approach. *Environment and Planning A*, 10(11), 1273–1285.

Hotelling, H. (1929). Stability in competition. *The Economic Journal*, 39(153), 41–57.

Huff, D. L. (1966). A programmed solution for approximating an optimum retail location. *Land Economics*, 42(3), 293–303.

Igwe, A., Onwumere, J., &Egbo, O. (2014). Efficient queue management in supermarkets: a case study of Makurdi Town, Nigeria. *European Journal of Business and Management*, 6(39), 185–192.

Jian, J., &Gao, Y. (2012). Status and optimization strategies based supermarket chain of the supply chain and distribution mode – distribution center Suguo Maqun as an example. *iBusiness*, 4, 335–340.

Jiang, Q, Xing, W., Hou, R., &Zhou, B. (2015). An optimization model for inventory system and the algorithm for the optimal inventory costs based on supply-demand balance. *Mathematical Problems in Engineering*, 1, 1–11.

Jiao, S. (2010). Application of dynamic random simulation in supermarket. Proceedings of the 2010 International Conference on Information Technology and Scientific Management, 1, 229–231.

Jingya, L., Yue, W., &Jiabin, L. (2017). Optimisation of intermodal transport chain of supermarkets on Isle of Wight, UK. *International Journal of Social, Behavioural, Educational, Economic, Business and Industrial Engineering*, 11(4), 856–863.

John, O., Daniel, H., &Henrik, P. (2019). Framework of last mile logistics research: a systematic review of the literature. *Sustainability*, 11(7131), 1–25.

Johnson, N., Mayne, J., Grace, D. and Wyatt, A. (2015). How will training traders contribute to improved food safety in informal markets for meat and milk? A theory of change analysis. IFPRI Discussion Paper 1451, IFPRI, Washington, DC.

Jorne, V., Jeroen, B., Philippe, D., Erik, D., &Liesje, D. (2012). Personnel scheduling: a literature review. *HUB Research Paper 2012/43*, 1–40.

Kilimci, Z., Akyuz, A., Uysal, M., Akyokus, S., Uysa, M., Bulbul, B., &Ekmis, M. (2019). An improved demand forecasting model using deep learning approach and proposed decision integration strategy for supply chain. *Complexity*, 7, 1–15.

King, P., &Park, T. (2004). Modelling productivity in supermarket operations: incorporating the impacts of store characteristics and information technologies. *Journal of Food Distribution Research* 35(2), 1–14.

Kithinji, F. (2015). *Impact of Information Technology on Inventory Management in Supermarkets in Nairobi City County*. Unpublished Master Dissertation, submitted at the University of Nairobi, Kenya.

Kubera, Y., Mathieu, P., &Picault, S. (2010). An interaction-oriented model of customer behaviour for the simulation of supermarkets. Proceedings of the 2010 IEEE/WIC/ACM International Conference on Web Intelligence and Intelligent Agent Technology, 2, 407–410.

Kumar, S. (2008). A study of the supermarket industry and its growing logistics capabilities, *International Journal of Retail & Distribution Management*, 36(3), 192–211.

Lesmono, D., &Limansyah, T. (2017). A multi item probabilistic inventory model, *Journal of Physics Conference Series*, 893(1), 1–7.

Li, B. (2013). A dynamic model for an optimal price promotion strategy of new products for retailers. *The Journal of Global Business Management*, 9(2), 42–52.

Makori, W. (2013). *Real-time Information Processing and Supply Chain Optimization among Supermarkets in Nairobi, Kenya*. Unpublished Masters Dissertation submitted at the University of Nairobi, Kenya.

Masatochi, S., Ichiro, N., Takeshi, M., Tomohiro, H. (2013). Purchase and transportation planning for food retailing in Japan. *Asia Pacific Management Review*, 18(1), 79–92.

Melachrinoudis, E. (1995). A microcomputer cashier scheduling system for supermarket stores. *International Journal of Physical Distribution & Logistics Management*, 25(1), 34–50.

Miwa, K., &Takakuwa, S. (2008). Simulation modelling and analysis for in-store merchandizing of retail stores with enhanced information technology. In Mason, S. J.,

Hill, R. R., Mönch, L., Rose, O., Jefferson, T., and Fowler, J. W. (Eds), *Proceedings of the 2008 Winter Simulation Conference*, Miami FL.
Mohamad, F., &Saharin, S. (2019). Application of Discrete Event Simulation (DES) for queuing system improvement at hypermarket. FGIC 2nd Conference on Governance and Integrity 2019, *KnE Social Sciences*, 330–346.
Nielsen (2015). Africa: how to navigate the retail distribution labyrinth. *Global Nielsen News and Insights*. Retrieved from https://www.nielsen.com/eg/en/insights/report/2015/africa-how-to-navigate-the-retail-distribution-labyrinth/#, The Nielsen Company. Accessed on 25 November 2019.
Njoike, C. (2015). *Applications of Customer Relationship Management and Data Mining in Predicting Customer Purchase Behaviour in Medium and Large Supermarkets in Kenya*. Unpublished Masters Dissertation, submitted at the University of Nairobi.
Oberoi, S. S. (2017). Profit maximizing probability inventory model under trade credit. *International Journal of Economics and Financial Issues*, 7(4), 408–410.
Patak, M., Branska, L., &Pecinova, Z. (2015). Demand forecasting in retail grocery stores in the Czech Republic. SGEM 2015 International Multidisciplinary Scientific Conferences on Social Sciences and Arts, Sofia, Georgia.
Rao, V. R., &Joseph, Thomas L. J. (1973). Dynamic models for sales promotion policies. *Operational Research Quarterly (1970–1977)*, 24(3), 403–417.
Selva, P. (2019). ARIMA model – complete guide to time series forecasting in Python. *Machine Learning Plus*. Retrieved from https://www.machinelearningplus.com/time-series/arima-model-time-series-forecasting-python/. Accessed on 1 September 2020.
Reilly, W.J. (1931). *The law of retail gravitation*. New York: Knickerbocker Press.
Shan, W., Yan, Q., Chen, C., Zhang, M., Yao, B., &Fu, X. (2017). Optimization of competitive facility location for chain stores. *Annals of Operations Research*, 273(3), 187–205.
Shetty, M., Nawada, V., Pai, K., &Kumar, R. (2018). Predicting sales in supermarkets. *International Research Journal of Engineering and Technology (IRJET)*, 05(03), 994–997.
Shilpa, P., Jagadeesh, D., &Arun, K. (2014). A study on transport cost optimization in retail distribution. *Journal of Supply Chain Management Systems*, 3(4), 31–38.
Signe, L., &Johnson, C. (2018). Africa's consumer market potential: trends, drivers, opportunities, and strategies. *African Growth Initiatives at Brookings*. Retrieved from https://www.brookings.edu/wp-content/uploads/2018/12/africas-consumer-market-potential.pdf. Accessed on 2 December 2019.
Simchi-Levi, D., &Zhao, Y. (2012). Performance evaluation of stochastic multi-echelon inventory systems: a survey. *Advances in Operations Research*, 5, 1–34.
Steeneken, F., &Ackley, D. (2012). A complete model of the supermarket business. *BP Trends*, 1–13.
Sternbeck, M., &Kuhn, H. (2014). Grocery retail operations and automotive logistics: a functional cross-industry comparison. *Benchmarking: An International Journal*, 21(5): 814–834.
Surjandari, I., Rachman, A., &Lusiani, M. (2012). Optimization of products shelf space allocation based on product price using multilevel association rules. 2012 2nd International Conference on Industrial Technology and Management (ICITM 2012), Singapore.
Taha, A. (2007). *Operations Research: An Introduction*. Pearson Prentice Hall, New Jersey.
Tekin, P., &Erol, R. (2017). A new dynamic pricing model for the effective sustainability of perishable product life cycle. *Sustainability*, 9(1330), 1–22.

Thiesing, F., &Vornberber, O. (1997). Sales forecasting using neural networks. *Proceedings International Conference in Neural Networks*,97(4), 2125–2128.

Tsai, C., &Huang, S. (2015). A data mining approach to optimize shelf space allocation in consideration of customer purchase and moving behaviours. *International Journal of Production Research*, 53(3), 850–866.

Valverde, J., &Succar, L. (2010). Controlling the supermarket service. *Reporte Técnico No. CCC-10-006*. Computer Science Department, National Institute of Astrophysics, Optics and Electronics, Mexico.

Wagner, J., Nickel, S., Rempel, J., &Verbenkov, M. (2016). Supermarket food procurement practices in Dar es Salaam: risks and benefits for rural smallholder farmers. *Undercurrent Journal*, XII(I), 36–48.

Xian, T., Hong, C., &Hawari, N. (2016). Modelling and simulation of queuing system for customer service improvement: a case study. The 4th International Conference on Quantitative Sciences and Its Applications (ICOQSIA 2016), Bangi, Malaysia

Zhou, X. (2017). Research on optimization of queuing system based on computer simulation. *2017* International Conference on Computer Technology, Electronics and Communication (ICCTEC), IEEE, Dalian, China.

Zufryden, F. S. (1986). A dynamic programming approach for product selection and supermarket shelf-space allocation. *The Journal of the Operational Research Society*, 37(4), 413–422.

8 Strategies used by local food suppliers to increase participation in modern food retailing in Tanzania

Felix Adamu Nandonde

Introduction

The global management consulting firm A.T. Kearney's (2014) report suggests that supermarket penetration in Tanzania is growing rapidly; however, 80% of the food items sold by these outlets is imported. That means that while Tanzania has witnessed a rapid rise in modern urban food retailing spearheaded by South African and Kenyan retailers, participation of local agri-food suppliers in modern food retailing is very low (see Nandonde, 2016). These findings contrast with the findings in a study by Snyder et al. (2015) in a survey in Dar-es-Salaam, which showed that 61% of packaged processed food sold in modern food stores were manufactured in Tanzania. Despite these contradictory findings, little is known about the strategies used by local food suppliers in increasing their participation in modern food retailing in Tanzania. Previous studies proposed understanding the response of local food suppliers following the emergence of modern food retailers that seem to prefer imported foods (Readorn, 2015; Snyder et al., 2015; Nandonde and Kuada, 2014)., The current study therefore intends to fill that knowledge gap.

Previous studies conducted in Africa on the agri-food business focused on the demand for processed food (Snyder et al., 2015), the criteria used by modem food retailers in the selection of local food suppliers (Nandonde and Kuada, 2016), changes introduced by agri-food processors (Reardon, 2015), and resources challenges to African food producers (Fafchamps, 1997). Other studies focused on the difficulties that local food suppliers in developing countries face in seeking inclusion in the modern food retail chains. Neven et al. (2006) studied consumer behaviour and food retailing in Kenya; Emongor (2008) studied the retailing impact in the Southern Africa Development Community (SADC) region. Others include Onzere (2012), who studied the impact of the emergence of modern retailers on fruits and vegetable suppliers in Uganda, and Sindi (2013), who investigated the implication of the emergence of supermarkets for the agri-food system and the rural poor in Kenya.

Other studies on Africa's food business focused on connecting African producers with markets within the European Union (EU). These studies concentrated on the procurement of fish and horticultural produce from Kenya, Uganda, Tanzania,

DOI: 10.4324/9780367854300-8

Ghana, and South Africa (see Dolan and Humphrey, 2000; Kadigi et al., 2007; Fold and Gough, 2008; Asfaw et al., 2010; Bukenya et al., 2012).

Although the relationship between the African growers and the EU retailers is very important for the economy of the continent, we submit that the changes in agri-food distribution currently taking place on the continent create additional opportunities for economic growth and poverty alleviation and therefore require academic and policy attention. As Atasoy (2013) argues, the lack of research in this area makes it difficult to assess the impact of these changes on production and consumption. Consequently, little is known on the response of local food processors in accessing modern food retailing in Africa following marginalisation. This study therefore intends to study the strategies used by local food suppliers in Tanzania to access modern food retail stores in the country and thus cover the knowledge gap in the discipline.

Participation levels among local food suppliers in the new emerging food retailing business in Tanzania remain minimal compared to the country's potential for food production. It is therefore important to understand the strategies used by the local food suppliers to increase their participation in the country. Thus, the study aims to answer the research question: what strategies are implemented by the local food suppliers to increase their participation in modern food retailing in Tanzania? This study used a case study approach and was guided by the resource-based view and network relationship theory to answer this question.

Literature review

The available evidence indicates that Tanzanian food processing is dominated by SMEs, which represents 97% of food processing activity (AfDB, 2014). Furthermore, the country's food processing industry is faced with many challenges, including low-level technology, inadequate raw materials, high operation costs, distribution bottlenecks, and insufficient working capital (MIT, 2012; AfDB, 2014; Tisimia, 2014). These obstacles appear to have influenced retailers to stock 80% of consumer goods in the form of imported products (A.T. Kearney, 2014). This means, for the local food suppliers to survive, access to resources such as finance and technology is very important.

According to the resources based view (RBV) theory, a firm's resources enable processors to formulate and implement strategies that help them achieve a competitive advantage (Wernerfelt, 1984; Barney, 1991). Since its inception, the theory has been used at different levels, from farming to retail distribution (see Schiefer and Hartman, 2008). Building on the understanding that resources are important in shaping competition, we used the resources based view to gain insight into the types of resources that local food suppliers in Tanzania need in order to enhance their inclusion in the modern food retail chain. The study also intended to gain insight into the availability of these resources and the manner in which they can be leveraged. However, in our assessment, resources-leveraging strategies in and of themselves are inadequate to understand the issues that this study seeks to address; this includes the factors that determine actors' support of each other in the value chain, and the manner in which the relationships between food suppliers and retailers can be maintained on a sustained basis.

The food business in most developing countries is generally characterised by opportunistic behaviours such as overpricing, false claims, and malpractice. These tendencies, that is, cheating, overpricing, and adulteration, have also been reported in other studies on the Tanzanian food business (see Bjerkas and Kagirwa, 1994; Gibbon, 1997; Kurwijila et al., 2005; Kabissa, 2014). Thus, according to studies (i.e. Mohr and Spekman, 1994; Sørensen, 2011), managing collaborations in buyer–supplier relationships requires mechanisms that safeguard the interest of partners and, at the same time, coordinate their transactions. Furthermore, food policies are very fragile in developing economies, and that local food suppliers are not well developed to meet market demand. In addition, the enforcement of contracts is almost negligible in many developing economies.

These challenges complicate supplier–retailer relationships. Under such conditions, Möller and Halinen's (2000) and Grönroos' (1994) assessments of network approaches in studying complex relationships in business are highly useful. The authors argue that the network-based retail marketing theory is most appropriate for understanding the complex relationships that characterise retail in developing countries because of a wide range of direct and indirect actors in the relationships. This argument encouraged our decision to explore the relevance of the network approach to the present study.

This study used theories such as marketing relationship theory (Dwyer et al., 1987; Hunt and Morgan, 1994a; Morgan and Hunt, 1994b;) and business network theory (Stern and Reve, 1980; Ander et al., 1994; Möller and Halinen, 2000; Grönroos, 1994, 1994b; Mattsson, 1997) in describing the relationships between buyers and suppliers and emphasising joint actions and flexibility among partners in achieving mutual goals.

Network theory provides insights into the dynamics of retailer–supplier interactions. Studies on retailer–supplier relationships in developed countries reveal reciprocal support. For example, the available empirical evidence shows that some European retailers invest in their relationships with food suppliers from developing economies. The forms of marketing support could be locating merchandising officers as advisers and providing financial support to cover promotion costs. Furthermore, studies show that retailers' support to small-scale suppliers of fresh vegetables is important for enhancing their supply to the modern food retailers (Andersson et al., 2015; Bloom, 2015). Retailers may also support local food suppliers in meeting the set standards and in improving the value chain through training and managerial skills.

Turning specifically to marketing activities, it is important to note that network theory sees marketing in terms of the coordination of the exchange of activities involving direct and indirect partners, with a view to mobilising and coordinating critical resources through a relationship with them (Möller and Halinen, 2000; Gummeson, 2002). In terms of food marketing, this approach has been used to study the management of relationships between suppliers and retailers in UK food value chains (Hingley et al., 2006; Hingley, 2005a; Wycherley, 2002; White

2000). Most previous studies, however, were based on a dyadic approach and were conducted in America and Europe. There have been some studies during the past decade on the buyer–seller relationship in developing economies, following the internationalisation of retail (see Elg et al., 2008; Ghauri et al., 2008).

During the last decade, studies on retail networking have included external factors such as socio-political influence (Elg et al., 2008). In countries such as Tanzania, institutions and political systems are critical to every aspect of business. In this regard, it is very important to look at the impact of economic and political factors on the formation of relationships because every organisation has to behave in a similar way based on the surrounding environment (Hadjikhani and Ghauri, 2001; Hadjikhani et al., 2008). In this regard, the current study extends network theory to include external factors in establishing business relationships in Tanzania. The area where the role of institutions is highly visible in developing countries is legal certification, which is frequently used as an indication of product quality. These certifications may come in the form of business licences, standards certificates, or health issues compliance certificates. Digal (2015) found that food safety certification is one of the important criteria for suppliers to access modern food retail.

In this regard, we argue that local food suppliers who lack important resources for producing high-quality products are likely to benefit from a stable relationship with modern food retailers who are assumed to have more resources. Furthermore, the influence of external actors is very important for this relationship to be meaningful in Tanzania business environment.

Methodology

The study used a critical realism qualitative case study approach to examine strategies used by local food suppliers to increase their participation in modern food distribution in Tanzania. The case study research strategy attempted to examine a contemporary phenomenon in its real-life context when the boundaries between the phenomenon and the context were not clear (Yin, 1981). As Yin (1981) observes, two factors make a case study approach important in a particular piece of research: The first is the situation in which one studies a new phenomenon. The second is an investigation in which one cannot separate the process and the actors. Since the emergence of modern food retail is a new phenomenon in Africa and the manner in which retailers decide on what to purchase from local suppliers is not well understood in developing economies, the study considered the case method as appropriate for this research. Nine cases were selected.

The cases used in the study comprised local food suppliers whose selection was based on age; three years was the minimum time for operation, as shown in Table 8.2. Food suppliers were selected after identification of the products of a particular firm in modern food stores. As Creswell (2013) and Plummer (1983) suggest, for qualitative research, it is very important to have participants who are marginal, great, or ordinary. In general, issues of whether or not to sell occur more at the firm level, and could be more than what participants would be ready to share. For this study, those without access to modern food retail distribution were marginalised, while the great were those with access to modern food retail stores. In that respect, this study took the initiative in finding some of the leading food brands that the researcher found in one store and not in other outlets.

Eleven managers of nine food processing companies were interviewed for the study. For collaboration of findings, seven retail branch managers were interviewed on strategies used by local food suppliers for increasing their participation. The retail firms interviewed include Nakumatt and Uchumi from Kenya and Game from South Africa. Local retail firms include Panone, Imalaseko, TSN, and Shop-N-Save. Furthermore, six participants from government institutions that regulate and promote the food industry in Tanzania were interviewed. The participants came from the Tanzania Food and Drugs Authority (TFDA), Tanzania Bureau of Standards (TBS), Tanzania Chambers of Commerce, Industries and Agriculture (TCCIA), and Small Industries Development Organisation (SIDO). These provided additional information on the food distribution situation in Tanzania.

As Patton (1987) argues, the key factor for selecting and making decisions about the appropriate unit of analysis is deciding on the unit one wants to discuss. It therefore becomes important to understand and identify contextual factors surrounding the unit of analysis (Grünbaum, 2007). Thus, the goal of the study was to explore strategies used by local food suppliers to increase their participation in modern food distribution in Tanzania. In that regard, this study employed relationships as a unit of analysis.

This study used a semi-structured interview for the selected case studies. The interview guidelines were used to guide the interviewer. Interview questions were developed from the previous literature on retail in Africa and the linkage of small-scale farmers (Sindi, 2013), and the impact of the emergence of supermarkets in a host country (Emongor, 2008; Onzere, 2012). Others include and the supplier–retailer relationship (Hingley, 2001, 2005, 2005). A voice recorder was used in the data collection process. The researcher asked for permission from the participants before the use of the voice recorder. The researcher told the respondents the reasons for recording them and explained the importance of the exercise for the study and, more specifically, the importance of recording at the data analysis stage. Some of the participants accepted, and some were rejected. In addition, a field notebook was used to record conversations for all interviews. Data were collected from September 2014 through February 2015.

The topic of the interviews included the types of food produced by retailers, the types of products one would like to buy but is not available in the country, the type of food requested by retailers, factors limiting the participation of local food suppliers in the modern food stores, and the strategies used by retailers to increase their participation. Data were collected in Arusha, Morogoro, and Dar-es-Salaam. The products used in this study included fresh and packaged food products. Processed foods selected for the study included maize flour, rice, sunflower cooking oil, rice, and dried beans. Fresh products included chicken meat, sausages, tomatoes sauce, beef, vegetables, and fruits. According to Green (2015), middle-income workers in Tanzania have increased the consumption of and the

Table 8.1 Sample description of the food suppliers that participated in the study

Case (Company)	Year started	Products	Number of employees	Participant position	Number of participants	Gender
Mzomo Services Limited	2004	Beef, fresh and frozen chicken	35	Managing Director (owner)	1	Male
Meat King Limited	1996	Beef, fish, pork, chicken, sausage	30	Managing Director (owner)	1	Female
Namazone Business Centre	2004	Vegetable and fruits supplier	3	Managing Director (owner)	1	Female
Happy Sausage Limited	1990	Beef, pork, sausage	43		1	Male
Kijenge Animal Products Limited	1984	Frozen chicken, animal foods	202	Senior Marketing officers	2	Males
Darsh Industries Limited	1998	Tomato paste and sauce, spices	200	Production Manager	1	Male
Monaban Farming and Trading Company Limited	1994	Wheat flour, maize flour, dried legumes, dried cereals	200	Director of Finance (relative)	1	Male
Foot Loose Tanzania Limited	2003	Maize flour, rice, dried legumes, cooking sunflower	6	Managing Director (owner)	1	Female
Basic Element Company Limited	2010	Maize flour	45	Marketing Manager and Operation Manager	2	Males

demand for packaged protein. Interviews were transcribed in Kiswahili first and then translated from Kiswahili into English. Transcripts were filed for manual analysis.

Qualitative data analysis

This study used a thematic analytical technique for data analysis. Thematic analysis can be defined as the means of searching for themes that emerged as significant in order to describe a particular phenomenon from particular qualitative data (Daly et al., 1997). This process requires an iterative reading of a whole transcript in order to understand and observe patterns that emerge from data. It is a form of pattern recognition within the data in which the emerging codes become the themes for analysis (Fereday and Muir-Cochrane, 2006).

There is no consensus on the terms used for qualitative data analysis (Creswell, 2013). For example, in some works, words like pattern and category are used interchangeably with the theme. Therefore, in this study, 'category' and 'theme' are used as different terms for clarity purposes. Furthermore, the study followed three stages in the thematic data analysis; these stages include codes, category, and theme. Thus, the interpretation will therefore be based on themes.

The first process in thematic qualitative data analysis is reducing the data in text format to display only the relevant words to the study. This process is known as textual coding. To start coding, the researcher used the framework, which was developed from the literature, to guide the analysis. This limits the problem of coding every single sentence in the original text (Attride-Striling, 2001). The second stage was looking for the codes that emerged from the proposed framework. The coding processes were conducted separately from the within-case analysis by reflecting on the research question in this study. The qualitative data were analysed manually and tabulation was used for each case. The cross-case analyses of each theme from the within-case analysis followed next. At this stage, some codes appeared in more than one theme.

'Theme' is a broad unit that combines to form a common idea (Creswell, 2013). In general, a theme combines codes and categories with the goal of giving the meaning of the study based on a particular context. That means that the interpretation of the meaning of a theme has to reflect social actors (Glasser and Strauss, 1967). The researcher started interpreting the data at this level to see if some of the themes were making sense, as previously argued. At this level, the focus was on the communality and differences within cases.

Findings

The extent modern food retailers do business with local food suppliers

The interview with participants from seven modern food retail stores shows that the percentage of food sold in the stores is increasing. For example, Table 8.4 shows that Nakumatt is estimated to sell about 45% of its fresh products and 20% of its processed products from local suppliers. The findings of this study correlate with the findings of a study conducted in Ghana by Andam et al. (2015), who found that international supermarket stock between 72 to 93 imported foods in the stores. Furthermore, our findings are in contrast with the findings in a study by Ijumba et al. (2015), who found that 70% of packaged food sold in modern food stores in Tanzania are locally processed. This difference is probably because our question is based on the percentage of sales comprised of the locally made food sold by them compared to imported products while previous studies based on counting the inventory stocked (see Ijumba et al., 2015).

Table 8.2 shows some of the typical food items supermarkets buy from Tanzania's food suppliers. Food items such as carrots, cabbages, chicken, eggs, and milk are procured in their fresh form from local suppliers. Processed food products such as juice, rice, maize flour, and cooking oil are also bought locally. The chain stores also import some meat from South Africa and apples and grapes from South Africa and Egypt.

Strategies used by local food suppliers to increase their participation

Table 8.4 provides an overview of the strategies used by local suppliers in order to be accepted by the supermarkets as major suppliers. As indicated in Table 8.4, the strategies that local suppliers use to make themselves attractive participants in the food distribution chain include network, innovation, outsourcing, sales support, production of a wide range of products, and the recruitment of experienced staff.

Table 8.2 Typical food procured from local food processors

Items	Products/Brands	Regions (Source of supply)
Fresh fruits and vegetables	Mchicha, carrots, cabbages	Tanga (Lushoto) and Dar-es-Salaam
Semi-processed	Sausage (Happy Sausage), liquid milk (Tanga Fresh, Asas diaries, Tan Dairies), chicken (Interchick)	Arusha, Tanga, Dar-es-Salaam
Maize flour	Variety	Dar-es-Salaam, Arusha
Rice	Felix Rice, Foot Loose and other brands	Dar-es-Salaam, Mbeya and Morogoro
Dried beans	Felix Dried Beans, Foot Loose Dried Beans and other brands	Dar-es-Salaam, Arusha
Juice	Azam Juice (Bakheressa Food Companies)	Dar-es-Salaam
Cooking oil	Sundrop (Murzah)	Dar-es-Salaam, Singida, Arusha
Eggs	Alaska eggs	Dar-es-Salaam

Table 8.3 Estimated percentage of food procured from local suppliers sold in supermarkets in Tanzania

Name of the retailers	Processed packed foods (%)*	Fresh foods (%)*
Nakumatt supermarket	20	45
Uchumi supermarket	50	50
Game supermarket	40	–
Shop-N-Save	15	70
TSN supermarket	20	65
Panone supermarket	20	–
Imalaseko supermarket	15	85

*This percentage is based on estimations of managers' experience based on their annual sales during the interview

Outsourcing of the value chain activities

Six of the food processors who participated in the study engaged in outsourcing food items they supply. For example, Basic Element Limited prefers to procure maize from specified suppliers whom the firms train on quality and maintenance of good standards. In order to have a supply of good quality items, participants initiated contract farming. This finding is in line with the findings in a previous study, which showed that quality is one of the factors influencing suppliers into engaging in outsourcing (Kaipia and Turkulainen, 2016). For example, the interview shows that Basic Element Limited trained officers of their maize suppliers on the quality of maize required by the firm. Similarly, Foot Loose supplied seeds to sunflower growers in Singida and Dodoma with the intention of improving the quality of the supplied seeds for oil pressing. A respondent from Basic Element Limited had this to say,

> Basic Element is currently engaged in a contract with one company, known as Rubuye Agro Farming. This company is working with farmers under contract farming. This company is located in Makambako, Iringa. This year, we had a bumper harvest, and maize is enough. Therefore, our silos are almost full. We used to receive between 60 tonnes to 90 tonnes of maize every day. Here, we have four silos with a storage capacity of 5,000 tonnes each.

The differences in the climatic conditions in different parts of Tanzania make outsourcing a reasonable economic proposition for the local suppliers. For example, sunflower and maize can be grown in different parts of the country. The variability allows for harvesting at different times in the year, and therefore improves the reliability of supplies without incurring huge inventory costs. The finding is similar to the findings in a study by Hsiao et al. (2011) in the Netherlands, who found that reliability influences food processors to outsource some value chain activities. On the other hand, there is a serious infrastructure bottleneck. Furthermore,

Table 8.4 Strategies used by local food suppliers to increase their participation in modern food retailing

Factors	Mzomo	Meat King	Happy Sausage	Namazone	Kijenge Animal	Monaban	Darsh Industries	Basic Element	Foot Loose
Outsourcing	√	√	√	√	x	X	√	x	√
Network	√	√	√	√	x	X	√	x	x
Business relationship	√	√	√	√	x	√	√	√	√
Innovation	√	√	√	x	x √	√	√	x	√
Experienced staff	√	√	√	x	√	√	√	√	X
Sales support	√	x	x	x	x	X	x	x	X
A wide range of products	√	√	√	√	√	√	√	√	√

the fact that agriculture in Tanzania is heavily dependent on rain means that the climatic advantages are somewhat reduced.'

However, outsourcing through contract farming arrangements is not without challenges. As the respondent at Mzomo Limited Services said,

> It is difficult to engage in contract farming. Farmers are not reliable ... If someone goes with money, they sell the chicken. For those with good relationships with us, we give those loans; we give them cash when they deliver the goods. They do not have to wait for the money. Therefore, they bring their goods to us. In addition, we pay a higher price when they bring their goods to us.

Business relationship

The interviews also show that becoming a supplier to a supermarket is not always based on rational economic analysis. Our findings are in line with the findings in previous studies that show that relationships that support the linkages of a supplier to retailers are based on personal relationships (Davies, 1994; Ghauri et al., 2008). Our study shows that social ties and network relationships appear to be important in some situations. In general, the supplier–retailer relationship is based on relational trust and calculative trust. The study shows that retailers are not supporting local suppliers financially or technologically. Furthermore, a business transaction is not controlled by contract, but rather it relies on a social agreement. Relational trust arises when social relations evolve to a stage where each partner can expect to act according to others' preferences and priorities (Poppo et al., 2016, p. 726). For example, if a former schoolmate or former employee of a supplier works in the supermarket, the chances of being selected increase significantly. For example, the owner of Mzomo Services Limited, who was a senior manager in two tobacco firms in Tanzania, admits that social relationships with employees in some of the supermarkets have simplified entry into the chains. There are also occasions when tribal linkages become important. However, previous studies show that frequent communication can lead to a good relationship between actors and which would allow the linkage of a supplier to the retailer. The findings of the present study show that social relationships are very important (Davies, 1994). A respondent from Mzomo Services Limited had this to say,

> Yes, we get access through someone who is our business partner, who is doing business with us and is linked to them. We operate through our network. But they started not to pay us, we stopped for a while, and then we started afresh. But they haven't paid us, ever since we started. It's fine, we know them. So it's networking, you know.

Similarly, the interview with the respondent from Namazone Business Centre indicated that the owner used a long-term network she established while in

Nairobi to become a supplier to the Nakumatt supermarket, Arusha branch. She explained the process this way,

> The man who connected us to this business is the one who is in charge of Fresh and Juicy for Uganda, Kenya, Tanzania, and Rwanda. It is true that Fresh and Juicy is the company that has a subtenant contract with Nakumatt ... When I was in Nairobi, I used to do business with Nakumatt. But that was due to support from my husband because he was a pilot. What kind of business? I used to sell to them flash discs and other IT stuff; therefore, I knew that Nakumatt was selling space, not products. When Nakumatt opened their store here, I said to myself that I would not continue with the IT business anymore. I would work with them by selling them my farm produce.

Local food suppliers also increased their participation by accepting the loss once the goods were delivered to the supermarket. In general, once a good is sold in an open market, the supplier is not liable for any loss related to damage or expiry that may occur to a buyer. But this system is not accepted by modern food retailers. That means for a supplier to be accepted he/she has to bear the loss related to damage while goods are in the custody of the modern retailers. Thus, acceptance of the loss by local food suppliers improved the relationship between them and modern food retailers.

The procurement manager of Uchumi Supermarket said,

> Yes, we have a return policy on expiry date and damages in transit. How do we share the loss? It depends. For example, damage can occur during transit. That one, the supplier has to change. Now we are managing that one before the expiry date. We can drop the price or return it. Or you can give us a new one.

Marketing Manager of Basic Element Limited said,

> ... in reality, it is not 30 days, because my pay is based on the completion of the supplied goods ... Last time, we received a call to exchange goods that amounted to Tsh 30,000, which was near the expiration date.

The use of experienced staff

Scholars indicate that characteristics of human resources, including all of the knowledge, experience, skills, and commitment, and their relationship with other external firms, give the firm a competitive edge (Barney and Wright, 1998; Wright et al., 1994). Recruitment of experienced staff enables local food suppliers to produce commodities that meet consumer demands. In general, food suppliers of maize flour, meat, and tomato paste have employed graduates with experience in food processing, and many of whom are foreigners. These employees seem to be the engine for the success of a number of food suppliers. Furthermore, food innovation initiatives of local food suppliers in meeting consumer demands and government requirements have recently increased local food suppliers' participation in modern distribution in Tanzania. The role of government institutions in supporting innovation processes is quite evident. This takes the form of training and support to enhance the standards of local food processors. The financial manager of Happy Sausage had this to say,

> Our quality control officer is a food scientist and a degree holder. We have a production manager who is a Kenyan and he has been with us for two years ... It's like what you have said, most Tanzanians don't understand meat processing. Six production managers have passed at this factory who were Kenyans.

The use of networking

Networking is another strategy used by local food retailers in increasing their participation in modern food distribution. The study shows that retailers use education, working, and tribal networks to increase their participation in modern food stores in Tanzania. For example, Namazone Business Centre became a supplier to Nakumatt by exploiting its owner's network – a network that enabled him to become a supplier while working as a corporate manager with AMREF in its Nairobi office. This is consistent with Barney's (1991) observation that social complexity in the form of managers' relationships gives firms a competitive strategy. Another study conducted in Tanzania found that personal relationships are important in developing relationships between actors in agribusiness value chains. In general, previous studies show that a network relationship is likely to enable actors to access resources. Interviews with food suppliers show that retailers do not support local food suppliers technologically and financially. Through this network, local food suppliers can access information on price and consumers' feedback on their products. The study shows further that local food suppliers use networking as the source of accessing market information.

A respondent from TFDA had this to say,

> We are working together with Helen Keller International, World Vision, and TuboresheChakula to facilitate this new innovative food idea of food fortification. We have trained food processors and our inspectors on food fortification. From January 2015, even imported foods will have to be fortified too.

Innovation

The interviews with modern food retailers show that the innovation factor tends to influence supermarkets' purchase of locally produced food items. Innovation was on extrinsic cues such as labelling, shape, and size. Studies on food retailing show a strong association between packaging and purchase decisions (Wells et al., 2007). Previous studies associate the low performance of locally processed foods with poor quality packaging, thus limiting them from accessing modern food stores. Studies in food innovation show that external actors are a major source of food innovation (Siriwongwilaichat and Winger, 2004). Similarly, this study shows that external players, such as NGOs and government institutions, are the major source of innovation in Tanzania. However, for innovation to be meaningful, having staff with technical skills is very important. In general, the ability to absorb new ideas depends much on the knowledge level and experience of staff in the firm. That means innovation factors correlate with the factor, such as the employment of experienced staff used by local food processors in Tanzania.

In the words of the Nakumatt Branch Manager,

> No ... errr ... Tanzanians have woken up, and they know their products, I swear to God. What I can say is that most of the local companies have involved professionals in the design of the packaging, not like in previous years.

A respondent from TCCIA had this to say,

> In most cases, we have to use the same companies for support for different projects, and it is true that you can find them supported by other organisations because most people do not like to participate by doing things like being members of business associations or at other events.

Sales support

The supermarket industry is relatively small; furthermore, many retailers are not willing to bear the cost of employing their own merchandising officers. For this reason, the supermarket industry does business with suppliers who can provide a nutritionist (or merchandising officer, as they call him/her) to answer questions customers may have about their products. The interviews with suppliers and retailers show that modern food retailers would like to work with local suppliers who are providing sales support to the final consumers. Previous studies show that locating merchandising officers helps firms to access new markets (Canavari et al., 2009). There are also situations when the supermarket has to drop local suppliers because either their items are of unacceptable quality or because consumers are not familiar with the items due to inadequate marketing efforts by the suppliers.

The respondent of Panone Supermarket said,

> We used to stock .... maize flour, but we dropped it because the product was not moving. You have to understand that when you stock an item, and it's not moving, it means that a supplier has not focused much on marketing the item. We simply remove that item. In short, most local processors don't invest in marketing their products by doing things such as locating them at gondola ends. You have to understand that when you supply to a supermarket, you the suppliers, and you should support retailer in how to market those items.

In general, only one local food supplier located his own merchandising officer to a number of modern food stores as the means of educating consumers about their products.

A wide range of products

The range of products a supplier produces can influence a retailer to source from a particular supplier. This shows that retailers would like to source from a single supplier, to allow control of the stock and the administration. Retailers considered sourcing from a supplier with multiple goods as a means of enabling the suppliers to commit to the retailer due to their relatively high sales value.

A respondent from Nakumatt said,

> Now we are dealing with suppliers who have a wide range of products and with the capacity to source from different parts of the country ...

A respondent from Foot Loose Limited said the following on the same issue,

> ... accepted to procure from me rice, green beans (choroko), and dried bean. They told me, we want to order rice in bulk. Can you do that? I said yes, I can supply to you rice too worry not. They started with an order of 3 million as an average for a week for rice.

Discussion

The empirical evidence shows that local food suppliers use seven strategies to get access to modern food retail in Tanzania. The strategies include outsourcing of value chain activities, business networking, business relationship, innovation, experienced staff, sales support, and production of a wide range of products. These important decisions are related to strategies and can enable the firms to build effective operations of delivering the goods demanded by modern food retailers. The cases illustrate how local food suppliers use factors from RBV and network theory perspectives to get access to modern food retail stores.

In general, from the RBV perspective, the data demonstrate that local food suppliers use an outsourcing strategy from producing inputs that are specialised and tailored to meet modern retailers' needs. Furthermore, local food suppliers employ experienced staff to reconfigure these resources into capabilities to seize the benefits from external networks such as government institutions (i.e. TFDA and TBS) on innovation ideas and training on food production.

Often the challenge of local food suppliers in developing economies is on not only producing products of high quality but also accessing modern food retailers. From a network relationship perspective, the cases provide evidence of how local food suppliers use relationships and networks to access modern food retail stores in Tanzania. For example, the use of relationships seems to be important for retailers to accept local food suppliers. The relationship is characterised by trade credit and return of the damaged or expiry products on the cost of suppliers. An interesting aspect of this relationship is that most of the firms involved do not use a contract to govern their operations. That means their relationship is based on trust with little support from modern food retailers to local food suppliers. Furthermore, the study shows that schoolmates and friends can be used to help local food suppliers to access modern food retail stores in Tanzania.

The result of our study provides broad support for the conceptualisation of strategies, which are important for the linkage of local food suppliers to modern food retail. Previous studies associated the linkage of suppliers to supermarkets with high-quality products and investment of high technologies machines on the suppliers' side (Dolan and Humphrey, 2004). This study suggests that to minimise problems of reliability for distribution of goods, local foods suppliers outsource some of the value chain activities. This strategy enables local food suppliers to concentrate on the main activities. In addition, the study shows further that relationships and networking are very important in enabling suppliers to access modern food distribution. Most of the previous studies in Africa confirm that personal relationship is a very important strategy in accessing resources; this is not surprising (Fafchamps, 2001; Fafchamps, 1997). Yet, this study shows that relational trust in business, which is formed at the early stage of business formation, has an effect on the linkage of a supplier to modern food retail stores. This finding contrasts with the finding in a study by Poppo et al. (2016), who found that calculative trust is very important in forming a relationship in vertical integration between suppliers and buyers.

Implications for the theory

This study adds to retail strategy management theory by specifying how new firms in food distribution operating in Africa rely on relationships. It offers three important theoretical implications. First, we integrated relationship theory and the resources based view to elucidate how local food suppliers from developing economies leverage the problem of resources by connecting with modern retail. We build on RBV and business network theory to show how firms with a lack of resources operating in food processing in developing economies get access to resources from external actors. Our results are consistent with the observations by other scholars (i.e. Fafchamps, 2001; Fafchamps, 1997) who highlighted the importance of personal relationships in accessing resources. To realise this objective, local food suppliers must work with late repayment and accept to bear the loss for damaged and expired goods. Nandonde and Kuada (2016) found that acceptance of late payment (trade credit) is one of the criteria used by retailers to include suppliers in their list in Tanzania. Our study found that modern food retailers do not support local food suppliers financially and technologically. However, there are two reasons that suggest the need for local food suppliers to continue with the relationship with modern food retailers. The first is price stability and the second is low-cost distribution.

Second, we identified the unique nature of establishing a personal relationship, such as being a schoolmate. The finding is similar to the finding in a study conducted in South Africa that found that being a family member and or a friend is most important in establishing business connections (Mitchell and Co, 2015). Prior research highlighted the importance of investment support in establishing a relationship. However, our study suggests that in a new context such as the one in Tanzania where law enforcement is quite challenging, actors rely on a personal trust relationship strategy.

Third, and of particular importance, is the role of networking in enabling local food suppliers to access some of the resources from the external actors. Due to liabilities of lack of financial resources, local food suppliers in Tanzania use networking with NGOs and government institutions to acquire knowledge and technology to produce food products and meet market standards. Therefore, our study indicates that getting access to resources institutions in developing economies depends on third party institutions and not direct actors such as retailers.

Implications for practitioners

A key implication of the study to practitioners in food distribution is that relationships and networks may enable firms to penetrate modern food distribution. Therefore, actors should not focus on price and improvement alone.

Despite the use of relationship and networking strategies being important for the linkage of local food suppliers in Tanzania, there are also challenges. Since local food suppliers are working with a large number of buyers (retailers) who prefer to buy on credit, a lack of relationship and networking strategy may create problems for local food suppliers in establishing a relationship with modern food retailers. To work in trade credit is a challenge to local food suppliers who have low-level working capital. This may force many local food suppliers into marginalisation. Another challenge is the failure of payment once the borrower's firms' collapse. For example, the collapse of Uchumi in Uganda and Tanzania caused chaos to many local food suppliers who were owed by the company. Local food suppliers should be aware of several mitigation strategies. First, payment should be made after the sales of the delivered goods and after a considerable time, let us say a month or so. Second, local food suppliers may prefer to work with wholesalers or distributors who pay cash, instead of selling directly to modern food retailers.

In this respect, policy implications of the study findings are as follows. Participation of local food suppliers in modern food distribution relationships through trade credit is very important. However, there is a consensus that African firms lack resources such as finance and human capital, which limits their potentials. These findings are in line with the suggestion in a study by Nandonde and Kuada (2016) that the government and financial institutions can foster this relationship between local food suppliers and modern retailers by providing loans against invoices issued by retailers to help local food suppliers minimise the impact of lack of working capital. Furthermore, the study shows that Tanzania's firms depend on international employees to work in their firms due to a lack of local workers in the labour market with experience in the food industry. However, recently the Tanzania government introduced stringent conditions for firms in that foreign employees must be paid more than US$3000. This condition limits and reduces local firms from employing staff from foreign countries such as Kenya and India. We understand the importance of providing employment to Tanzanians; however, some of the sectors, such as the food processing industry, need special treatment for them to grow.

Limitations and future research

The study has its limitations. The selection of cases was subjected to certain potential biases. First, only those who supplied modern retail stores were contacted to participate in the study. That means some of the suppliers who were marginalised failed to share their experiences. This is due to the lack of a reliable database. The second limitation was the response bias of only those individuals who were interested in participating in the study. We understand that some of the respondents who declined to participate in our study would have made our study more informative. Finally, the data include only food processors who distributed directly to modern food retail stores. That means we did not include some of the suppliers who were distributing through distributors or wholesalers. In this respect, these biases prevented the current study from observing a full range of values on strategies used by local food suppliers to increase their participation in modern food distribution in Tanzania. However, the methodology was suitable for the study of the new phenomenon (Deshpande, 1983).

The study builds on RBV and business relationship theories to determine strategies used by local food suppliers to increase their participation in modern food distribution in Tanzania. Future research could extend the analysis of strategies used by local food suppliers to increase their participation in modern food retail by assessing the roles of sales employees. Previous studies in Tanzania show that establishing relationships relates to ethnicity; this means, Tanzanian-Asians are perceived to be more efficient in relationship formation. One of the findings of this study shows that relationships and networking are among the strategies that allow local food suppliers to get access to modern food retailers in Tanzania (Kristiansen, 2004; Jensen and Kristiansen, 2004). In this regard, future research should focus on the role of strategy type preferred between non-native and native Africans.

Acknowledgement

A large part of this chapter originated in the data collected during PhD study at Aalborg University by the author and was financed by DANIDA. Therefore, I would like to take this opportunity to thank DANIDA for their support.

References

AfDB (2014). Eastern Africa' manufacturing sector: promoting technology, innovation, productivity and linkages. Available at: http://www.afdb.org/fileadmin/uploads/

afdb/Documents/GenericDocuments/Eastern_Africa%E2%80%99s_Manufacturing_Sector_-_Promoting_Technology_-_Tanzania_country_report_November_2014.pdf (Accessed 19 January, 2016).
Andam, K., Al-Hassan, R.M., Asante, S.B., & Diao, X. (2015). Is Ghana making progress in agro-processing? Evidence from inventory of processed food products in retail shops in Accra, IFPRI. Working Paper 41, Washington.
Anderson, J.C., Håkansson, H., & Johanson, J. (1994). Dyadic business relationships within a business network context. *The Journal of Marketing*, 58(4), 1–15.
Andersson, C.I., Chege, C.G., Rao, E.J., & Qaim, M. (2015). Following up on smallholder farmers and supermarkets in Kenya. *American Journal of Agricultural Economics*, 97(4), 1247–1266.
Asfaw, S., Mithöfer, D., & Waibel, H. (2010). What impact are EU supermarket standards having on developing countries' export of high-value horticultural products? Evidence from Kenya. *Journal of International Food & Agribusiness Marketing*, 22(3–4), 252–276.
Atasoy, Y. (2013). Supermarket expansion in Turkey: shifting relations of food provisioning. *Journal of Agrarian Change*, 13(4), 547–570.
A.T.Kearney (2014). Seizing Africa's retail opportunities: the 2014 retail development index. Available at: https://www.atkearney.com/documents/10192/4371960/Seizing+Africas+Retail+Opportunities.pdf/730ba912-da69-4e09-9b5d-69b063a3f139 (Accessed 19 January, 2016).
Attride-Stirling, J. (2001). Thematic networks: an analytic tool for qualitative research. *Qualitative Research*, 1(3), 385–405.
Barney, J. (1991). Firm resources and sustained competitive advantage. *Journal of Management*, 17(1), 99–120.
Barney, J.B., & Wright, P.M. (1998). On becoming a strategic partner: the role of human resources in gaining competitive advantage. *Human Resource Management*, 37(1), 31–46.
Bjerkas, T., & Kagirwa, J. (1994). Business ethics and legal norms: a comparative study between Norway and Tanzania. Research Report No. 5, AdgerCollge and Mzumbe University, Morogoro.
Bloom, J.D. (2015). Standards for development: food safety and sustainability in Wal-Mart's Honduran Produce Supply Chains. *Rural Sociology*, 80(2), 198–227.
Bukenya, J.O., Obuah, E., & Hyuha, T.S. (2012). Demand elasticities for East African fish exports to the European Union. *Journal of African Business*, 13(1), 70–80.
Canavari, M., Lombardi, P., & Spadoni, R. (2009). Evaluation of the potential interest of Italian retail distribution chains for Kamut-based products. *Journal of Food Products Marketing*, 16(1), 39–59.
Creswell, J.W. (2013). *Qualitative Inquiry and Research Design*, 3rd ed., Sage, London.
Daly, J., Kellehear, A. and Gliksman, M. (1997). *The Public Health Researcher: A Methodological Approach*. Oxford University Press, Melbourne, Australia.
Davies, G. (1994). Maintaining relationships with retailers. *Journal of Strategic Marketing*, 2(3), 189–210.
Deshpande, R. (1983). 'Paradigms Lost': on theory and method in research in marketing. *The Journal of Marketing*, 47(4), 101–110.
Digal, L.N. (2015). Modern retail food sector in the Philippines: dominance of large domestic retailers and their effects on the supply chain. *The International Review of Retail, Distribution and Consumer Research*, 25(4), 407–430.

Dolan, C., & Humphrey, J. (2000). Governance and trade in fresh vegetables: the impact of UK supermarkets on the African horticulture industry. *Journal of Development Studies*, 37(2), 147–176.

Dolan, C., & Humphrey, J. (2004). Changing governance patterns in the trade in fresh vegetables between Africa and the United Kingdom. *Environment and Planning A*, 36(3), 491–509.

Dwyer, F.R., Schurr, P.H., & Oh, S. (1987). Developing buyer-seller relationships. *The Journal of Marketing*, 52(2), 11–27.

Elg, U., Ghauri, P.N., & Tarnovskaya, V. (2008). The role of networks and matching in market entry to emerging retail markets. *International Marketing Review*, 25(6), 674–699.

Emongor, E. (2008). The impacts of South African supermarkets on agricultural and industrial development in the Southern African development community. Unpublished PhD thesis, University of Pretoria, Pretoria.

Fafchamps, M. (1997). Trade credit in Zimbabwean manufacturing. *World Development*, 25(5), 795–815.

Fafchamps, M. (2001). Networks, communities and markets in Sub-Saharan Africa: implications for firm growth and investment. *Journal of African Economies*, 10(suppl 2), 109–142.

Fereday, J., & Muir-Cochrane, E. (2006). Demonstrating rigor using thematic analysis: a hybrid approach of inductive and deductive coding and theme development. *International Journal of Qualitative Methods*, 5(1), 80–92.

Fold, N., & Gough, K.V. (2008). From smallholders to transnationals: the impact of changing consumer preferences in the EU on Ghana's pineapple sector. *Geoforum*, 39(5), 1687–1697.

Ghauri, P.N., Tarnovskaya, V., & Elg, U. (2008). Market driving multinationals and their global sourcing network. *International Marketing Review*, 25(5), 504–519.

Gibbon, P. (1997). The relations: a political economy of the marketing chain for Dagaa in Tanzania. CDR Working Paper, 97.2.

Glaser, B.G., & Strauss, A.L. (1967). *The Discovery of Grounded Theory*. Aldine, New York.

Green, M. (2015). Making Africa middle class: from poverty reduction to the production of inequality in Tanzania. *Economic Anthropology*, 2(2), 295–309.

Grönroos, C. (1994). From marketing mix to relationship marketing: towards a paradigm shift in marketing. *Management Decision*, 32(2), 4–20.

Grünbaum, N.N. (2007). Identification of ambiguity in the case study research typology: what is a unit of analysis? *Qualitative Market Research: An International Journal*, 10(1), 78–97.

Gummesson, E. (2002). Relationship marketing in the new economy. *Journal of Relationship Marketing*, 1(1), 37–57.

Hadjikhani, A., & Ghauri, P.N. (2001). The behaviour of international firms in socio-political environments in the European Union. *Journal of Business Research*, 52(3), 263–275.

Hadjikhani, A., Lee, J.W., & Ghauri, P.N. (2008). Network view of MNCs' socio-political behaviour. *Journal of Business Research*, 61(9), 912–924.

Hingley, M. (2001). Relationship management in the supply chain. *The International Journal of Logistics Management*, 12(2), 57–71.

Hingley, M., Lindgreen, A., & Casswell, B. (2006). Supplier-retailer relationships in the UK fresh produce supply chain. *Journal of International Food & Agribusiness Marketing*, 18(1–2), 49–86.

Hingley, M.K. (2005a). Power to all our friends? Living with imbalance in supplier–retailer relationships. *Industrial Marketing Management*, 34(8), 848–858.

Hsiao, H.I., Kemp, R.G., van der Vorst, J.G., & Omta, S.W.F. (2011). Logistics outsourcing by Taiwanese and Dutch food processing industries. *British Food Journal*, 113(4), 550–576.

Hunt, S.D., & Morgan, R.M. (1994). Relationship marketing in the era of network competition. *Marketing Management*, 3(1), 18–28.

Ijumba, C., Snyder, J., Tschirley, D., & Reardon, T. (2015). *Stages of Transformation in Food Processing and Marketing: Results of an Initial Inventory of Processed Food Products in Dar es Salaam, Arusha, and Mwanza*. Tanzania Policy Research Brief.

Kabissa, J.C.B. (2014). *Cotton in Tanzania: Breaking the Jinx*. Tanzania Education Publishers, Bukoba.

Kadigi, R.M., Mdoe, N.S., Senkondo, E., & Mpenda, Z. (2007). Effects of food safety standards on the livelihoods of actors in the Nile perch value chain in Tanzania (No. 2007: 24). DIIS Working Paper.

Kaipia, R., & Turkulainen, V. (2016). Managing integration in outsourcing relationships – The influence of cost and quality priorities. *Industrial Marketing Management* (in press).

Kristiansen, S. (2004). Social networks and business success. *American Journal of Economics and Sociology*, 63(5), 1149–1171.

Kurwijila, R.L., Richard, L., & Ryoba, R. (2005). Evaluation of extent of water adulteration of milk produced and marketed in Morogoro municipality, Tanzania. *Tanzania Journal of Agricultural Sciences*, 6(2), 104–107.

Mattsson, L.G. (1997). 'Relationship marketing' and the 'markets-as-networks approach' – a comparative analysis of two evolving streams of research. *Journal of Marketing Management*, 13(5), 447–461.

MIT (2012). *National Baseline Survey Report: Micro, Small and Medium Enterprises in Tanzania*. Available at: http://www.fsdt.or.tz/fileadmin/downloads/MSME_National_Baseline_Survey_Report_2012.pdf (Accessed 19 January, 2015).

Mitchell, B.C., & Co, M.J. (2015). Entrepreneurial networks: findings from a South African study. *South African Journal of Economic and Management Sciences*, 7(4), 589–600.

Mohr, J., & Spekman, R. (1994). Characteristics of partnership success: partnership attributes, communication behaviour, and conflict resolution techniques. *Strategic Management Journal*, 15(2), 135–152.

Möller, K., & Halinen, A. (2000). Relationship marketing theory: its roots and direction. *Journal of Marketing Management*, 16(1–3), 29–54.

Morgan, R.M., & Hunt, S.D. (1994). The commitment-trust theory of relationship marketing. *The Journal of Marketing*, 58(3), 20–38.

Nandonde, F.A. (2016). Integrating local food suppliers in modern food retail in Africa: the case of Tanzania. Unpublished PhD thesis submitted at Aalborg University, Denmark.

Nandonde, F.A., & Kuada, J. (2014). Empirical studies on food retailing in developing economies. International Food Marketing Research Symposium, 19–20, June, Aaurhus, Denmark, Conference Proceeding.

Nandonde, F.A., & Kuada, J. (2016). Modern food retailing buying behaviour in Africa: the case of Tanzania. *British Food Journal*, 118(5), 1163–1178.

Neven, D., Reardon, T., Chege, J., & Wang, H. (2006). Supermarkets and consumers in Africa: the case of Nairobi, Kenya. *Journal of International Food & Agribusiness Marketing*, 18(1–2), 103–123.

Onzere, S.N. (2012). Emerging food retailers and the development of hybrid food retail institutions in Ugandan produce supply chains. Unpublished PhD thesis submitted at Iowa State University.

Patton, M.Q. (1987). *How to Use Qualitative Methods in Evaluation*. Sage, London.

Plummer, K. (1983). *Documents of Life: An Introduction to the Problems and Literature of Humanistic Method*. Unwin Hyman, London.

Popo, L., Zhou, K.Z., & Li, J.L. (2016). When can you trust, 'trust'? Calculative trust, relational trust and supplier performance. *Strategic Management Journal*, 37(4),724–741.

Reardon, T. (2015). The hidden middle: the quiet revolution in the midstream of agri-food value chains in developing countries. *Oxford Review of Economic Policy*, 31(1), 45–63.

Schiefer, J., & Hartmann, M. (2008). Determinants of competitive advantage for German food processors. *Agribusiness*, 24(3), 306–319.

Sindi, J.K. (2013). Essays on access to market through collective action: analyses of factors affecting the formation, success, and impact of farmer marketing groups in Kenya. Unpublished PhD Dissertation, submitted to Michigan State University.

Siriwongwilaichat, P., & Winger, R.J. (2004). Technical knowledge for food product innovation in Thailand. *Agribusiness*, 20(3), 233–252.

Snyder, J., Ijumba, C., Tschirley, D., & Reardon, T. (2015). Local response to the rapid rise in demand for processed and perishable foods: results of an inventory of processed food products in Dar es Salaam. Innovation Lab for Food Security, Michigan State University, East Lansing, MI, Tanzania Policy Research Brief, (2).

Sørensen, O.J. (2011). The global value chain: formation, organisation and management perspectives. A paper presented at DDRN Conference on Global Value China and Sustainable Development, Technical University of Denmark, Lyngby, May 24–25.

Stern, L.W., & Reve, T. (1980). Distribution channels as political economies: a framework for comparative analysis. *The Journal of Marketing*, 44(3), 52–64.

Tisimia, V.K. (2014). Growth of agro-processing firms and their influence on employment creation, Tanzania. Unpublished PhD thesis submitted at Sokoine University of Agriculture.

Wells, L.E., Farley, H., & Armstrong, G.A. (2007). The importance of packaging design for own-label food brands. *International Journal of Retail & Distribution Management*, 35(9), 677–690.

Wernerfelt, B. (1984). A resource-based view of the firm. *Strategic Management Journal*, 5(2), 171–180.

White, H.M. (2000). Buyer-supplier relationships in the UK fresh produce industry. *British Food Journal*, 102(1), 6–17.

Wright, P.M., McMahan, G.C., & McWilliams, A. (1994). Human resources and sustained competitive advantage: a resource-based perspective. *International Journal of Human Resource Management*, 5(2), 301–326.

Wycherley, I. (2002). Managing relationships in the UK organic food sector. *Journal of Marketing Management*, 18(7–8), 673–692.

Yin, R.K. (1981). The case study crisis: some answers. *Administrative Science Quarterly*, 26(1), 58–65.

9 Exploring the relationships between supermarkets and local suppliers in developing countries
Evidence from Tanzania

Daniel Wilson Ndyetabula

Introduction

The share of supermarkets in food retailing in developing countries has increased significantly in the last two decades (Rao and Qaim, 2011). For example, supermarkets already have a 55% share of national food retail in South Africa, similar to the share in Argentina, Chile, and the Philippines (Reardon et al., 2009). This phenomenon goes parallel with the rise in supermarkets in developing countries, especially in Eastern and Southern Africa (das Nair, 2018). Since the late 1990s, the number of supermarkets has increased accompanied by more efficient management systems that benefit from economies of scale and sales of food at relatively low prices (Timmer, 2009). According to Weatherspoon and Reardon (2003), the increase of supermarkets in Africa has been caused by urbanisation and, to some extent, the rise of the middle class. As Louw et al. (2008) indicate, population increase in developing countries is triggered by rapid urbanisation, which is expected to continue during the next three decades due to an increase in global disposable income. As the World Urbanisation Prospectus by the United Nations (2004) indicates, population growth will be particularly rapid in the urban areas of developing countries, averaging 2.3% per year from 2000 to 2030.

Africa is not exempt from this rapid urbanisation. In South Africa and Tanzania, about 59.8 and 26% of the populations, respectively, reside in urban areas (World Bank, 2008). According to Louw et al. (2008) and UN-Habitat (2005), this could rise to 62.2 and 30%, respectively, by 2030. Today, urbanisation influences new consumption patterns and preferences for high quality and easy to cook foods. As a result, supermarkets find these patterns and people's preferences as a catalyst for growth and prosperity. Supermarkets, retail chains, and agri-processors have now become important players in the food sector (Reardon et al., 2018).

Paradoxically, the rapid rise and spread of supermarkets in developing countries occur while the institutional setting in these countries is fragile in terms of food policies and regulations (Reardon and Gulati, 2008; Timmer, 2009). Some African countries such as Tanzania have introduced regulations that limit importations of some food items while the domestic supply chain is not well advanced. For example, Weatherspoon and Reardon (2003) demonstrate that the emergence

DOI: 10.4324/9780367854300-9

of multinational supermarkets has created anxieties among policymakers that domestic producers might be marginalised by supermarkets' importing their supplies. This has led to the adoption of regulations that require supermarkets in Tanzania to source up to 40% of their supplies locally from Tanzanian producers. In 2004, Kenya banned the importation of chicken in a situation that shocked operations of such food businesses as KFC and Subway, since domestic supplies of chicken were not up to the standards required by these fast food vendors. Against this background, studying the rapid rise and spread of supermarkets in developing countries is imperative. As Weatherspoon and Reardon (2003) argue, the rise of supermarkets in Africa matters for the development of both the urban and the rural poor. This is because supermarkets are rapidly taking over food markets, which poor rural farmers need to be connected to for selling their produce in their efforts to overcome income poverty.

In this chapter, we draw lessons from the supply relationship between the supermarkets previously existing in Tanzania, particularly Shoprite supermarket and its suppliers of fresh produce. The lessons are intended to shed light on the manner in which supermarkets strategically collaborate with local suppliers to ensure consistency in the availability of the required food products. Literature has indicated that the supply relationship between supermarket chains and small farmers (herein conceptualised as fresh produce suppliers) in the developing world represents a key intersection of current critical dimensions of economic theory and policy. This is especially in terms of participation of the rural poor in local markets, possibilities for rural entrepreneurship, and contracts between small growers and large buyers (Michelson et al., 2012; Zonin et al., 2014).

According to Michelson et al. (2012), previous studies on the relationship between farmers and supermarkets focused on understanding whether and why supermarkets source from small farmers. Some studies (Maertens and Swinnen, 2009) found that supermarkets source from small farmers mainly because the former aim to establish a welfare impact on small farmers. Furthermore, they strategically use collaboration and inclusion to ensure consistency in their operations. For example, a number of studies (see, for example, Rao et al., 2012; Giovannucci et al., 2001; Haantuba, 2003; Freidberg, 2003) have shown how small-scale farmers/suppliers have been included in the formal food system. The conceptualisation in this chapter prompts the argument that the supply relationship in the agri-food business in developing countries is a function of close collaboration, involvement, and co-existence between local suppliers and supermarkets.

The rest of the chapter contains a brief overview of the history of supermarkets in developing countries and their growth/spread in developing countries. This is followed by the description of the mechanisms supermarkets use to forge relationships with suppliers (small farmers and producers in this case), focusing on two strategies: changing power relations and transforming agri-food systems. Both the former and the latter aim to explore the role supermarkets play in the agri-food value chain to ensure the sustained supply of required products while meeting public regulations and consumer needs for agri-food products. The two focus areas are part of the value chain framework used to inform the study. The chapter concludes with the presentation and discussion of Shoprite's relationship with local suppliers in Tanzania.

A brief history of the supermarkets and their spread in developing countries

Supermarkets are defined as departmentalised stores, usually with 30,000 square feet or smaller selling space (Latella and Morrissey, 2006). They are also described as grocery stores, which are self-service, offering a wide range of food and household merchandise, organised into departments. Supermarkets are larger and have a wider selection than traditional grocery stores. Supermarkets comprise meat, fresh produce, dairy, and baked goods departments along with shelf space reserved for canned and packaged goods as well as for various non-food items such as household cleaners, pharmacy products, and pet supplies. Most supermarkets also sell a variety of other household products, which are consumed regularly, such as alcohol (where permitted), medicine, clothes, and some sell a much wider range of non-food products.

According to Lawrence and Burch (2007), what we refer to as supermarket possesses most of the following features:

- much larger in size and greater throughput than the small local grocery store which preceded it
- a wide variety of goods for sale, with foodstuffs as the most significant commodity lines
- consumers self-serving from goods displayed on open shelves
- requiring customers to pay for goods at a designated location (the checkout)
- part of the chain of similar outlets, which may be owned or franchised by one company, or may be part of a cooperative buying agency.

Reardon and Gulati (2008) indicate that the concept of supermarket originated in the US in the early 1900s and spread out of the attempts by US retailers to find new ways of selling goods (Ellickson, 2011). Before 1900, the traditional food system in the US was similar to India's food system, dominated by wet markets, tiny mom and pop stores, street hawkers, and home delivery. When the supermarket was introduced for the first time, the most interesting innovation was the concept of self-service, which according to Lawrence and Burch (2007), was first introduced in 1916 by Clarence Saunders in his Memphis 'Piggly Wiggly' store. The self-service innovation involved three innovative features, which were designed to allow customers to move around the store, rather than queuing behind a counter, it facilitated customer inspection and interaction with the items on sale, and it focused on sales at a 'checkout' – the point of store exit (ibid.).

Literature on the history of the supermarkets (Ellickson, 2011; Reardon and Gulati, 2008) indicates that there is a dispute over which store can claim the title of being the first fully-fledged supermarket in the world. According to Lawrence and Burch, the first store opened in a garage in Queens, New York, in 1930 with the famous slogan 'pile it high, sell it low', which was an immediate success in providing cheap food in Depression-era America. Six years later, Cullen had 17 supermarkets with an annual turnover of approximately US$6 million (ibid.). In adopting the principle of mass merchandising (selling high volumes at relatively low-profit margins), King Kullen became a model for future supermarket operations.

Lawrence and Burch (2007) reveal further that when Kullen supermarket operations were expanding in the US, the physical size of the supermarkets grew as retailers attempted to increase throughput (making a profit via high volume sales) and reduce store overheads. After the Second World War, the number of supermarkets in the US expanded rapidly because of the growing economic prosperity and increased suburbanisation. Consequently, US retailing methods began to spread to other developed countries such as the UK, Canada, and many places in Europe before it spread to other countries in the world. Reardon et al. (2004) navigate through four diffusion patterns thereafter. The patterns are classified chronologically in terms of the earliest to the latest adopters of supermarkets in different regions ranging from Latin America to Asia to Africa. As Reardon et al. (2004) put it, the diffusion pattern roughly reflects the order of income, urbanisation, infrastructure, and policies that favour the growth of supermarkets.

According to scholars (i.e. Traill, 2006; Reardon et al., 2004), the first diffusion pattern of supermarkets in developing countries was led by Latin American countries, especially Brazil, Argentina, Chile, Costa Rica, Colombia, and Mexico. Before the 1980s, only niche markets in big cities were targeted by the small number of domestic capital supermarkets that existed at the time. In 1990, the niche retail market in Latin American big cities comprised a maximum of 10 to 20% of National Food Retail Sales. By 2000, supermarkets had risen to occupy 50 to 60% of national food retail among the Latin American countries. This almost approached a 70 to 80% share in the US, an indication of the fast growth in a single decade to reach the level that was reached by the US in five decades. Currently, the average supermarket share of retail food sales for the six leading Latin American countries is 30 to 70%, with Brazil having the biggest share, followed by Argentina, Chile, Costa Rica, Colombia, and Mexico. These countries account for 85 and 75% of income and population, respectively, in Latin America.

The second diffusion pattern was experienced in Southeast Asia. In this region, the development and spread of supermarkets were similar to that of Latin America. The diffusion started five to seven years (on average) after the spread of supermarkets in Latin America. The growth of supermarkets in South-East Asia was faster than the growth of its counterpart in Latin America. On average, the food retail share over several Southeast Asian countries, Indonesia, Malaysia, and Thailand was 33%, and 63% in the Republic of Korea and Taiwan. The supermarket subsector in China is the fastest-growing in the world. Its diffusion started in the early 1990s, but in 2003 China had US$55 billion of sales and 30% of urban food retail. Currently, the supermarket subsector in China is growing by 30 to 40% annually (Reardon et al., 2004)

Table 9.1a Projected background data on supermarkets for 2002 and 2015

Country	Supermarket share of retail food market % c. 2002	Income per capita (US$) 2002	Projected income per capita 2015	Urbanisation % 2002	Projected urbanisation % 2015
Argentina	54	2,797	4,143	89.9	92.1
Austria	67	25,536	37,464	65.8	79.4
Bangladesh	1	351	530	23.9	29.5
Belgium	89	23,749	33,447	97.2	97.5
Brazil	49	2,593	3,951	82.4	88.4
Bulgaria	23	1,944	3,746	69.4	74
Chile	62	4,115	7,328	86.6	90.2
China	11	989	2,109	37.7	49.8
Colombia	47	1,850	2,693	76	81.3
Costa Rica	55	4,271	5,717	60.1	66.8
Croatia	42	5,025	8,383	58.6	64.6
Czech R	55	6,808	11,645	74.2	75.7
Denmark	75	32,179	43,628	82.1	86.8
Egypt	10	1,354	2,047	42.1	44.9
Finland	74	25,295	39,560	61	62.1
German	79	24,051	35,525	87.9	90
Greece	65	12,494	19,883	60.6	65.2
Honduras	42	966	1,286	45.2	51.3
Hungary	48	6,481	13,036	64.7	70
India	2	487	827	28.1	32.2
Italy	54	20,528	30,175	67.3	69.2
Kenya	10	393	497	38.2	51.8
Mexico	45	6,320	9,648	75.2	78.8
Morocco	5	1,218	1,840	56.8	64.8
Norway	70	41,974	56,521	77.6	86.4
Pakistan	1	408	521	33.7	39.5
Paraguay	35	100	1,109	56.6	64.3
Poland	44	4,894	9,237	61.8	64
Portugal	70	11,948	17,977	54.1	60.9
Romania	8	2,052	3,633	54.5	56.4
Russia	10	2,405	3,989	73.3	74.3
Slovakia	49	4,403	8,007	57.2	60.8
South Africa	55	2,299	3,340	56.5	62.7
Spain	60	15,961	25,302	76.4	78.1
Sweden	80	26,929	39,546	83.3	84.3
Switzerland	74	36,687	49,402	67.6	68.7
Tunisia	5	2,149	3,397	63.4	68.1
Turkey	37	2,638	4,334	65.8	71.9
UK	88	26,444	36,774	89	90
US	90	36,006	48,485	79.8	83.6

Source: Traill (2006)

The most recent pattern of supermarket diffusion was witnessed in Africa, especially in Eastern and Southern Africa. According to Weatherspoon and Reardon (2003), the general pattern of development of the supermarkets in Africa in the past decade occurred mostly in the largest and/or richest African countries. A similar trend was happening in Latin America and South-East Asia (Reardon et

Table 9.1b Projections of the spread of supermarkets to 2015

Country	Actual share c. 2002 %	Income effect 2015 %	Urbanisation effect 2015 %	Combined effect 2015 %
Argentina	54	61	53	60
Austria	67	80	65	77
Bangladesh	1	1	2	2
Belgium	89	99	89	99
Brazil	49	58	47	56
Bulgaria	23	30	23	30
Chile	62	73	61	72
China	11	15	16	23
Colombia	47	53	46	52
Costa Rica	55	60	56	61
Croatia	42	47	43	48
Czech R	55	68	55	67
Denmark	75	85	73	83
Egypt	10	11	11	12
Finland	74	90	75	91
German	79	91	78	90
Greece	65	75	66	76
Honduras	42	45	45	48
Hungary	48	62	48	62
India	2	3	4	5
Italy	54	65	54	65
Kenya	10	11	14	15
Mexico	54	55	44	54
Morocco	5	6	5	7
Norway	70	82	66	77
Pakistan	1	1	1	1
Paraguay	35	37	36	38
Poland	44	54	44	54
Portugal	70	79	72	81
Romania	8	10	8	10
Russia	10	15	10	15
Slovakia	49	58	50	59
South Africa	55	63	57	65
Spain	60	72	60	72
Sweden	80	93	80	93
Switzerland	74	84	74	84
Tunisia	5	7	5	7
Turkey	37	41	37	41
UK	88	97	88	97
US	90	99	89	98

Source: Traill (2006)

al., 2004). The fastest transformation occurred in South Africa and Kenya among the larger, relatively richer, and more organised markets. South Africa was the first wave country regarding supermarket development. As Louw et al. (2008) indicate, by the end of 2007, the South African supermarket chain had 4,219 stores and 93.8% of the market share of retail sales. According to Reardon et al. (2004), supermarkets in South Africa increased significantly from the end of apartheid in 1994.

African countries that experienced a rapid increase of supermarkets were mostly those that were receiving Foreign Direct Investment (FDI) from South Africa in particular and more recently from Kenya. These include Zimbabwe, Zambia, Namibia, Botswana, Swaziland, Lesotho, and recently Madagascar, Mauritius, Angola, and Mozambique – hence Southern Africa and most recently Tanzania and Uganda – hence Eastern Africa (Weatherspoon and Reardon, 2003; Dakora et al., 2010; Louw et al., 2008). According to Neven and Reardon (2004), Kenya was another country in the East African region with rapid growth and spread of the supermarket subsector. The country has over 300 supermarkets and a 20% share of supermarkets in urban food retail.

Supermarkets are growing steadily in other African countries such as Zimbabwe, Zambia, Tanzania, and Uganda. As indicated previously, the rate of the spread of supermarkets in developing countries is an issue of topical interest because of their potential impact on farming and the food business. Furthermore, supermarkets have some influence on the inclusion and exclusion of smallholder farmers in developing countries. For example, the unstable regulatory and policy landscape of the supermarket subsector has necessitated the rise of formal and informal supply relationships between supermarkets and small-scale agri-food producers. Supermarkets have thus created distinctive standards that involve environmental, social, and economic responsibilities associated with sustainability and profit maximisation (Zonin et al., 2014). In the perspective of developing countries where upstream activities of the agri-food supply chain are dominated by small-scale producers, the impact of distinctive standards has mostly been the exclusion of smallholders in the supply chain. In very few cases, such as Transkei in South Africa, the relationships between supermarkets and small-scale farmers resulted in farmers' inclusion.

Supermarket relationships with suppliers

Changing power relations

In the mid-1970s, agriculture was vertically integrated such that food production, distribution, and retailing were organised on a global scale by the major food manufacturers such as Nestle, Heinz, and Unilever. This level of corporate control over the food industry stimulated academic debate about numerous issues such as industry profiteering, the impact of rural communities, consumers and the environment, and most interestingly the future role of small-scale farming (Lawrence and Burch, 2007; Burch and Lawrence, 2005; Zonin et al., 2014). The debate also resulted in interesting questions on who drives the supply (Vagneron et al., 2009; das Nair et al., 2018). The conceptions about who drives the chain have changed substantially in recent years. Dolan (2004) found an interesting chain driving the changes between the 1970s and 1990s when studying the linkages between producers and exporters of fresh vegetables in some African countries and leading importers and retailers in the UK. She established that in the 1970s, the chain was governed through an arm's-length market relationship, in the sense of a clear dominance structure; the driving the supply chain was not necessarily a constitutive element where power and coordination within the chain were found in one firm; rather, certain chains were decisively marked by different actors. Other authors (Humphrey and Schmitz, 2002) reported similar findings in their studies on value chain drivers. In another study, Dolan (2004) found that by the late 1990s, the agri-food supply chain was predominantly driven by supermarkets.

The eventualities of the debates about the chain's driving power had partial integration of the agri-food sector but vertical coordination. According to Fox and Vorley (2004), it is not the manufacturers that have come to exercise control, but supermarkets, fast food outlets, the foodservice industry, and large players in the food distribution system that are exercising control within the agri-food supply chain. Supermarkets are dominating the control and have an influence in the restructuring of the agri-food supply chains. Their control goes beyond the issues of market share. Their power is well defined and has moved beyond supermarkets' traditional responsibility of food distribution. Currently, supermarkets strongly influence the patterns of production and consumption of agri-food products (Fox and Vorley, 2004; das Nair and Chisoro, 2015). In food production, supermarkets play a major role in setting safety, quality, and environmental sustainability standards for suppliers who are mostly small farmers in the case of developing countries (Lawrence and Burch, 2007; Liverpool-Tasie et al., 2017). This is one avenue of either the inclusion or exclusion of smallholder farmers in supplying agri-food products to supermarket multinationals in developing countries (Rao et al., 2012). Research (Dakora et al., 2010) has revealed that due to their characteristic of being small with poor resource investment in their farming business, farmers (who are mostly suppliers to the supermarkets) in developing

Table 9.2 Trend in market share of major supermarkets in South Africa

Supermarket chain	Market share (%)			
	1993	2003	2004	2007
Shoprite Checkers	43.4	29.4	27.8	25.1
Pick n Pay	22.5	35.4	35.2	24.1
Spar	18.5	26.1	26.3	13.0
Woolworths	4.2	6.9	7.1	11.4
Others	11.6	2.2	3.6	26.4
Total	100	100	100	100

Source: Louw et al., (2008)

countries have largely found themselves marginalised and/or excluded from the agri-food supply chain. The liability of small suppliers' farming business results in non-compliance to safety and quality requirements set by the supermarkets. However, in other cases, the requirements set by supermarkets have forged supply relations that ensure a constant supply of agri-food products to supermarkets and which accrue benefits to smallholder farmers in terms of avenues for product sales.

Another dimension that supermarkets strongly influence is food consumption, which according to Harvey et al. (2002) is influenced by a new form of convenience food such as ready meals. For example, supermarkets own over 95% of brand lines of home ready meals in developed and developing countries. All these are a product of innovation by supermarkets rather than established food manufacturers. With this rapid trend of supermarkets dominating the agri-food supply chain, it can be argued that the traditional dominance of food markets by the food-manufacturing sector is being challenged by the development of supermarkets. This is the case especially in developing countries where the relationships between supermarkets and small-scale suppliers are monopolistic (i.e. numerous suppliers confronted by few buyers). According to Lawrence and Burch (2007), this situation puts small-scale suppliers in a weak position, which is further exacerbated by the flexible sourcing capacities displayed by the supermarkets.

Indeed supermarkets are emerging as food authorities, and which, according to Fox and Vorley (2004), assume a powerful role as the gatekeepers of food standards, though they do not address all the issues of consumer health as alluded to by Lawrence and Burch (2007). Nevertheless, because of the growing retail power in the agri-food supply chain, supermarkets will eventually become strong determinants of what is produced, where it is produced and sold, and what is the standard of the produced agri-food products (Von Broembsen, 2016).

Transformation of the agri-food system

In studying supermarkets and agri-food systems, the most relevant and widely used approach is the commodity and/or value chain approach in which a particular agri-food product or commodity is traced through the entire agri-food supply chain (Gereffi and Lee, 2012). As Delforce et al. (2005) indicate, this is usually accomplished by tracing a product from the point of production (usually a farm in the case of a developing country) through systems of processing, wholesaling, distribution to retailing. In value chain studies (Trienekens, 2011), all activities, which are associated with moving a product from the point of production to the points of consumption, are referred to as value-adding activities – hence the concept of the value chain. Both the value-adding activities and actors (i.e. companies, consumers, and other stakeholders) are the basic building blocks for the formation and analysis of the value chain (Sørensen, 2009).

The genesis of value chain literature is the fall in the central planning era and the privatisation of parastatals, and the opening and liberalising of economies internationally. According to Sørensen (2009), this situation resulted in the opening of the global field for multinational companies (MNCs) to organise their activities more freely within as well as across countries. Consequently, many countries formulated FDI platforms to attract MNCs. With this new situation, research started to conceptualise industry systems by studying the global commodity chain (Gereffi, 1994), global production network (Dickens, 2007), global supply chain (Skjøtt-Larsen et al., 2007), and global value chain (Sørensen, 2009; Gibbon and Ponte, 2008). Apparently, the global commodity chain (GCC) and/ or global value chain (GVC) are the two concepts that are commonly used and agreed upon in the literature. The widely used and agreed upon concepts of GCC and GVC form the basis of the two approaches used in tracing products from the point of production to consumption.

The first approach (GCC approach) is based upon Wallerstein's world system theory, which according to Lawrence and Burch (2007) attempts to contextualise modern social change by looking historically at the world division of labour characterised by exploitation and unequal exchange in various levels of specialisation. Lawrence and Burch (2007) assert further that from this perspective, Gereffi and Korzeniewicz (1994) applied Wallerstein's insights to the analysis of supply chains, with the argument that differential access to markets and resources was central to the understanding of global profit-making and global inequalities.

The second approach is based on the ways in which products acquire value as they are progressively transformed. Over the past decade, this approach has steadily gained momentum and enabled researchers (Humphrey and Schmitz, 2002; Trienekens, 2011) to identify power regimes in the production and distribution of particular commodities, focusing on production practices and governance structures. With this focus, an important question about value chain governance arises. The term value chain governance is associated with the works of scholars (i.e. Gereffi, 1994; Gibbon and Ponte, 2008) who indicate that value chain governance has to do with identifying drivers and their functional positions along the chain. These are those who are able to drive the value chain in different ways and to a different degree. Focusing on the number and types of actors in the value chain, spatial distribution, and organisation of value chains, Gereffi (1994) identifies two types of value chain, namely producer-driven and buyer-driven commodity chains.

Producer-driven chains are controlled by large multinational companies in industries where economies of scale and learning matter and where capital and technology form barriers of entry (Sørensen, 2009). On the other hand, the buyer-driven chains are controlled by retailers who are in contact with the final consumers (Humphrey and Schmitz, 2002). The retailers, such as supermarkets, are in control of design, marketing, and logistics (Vagneron et al., 2009). In agri-food chains, these retailers use middlemen to link to small-scale producers. At the global level, most agri-food value chains are characterised by buyer-driven commodity chains (Fr, 2007). For example, in developing African countries such as Tanzania, Kenya, and Uganda, leading firms and retailers are linked to small-scale producers of agri-food products and are in control of such activities as design, marketing, and logistics (Dolan, 2004). In fresh vegetables, for example, it is argued that UK supermarkets are sourcing these vegetables from Africa and have control over the chain even though they focus their activities on retailing. The advantage of this kind of link to developing countries is that the buyer is responsible for the reduction of transaction costs to small-scale producers (suppliers). It also plays a major role in the inclusion of farmers (suppliers) while strategically ensuring quality product sales to consumers.

Reduced transaction costs to suppliers play an important role in coordinating activities in the value chain. These costs are high when the value chains are producing non-standard products, that is, products with integral product architectures and products whose output is time-sensitive (Baldwin and Clark, 2000). These costs are high because suppliers create risks to the buyer, and so buyers have to develop monitoring strategies.

Another reason is that vertical coordination requires simultaneous innovation at various points of the value chain. Firms have to incur these costs in order to be able to monitor and enforce the purchase of non-standard products. As Fromm (2007) demonstrates, when buyers pursue a strategy of product differentiation (i.e. packaging, labelling, varieties, processes), the need to work directly with suppliers on issues such as product design, specification, delivery schedule, and handling increases.

The importance of value chain governance to developing countries cannot be overemphasised. Humphrey and Schmitz (2002) indicate that value chain governance is important since it enhances market access, distribution of gains, and fosters technical assistance to developing countries. As for market access, the dismantling of trade barriers by developed countries does not give producers in developing countries automatic access to the market since the chains to which these producers work are governed by a limited number of buyers (Humphrey and Schmitz, 2002). On the issue of fostering technical assistance, the relationships between lead firms and SMEs (e.g. TNC-SME) are an entry point to provide effective technical assistance to developing country producers.

The once existed Shoprite's supply relationship with local farmers in Tanzania

Firm's background

Shoprite is a South African based group of companies whose establishment history dates back to 1979 when the group acquired a supermarket chain in the Western Cape. It started with eight stores and a turnover of US$0.94 million, which grew to US$2.6 billion in roughly two decades. Shoprite has a number of subsidiary and franchise companies such as Checkers Hyper, Usave, OK House and Home, OK power express, Checkers, and OK Franchise Division. Since its inception in South Africa, Shoprite has been growing through mergers and acquisitions, a strategy, according to Dakora et al. (2010), that has been subjected to modifications to accommodate Shoprite's internationalisation of its activities.

Shoprite's internationalisation process is through FDI and derives its impetus from the strategy of opening its own stores in the countries where it operates. According to Dakora et al. (2010), this strategy allows the company to have absolute control over its operations by managing the operations from its central office. Out of the 984 stores that the Shoprite group of companies own, 100 stores are supermarkets operating in 16 countries other than South Africa. The countries in which Shoprite internationalised its activities up until 2014 include Namibia, Zambia, Ghana, Uganda, Kenya, Nigeria, Botswana, Mozambique, Lesotho, Swaziland, Angola, Mauritius, Madagascar, and Tanzania. The internationalisation to these countries has taken Shoprite two decades since its establishment.

Shoprite was first introduced in Tanzania in December 2001 with an outlet along Pugu Road in Dar-es-Salaam, which became the headquarters of Shoprite-Tanzania. Shoprite operated in Tanzania for 13 years before it was sold in 2014 to a Kenyan retailer Nakumat. From one branch, the company grew to five major outlets, four in Dar-es-Salaam and one in Arusha in almost a decade. This happened while other domestic and international supermarkets (such as TSN and Uchumi, respectively) were rapidly expanding.

Shoprite's entry mode to Tanzania and its supply relation with farmers

Shoprite's mode of entry to Tanzania was the direct 'wholly owned' in which all its operational activities were organised from their headquarters in Cape Town.

Table 9.3 FDI by Shoprite in food retailing in other African countries in 2003

Country	Number of supermarkets	Remarks
Botswana	3	Plus 1 Megasave, a large-format discount store serving small-scale retailers wholesale as well as consumers
Egypt	3	Started in 2001
Lesotho	2	Plus 1 Megasave
Malawi	2	
Mauritius	1 hypermarket	2 supermarkets opened in 2003
Madagascar	5	Bought the champion supermarkets chain of five supermarkets and one distribution centre in 2002
Mozambique	3	
Namibia	18	Plus 11 Megasave stores
Swaziland	2	Plus 2 Megasave stores
Tanzania	5	Of which three bought from Pick n Pay in 2002
Uganda	1	
Zambia	18	Since 1996 following the privatisation of state-run retail
Zimbabwe	1	

Source: Modified from Weatherspoon and Reardon (2003).

In this regard, Shoprite had control of day-to-day activities. Literature (Doole and Lowe, 2004) indicates that this mode of entry is expensive (as it requires more resource commitment, including management of time and finance) and therefore it is used only when companies are sure that their products would (in the long run) perform better in a foreign market. Although expensive, Shoprite's wholly owned mode of entry to Tanzania was driven by the fact that:

- Tanzania is politically stable, and therefore if the product performs better, the company would realise long-run positive returns on investment.
- Tanzania investment policy allows MNCs investing in Tanzania to have full ownership and control of their companies to meet their strategic objectives.

In its efforts to empower the domestic producers of agri-food products and promote Tanzania's labour force, the Government of Tanzania, through its agencies and departments (such as the Ministry of Agriculture, the Ministry of livestock, the Ministry of Trade and Industry, and the Ministry of Labour), encourage distributors and retailers such as supermarkets to invest in Tanzania. This was thus done to source agri-food produce from local suppliers or producers and to provide employment to qualified Tanzanians for related operations. As is the case in other countries, such as Zambia, Shoprite responded positively to this by employing more than 200 Tanzanians in its three stores. Most importantly, local small-scale farmers in regions such as Iringa were supported to upgrade their production systems and products to supply to Shoprite stores. About 75% of the fresh agri-food products that Shoprite procured and distributed in Tanzania were locally produced by farmers in the Coast, Morogoro, Tanga, Iringa, Dar-es-Salaam, Arusha, and other regions. The remaining gaps for fruits and vegetables were filled by imports mainly from South Africa and China.

Shoprite had three different alternatives to procure its fresh supplies of agri-food products, namely direct purchase from producers, purchase through distribution firms or entrepreneurs, and purchase through a group of producers. In the former, Shoprite had a direct relation with producers in terms of traceability in which supplies were traced to the farms/gardens from which they grew their products. The company was supporting producers through the provision of extension services and product specifications, which helped farmers meet Shoprite requirements. This specifically applied to green vegetable farmers in Morogoro and fruit farmers in Iringa. Shoprite established and strengthened its relation with producers by involving itself in fruit (apples) production projects in the Iringa region. In this project, Shoprite provided credit to farmers in terms of inputs and factored the same in the final payment when farmers were paid for their produce. In this case, Shoprite made efforts to contract producers and/or suppliers to ensure sustainable and reliable supplies through formal contracts.

In addition to contracts, Shoprite established mutual relations with producers/suppliers, particularly in terms of the availability and quality of the products supplied. To encourage a constant and consistent supply culture, Shoprite paid producers/suppliers upon delivery of their produce.

The second alternative, Shoprite had a corporate and supply agreement with such distributors as the Azam Group of companies, Azania Millers, and Mohammed Enterprises for the processed agri-food products, such as fruits, maize, and edible oil. This mode of sourcing was applied in situations where producers were too small to meet the individual quantities required by Shoprite. Shoprite was receiving a number of processed agri-food and spicy products from a number of women groups in Tanzania. Before accepting the products, Shoprite specified the product quality attributes from cooperative groups such as Tanzania Food Processors' Association (TAFOPA).

Most of the products were procured fresh and in bulk packages. They were received independently at every Shoprite outlet in either Dar-es-Salaam or Arusha, depending on the spatial location of the suppliers. Shoprite used to do the final packing and display of the products for sale. In the case of the final packed products, Shoprite would give pre-defined specifications to suppliers, particularly on the weight, date of expiration, and the barcode. Regarding the finally displayed products, the emphasis was on the quality and constant supply (availability) rather than on the size of the products.

Shoprite's objective of involving farmers in the production and procurement of agri-food products was twofold: first, to respond to the government's call for purchasing most of the fresh agri-food products domestically and ensure inclusion of Tanzanian fresh produce farmers in agri-food supply chains; second, to explore the possibilities of reducing sourcing costs through consistent supply relations with domestic suppliers. Largely, these objectives were attained since Shoprite was able to source up to 75% of its fresh agri-food supplies from within Tanzania. However, the process of establishing a relationship among value chain actors faced with opportunistic behaviour. Farmers who entered into a contract with Shoprite did not honour contracts. They displayed a high degree of opportunism by taking the most optimal deals. Driven by prices and the need to repay back input credits, farmers would sell some of the produce to the alternative markets (mostly middlemen) at their disposal. Another challenge was to do with the seasonality of fresh produce in Tanzania because of poor investment. Currently, the production of fresh produce is dismally consolidated in Tanzania, making the subsector prone to weather cycles of drought. Largely, this disrupted the consistent supply of fresh agri-food products from within Tanzania, a situation that prompted the importation of such products from neighbouring countries such as Kenya and South Africa.

The retail market situation, competition, and consumers

As reflected in the preceding sections, the retail market structure in Tanzania is slowly changing from normal district/municipal markets to departmentalised stores and supermarkets. This is occurring mainly in areas where urbanisation and household incomes are increasing. Several retail chains are emerging and being located in popular places in the cities and towns. Uchumi from Kenya, Game from South Africa, Nakumat from Kenya, Shoppers plaza, and TSN from Tanzania are the other supermarket chains in Tanzania similar to Shoprite.

Local suppliers in developing countries   165

In specific streets and localities, kiosks and small individual shops (not in a chain fashion) are rapidly growing. These are mainly standalone shops or kiosks found in the proximity of the households. Even though the retail market structure might blossom, there is still a culture of buying from informal markets (which are either periodic, district, or municipal markets). Characteristically, these markets have low-quality infrastructures and sell substandard products. However, consumers are still mostly buying from these markets.

Prices of goods are perhaps relatively lower in normal markets than in supermarkets. Consumers therefore tend to look for where they can buy to maximise their purchasing utilities, although transaction costs may be high in local and informal markets. In this case, the normal markets are interestingly considered as threatening competitors to supermarkets due to the consumer behaviour of preferring to buy from local kiosks. It appears, therefore, that supermarkets are currently not competitors against each other. Instead, local kiosks and outlets in the vicinity of cosmopolitan consumers provide such competition to supermarkets.

In Tanzania, Shoprite undertook a customer counting exercise by determining the rate and extent of product picking from the shelves. The results indicated that the number of customers buying from the supermarket was increasing. However, the culture of buying from the normal market was still very high in Tanzania. Another dimension that may have contributed to the tendency of consumers to buy from normal markets is the complicated transport system in such big cities as Dar-es-Salaam. The city experiences heavy traffic that makes consumer's trips to supermarkets very challenging, as it is not easy to drive to where the stores are due to traffic problems.

Discussion

While there have been several long term farmer–buyer relationships in commercial crops (such as sugar, cotton, coffee, tobacco, cashew nut, tea, and pyrethrum) through contract farming arrangements, this practice is occurring in fresh agri-food produce, such as fruit and vegetables, in Tanzania. Supermarkets have been sourcing fresh produce internationally from neighbouring countries where the value chains are more consolidated. In Tanzania, the retailer–local supplier relationships were not common until recently when multinational supermarket chains such as Shoprite ventured in with sporadic joint production projects with farmers. Since the practice is just beginning, it would be useful to draw some lessons from Shoprite's case.

The first lesson brings us back to our initial argument about the supply relationship between small-scale farmers and supermarkets being a function of the inclusion of the smallholders. It was possible for Shoprite to attain 75% of the domestic supply of fresh agri-food products through contractual arrangements with farmers in their collaborative fruit and vegetable production project. In respect to the ongoing transformation in the agri-food system where power and control shift from manufacturers to retailers and supermarkets, smallholder farmers need to hold on to the initiatives that enable them to forge contractual supply arrangements with supermarkets. These changes provide potential supply opportunities for some small-scale farmers to broaden and strengthen their markets. To other small-scale farmers, the changes imply challenges and the risk of exclusion. The major challenge will of course lie in linking small-scale producers and supermarkets to the emerging supply relationship channels. However, the approach similar to the one used by Shoprite in Tanzania (getting hold of small-scale farmers as they come to ask for supply deals) may be adopted.

The second lesson that is worth noting is that although there are several players in the agri-food supply chain, supermarkets and retailers are emerging as architects of the dynamics of the supply chains. Through their links with the upstream actors of the value chain (small-scale producers), they provide a market for small-scale farmer produce. What may prevent small-scale producers from benefiting from this lucrative market possibility is the poor development of the production capacity and trade deficiency.

Another lesson that may be drawn from the debate is on the impact of supermarkets on poor farmer development (Weatherspoon and Reardon, 2003). Admittedly, this chapter does not explicitly articulate the ultimate impact of the relation that Shoprite established with farmers in Tanzania. However, we argue that the gains for small-scale suppliers can be explained by both their assured access to markets and the upgraded products as required and/or specified by the retailers. The ultimate effect of this gain will be strongly reflected in the net benefits to consumers through prices, time costs, and food safety.

Strangely, Shoprite's case suggested that local shops and informal markets appear to emerge as competitive threats to supermarkets in Tanzania. This can be a good lesson since competition is literally a function of market disequilibrium (when there is more supply than the market demands). The concept is well understood when a certain industry is composed of firms of similar size in terms of technology, capital, production, and perhaps distribution strategies. However, in the case of retail food chains in Tanzania, such firms appear not to be competitors yet. Instead, competition pressure comes from numerous, small, and unorganised retail markets and local shops. Expectedly, the competition would be, for example, between Shoprite and similar firms such as Uchumi supermarkets, Shoppers Plaza, and/or TSN in the retail industry, but what we see is the competition between small unorganised kiosks/normal markets and departmentalised stores. This is an interesting phenomenon to investigate further. Several dimensions may explain why supermarkets in Tanzania are yet to see themselves as competitors and why is competition pressure coming from unorganised markets (most of which suffer the liability of smallness). One such explanation could be that there is still market potential influenced by growing urbanisation and incomes; that is, the entrepreneurial density is still low and there are therefore ample opportunities to invest in the retail sector. Consumers are usually rational and act in favour of their maximised utilities. This is one of the possibilities that may explain their strong and continued culture of buying from unorganised markets. Additionally, their struggle for prices, convenience, as well as consumers' perception and culture, may also explain why competitive pressure is more from local shops and markets.

Conclusion

This chapter explored the relationship not in terms of institutional and economic conditions or the impact these relations have had on the inclusion or exclusion of farmers but through the lenses of the growing power of retailers in the supply chain and changing agri-food systems. It is apparent from the chapter that supermarkets are ever-growing in developing countries and are governing the dynamics of the supply chains.

This is an emerging trend in agri-food supply chains and through which we witness an increasing role for supermarkets as the orchestrators of the dynamics of the supply chains. Today, supermarkets are increasingly linking to upstream value chain activities through their supply relationship with producers of fresh agri-food products. In this regard, there are more opportunities than limitations for small-scale farmers (suppliers) in terms of access to markets for their produce. This is because there is a growing necessity for the supermarkets to source their supplies from domestic producers, and at the same time there is an increasing necessity to increase the production of agri-food products to meet the ever-growing urban market for agri-food products. As the supermarket revolution has reached a critical point that concerns researchers and policymakers, a heated debate has recently emerged as to what policy measures are the best in enhancing a more inclusive relationship between supermarkets and small-scale producers in developing countries. Because of this exploratory chapter, this may be one of the interesting topics for further investigation.

References

Burch, D., and Lawrence, G. (2005). Supermarket own brands, supply chains and the transformation of agri-food system. *International Journal of Sociology of Agriculture and Food*, 13(1): 1–18.

Dakora, E. A. N., Bythewaym, A., and Slabert, A. (2010). The Africanisation of South African retailing: a review. *African Journal of Business Management*, 4(5): 748–754.

das Nair, R., and Chisoro, S. (2015). The expansion of regional supermarket chains: changing models of retailing and the implications for local supplier capabilities in South Africa, Botswana, Zambia, and Zimbabwe. WIDER Working Paper 2015/114.

das Nair, R., Chisoro, S. and Ziba, F. (2018). Supermarkets' procurement strategies and implications for local suppliers in South Africa, Botswana, Zambia and Zimbabwe. *Development Southern Africa*, 35(3): 334–350.

Delforce, R., Dickson, A., and Hogan, J. (2005). Australia's food industry: recent changes and challenges. *Australian Commodities*, 12(2): 379–390.

Dicken, P. (2007). *Global Shift: Mapping the Changing Contours of the World Economy* (4th ed.). Sage Publications, London.

Dolan, C. S. (2004). On farm and pack-house: employment at the bottom of a global value chain. *Rural Sociology*, 69(1): 99–112.

Doole, I., and Lowe, R. (2004). *International Marketing Strategy: Analysis, Development and Implementation* (4th ed.). Cengage Learning, London.

Ellickson, P. B. (2011). The evolution of the supermarkets industry from A&P to wal-mart. A paper prepared for the Grocery Store Anti-Trust Conference Organized by Federal Trade Commission. Rochester, NY.

Fox, T., and Vorley, B. (2004). *Stakeholder Accountability in the UK Supermarket Sector: Final Report of the Race to the Top Project*. International Institute for Environment and Development. London.

Freidberg, S. (2003). The contradictions if clean: supermarket ethical trade and African Horticulture. *Gatekeeper Series No. 109*. International Institute for Environment and Development (IIED): 1–18.

Fromm, I. (2007). *Upgrading in Agricultural Value Chain: The Case of Small Producers in Honduras*. Germany Institute of Global and Area Studies (GIGA) Working Paper 64/2007.

Gereffi, G. (1994). The organization of Buyer-driven global commodity chains: how US Retailers shape overseas production networks. In G. Gereffi and M. Korzeniewicz (eds.). *Commodity Chains and Global Capitalism*. Greenwood Press, Westport.

Gereffi, G. and Korzeniewicz, M. (eds.) (1994). *Commodity Chains and Global Capitalism*. Greenwood Press, USA.

Gereffi, G. and Lee, J. (2012). Why the world suddenly cares about global supply chains. *Journal of Supply Chain Management*, 48(3): 24–32.

Gibbon, P and Ponte, S. (2008). Global value chains: from governance to governmentality. *Economy and Society*, 37(3): 365–392.

Giovannucci, D. P., Sterns, P. A., Eustrom, M., and Haantuba, H. (2001). The impact of improved grades and standards for agricultural products in Zambia. East Lansing, MI: Michigan States University and United States Agency for International Development, PFID-F & V Report No. 3.

Haantuba, H. (2003). Linkages between smallholder farm producers and supermarkets in Zambia. Consultant Report to Food and Agriculture Organisation, Draft 3.

Harvey, M., Quilley, S., and Beynon, H. (2002). *Exploring the Tomato, Cheltenham*. Edward Elgar, UK and Northampton, MA.

Humphrey, J. and Schmitz, H. (2002). *Developing Country Firms in the World Economy: Governance and Upgrading in the Global Value Chains*. Institut für Entwicklung un Frieden der Gerhard-Mercator-Universität Duisburg.

Latella, R. W. and Morrissey, J. (2006). *Supermarket Industrial Overview*. Retail Industry Group. Cushmen and Wakefield, USA.

Lawrence, G., and Burch, D. (2007). Understanding supermarkets and agri-food supply chains. In Burch, D., and Lawrence, G. (eds). *Supermarkets and Agrifood Supply Chains: Transformation in the Production and Consumption of Food*. Edward Elgar Publishing Limited, UK.

Liverpool-Tasie, L., Reardon, T. and Abagyeh-Igbudu, I. (2017). Rapid agri-food system transformation in Sub-Saharan Africa: evidence from processed food inventories in Nigeria. Selected presentation presented at the Annual Meetings, Agricultural and Applied Economics Association, Chicago, IL.

Louw, A., Jordaan, D., Ndanga, L., and Kirsten, J. F. (2008). Alternative marketing options for small-scale farmers in the wake of changing agri-food supply chains in South Africa. *Agrikon: Agricultural Economics Research, Policy and Practice in Southern Africa*, 47(3): 287–308.

Maertens, M., and Swinnen, J. (2009). Trade, standards, and poverty: evidence from Senegal. *World Development*, 37(1): 161–178.

Michelson, H., Readon, T., and Perez, F. (2012). Small farmers and big retailers: trade-offs of supplying supermarkets in Nicaragua. *World Development*, 40(2): 342–354.

Neven, D. and Reardon, T. (2004). The rise of Kenyan supermarkets and the evolution of their horticultural product procurement systems. *Development Policy Review*, 22(6): 669–99.

Rao, E. J. O., and Qaim, M. (2011). Supermarkets, farm household income, and poverty: insights from Kenya. *World Development*, 39(5): 784–796.

Rao, E. J. O., Brummer, B., and Qaim, M. (2012). Farmer participation in supermarket channels, production technology and efficiency: the case of vegetables in Kenya. *American Journal of Agricultural Economics*, 94(4): 891–912.

Readon, T., Barrett, C. B., and Swinnen, J. F. M. (2009). Agrifood industry transformation and small farmers in developing countries. *World Development*, 37(11): 1717–1727.

Readon, T., and Gulati, A., (2008).*The Rise of Supermarkets and their Development Implications*. IFPRI Discussion paper Number 00689. International Food Policy Research Institute. Washington, DC.

Readon, T., Timmer, P., and Berdegue, J. (2004). The rise of supermarkets in developing countries: induced organizational, institutional, and technological change in agri-food systems. *Electronic Journal of Agricultural and Development Economics*, 1(2): 168–183.

Reardon, T., Echeverria, R., Berdegue, J., Minten, B., Liverpool-Tasie, S., Tschirley, D and Zilberman, D. (2018). Rapid transformation of food systems in developing regions: highlighting the role of agricultural research & innovations. *Agricultural Systems*. 10.1016/j.agsy.2018.01.022.

Skjøtt-Larsen, T., Schary, B. P., Mikkola, J. H., and Kotzab, H. (2007). *Managing the Global Supply Chain*. (3rd ed.). Copenhagen Business School Press, Copenhagen.

Sørensen, O. J. (2009). Formation, organization, and management of the (global) value chain in a theoretical perspective. Working Paper Number 52. International Business Economics. Aalborg University. Denmark.

Timmer, C. P. (2009). Do supermarkets change the food policy Agenda? *World Development* 37(11): 1812–1819.

Traill, B. W. (2006). The rapid rise of supermarkets? *Development Policy Review*, 24(2): 163–174.

Trienekens, J. H. (2011). Agricultural value chains in developing countries: a framework for analysis. *International Food and Agribusiness Review*, 14(2): 51–83.

UN – Habitat (2005). *Human Settlements Indicators*. Database Version 4 (Hsdb4–99). United Nations Human Settlements Programme (UN-Habitat).

United Nations (2004). *World Urbanisation Prospectus: The 2003 Version*. Department of Economics and Social Affairs/Population Division, New York.

Vagneron, I. Faure, G. and Loeillet, D (2009). Is there a pilot in the chain? Identifying the key drivers of change in the fresh pineapple sector. *Food Policy*, 34(5): 437–446.

Von Broembsen, M. (2016). You can't bite the hand that feeds you: the commercial and contractual relations between the four large South African food retailers and their SME suppliers. REDI3x3 Working paper Number 22.

Weatherspoon, D. D., and Readon, T. (2003). The rise of supermarkets in Africa: implications for agri-food systems and the rural poor. *Development Policy Review*, 21(3): 333–355.

World Bank (2008). *World Development Report 2008-Agriculture for Development*. International Bank for Reconstruction and Development, Washington, DC.

Zonin, V. J., Winck, C. A., Zonin, W. J., Leonardi, A. and Machado, J. A. D. (2014). Supermarket chains and small farmers in Africa: a new look from the perspective of new institutional economics. *African Journal of Agricultural Research*, 9(3): 353–362.

10 Understanding the role of service providers on the development of supermarkets in Africa

Edward A. N. Dakora

Introduction

Supermarket chains, including Carrefour, Shoprite Holdings, Woolworths, Pick n Pay, Spar, and Choppies, have spread across various parts of the African continent. Earlier scholars on this subject have called it a revolution, emphasising its process of development to be akin to what occurred in other regions, notably Asia and South America (Reardon, Timmer, Barrett, and Berdegue, 2003; Weatherspoon and Reardon, 2003).

The spread of supermarkets in Africa was rather rapid (Weatherspoon and Reardon, 2003) and propelled by South African supermarkets (Dakora, Bytheway, and Slabert, 2010; Crush, 2018). The fall of Apartheid opened up South Africa (SA) to the world with new market opportunities for South African businesses (which were already hungry for new markets). The coincidence of the fall of Apartheid and the readiness of the supermarkets contributed to the speed of the supermarket revolution in Africa. Familiarity with the neighbouring countries alone made the expansion into immediate countries almost easier (cf. Dakora et al., 2010).

Previous studies on the internationalisation of South African retailers (cf. Reardon, Timmer, Barrett, and Berdegue, 2003; Weatherspoon and Reardon, 2003) have paid attention to the impact of this expansion on farmers and producers. Thus, these studies on supermarket internationalisation have paid less attention to the role of services providers in the retailers' home countries. We understand that previous studies have looked at the role of home countries service providers on retailers' internationalisation, focusing on America and Europe. The current study intends to fill this knowledge gap by focusing on South African retailers. The study argues that with the emergence of SA retailers, the home country's service providers helped them to expand their operations across the continent and helped in scaling up the supermarket revolution in Africa alone.

This argument is plausible because there are many challenges reported by other scholars (cf. Reardon and Hopkins, 2006; Dakora et al., 2010; das Nair and Shingie, 2016). These challenges would have made it impossible for supermarkets to traverse this less familiar territory of internationalisation alone. The chapter reports on the support services provided by other companies, mostly South African, that facilitated the South African supermarket retail expansion project.

DOI: 10.4324/9780367854300-10

The study uses the supermarket value chain as an analytical lens for understanding the contribution of these support service providers.

The narrative that South Africa led the retail revolution is further reflected in several ways. First, this phenomenon was orchestrated by South Africa's neo-liberal regional re-integration agenda (Miller, 2008), and the re-awakening of the African renaissance mantra (Dakora et al., 2010). As will be discussed later, these events led to a wave of South Africa's corporate investment in the Southern African Development Community (SADC) region and beyond (notably Shoprite, Telkom, etc.). Second, before the end of Apartheid in 1994, the South African retail system was already reaching market saturation limits, and there was a need for seeking market opportunities elsewhere (especially because these businesses were mainly white-owned and thereby limited to white urban and white suburbs). Therefore, South Africa's reconnection with the rest of the continent came at an opportune moment for retailers to expand.

Third, most African countries have been implementing economic reforms in order to attract Foreign Direct Investments (FDIs) to boost their local economies. At the same time, there has been rampant urbanisation, leading to the emergence and growth of the so-called middle-class income earners. All of these economic changes accorded South African companies the opportunity of investing in the provision of products and services and the development of infrastructure in the rest of the continent.

A combination of these factors provided fertile ground for South African supermarkets to expand their operations into the neighbouring countries and beyond. It is clear that these supermarkets were already large and sophisticated, but they lacked international experience. What was also apparent was that the supermarkets needed the support of other stakeholders, especially for market research and logistics. Therefore, other South African businesses provided them with support services in facilitating their internationalisation programme, making this supermarket revolution a collaborative effort. Literature is silent on this collaborative aspect of the South African supermarket operations in the rest of Africa. The question is how this support (if any) influenced the development and control of the supermarket value chain in the continent.

The remainder of the chapter is organised as follows: after the introduction, the second part presents the literature on supermarkets in Africa, focusing on South Africa's supermarket expansion within the continent. The third part puts the supermarket revolution in Africa into perspective; the fourth part discusses the supermarket value chain and its challenges, where the nature of stakeholder relations with such the value chain is further explained. This is aimed at picking out ideas that could assist in the analysis of the data. The rest of the chapter presents the methodology and analysis of the data and the conclusion.

Literature on supermarkets in Africa

Since the beginning of the 21st century, Africa has been seen as the next frontier for growth, presenting business development opportunities (Leke and Signé,

2019). The retail industry is one of the areas that attracted significant FDIs from international retailers, including South African retailers in most other African countries. This development appears to have stimulated local economies in some ways (cf. Weatherspoon and Reardon, 2003).

The rapid increase of supermarkets in Africa has been made possible through urbanisation and the rise of the middle class with disposable income (Weatherspoon and Reardon, 2003). Scholars observe further that supermarkets are extending their operations into the more impoverished neighbourhoods, a shift from being a luxury to a necessity. This turn of events has been experienced by rural communities also, as observed in South Africa.[1]

An interesting example is that when Woolworths withdrew its retail clothing operations from Nigeria (citing challenges), Shoprite opened a new store in the city of Kano, in Northern Nigeria, which is one of the most troubled regions in the country. Similarly, Massmart (Walmart), the second-largest retailer in South Africa, plans to extend its Pan-African expansion drive by opening 20 new stores in Ghana, Kenya, Mozambique, and Swaziland in the next three years (Bavier, 2018).

Modern supermarket expansion within Africa is still gaining ground, especially because of the market opportunities the continent continues to offer. These include, as mentioned earlier, sustained urbanisation, a growing population, especially among the youth, a growing middle class, and the associated quest for better products and services. As estimated by AT Kearney (2014), about 900 million people live in Africa, with an urbanisation rate of 3.6%. The report further reveals that the average GDP is nearing 6%, with about seven sub-Saharan Africa economies ranking among the ten fastest-growing economies globally. Similar reports estimate that by 2020 about 128 million African households will have a disposable income, by 2030 50% of African populations will be living in the cities, and that by 2040 the working class will reach 1.1 billion people (McKinsey, 2012).

The new initiatives are likely to push this further, such as the African Union's (AU) vision 2063 agenda. This vision envisages achieving regional integration through trade and free movement of people, and a free trade collation that could be the biggest free trading bloc since the establishment of the World Trade Organisation (WTO) (Allison, 2018). These initiatives, if implemented, will do away with some of the many and conflicting economic blocs on the continent, bringing uniformity around trade regulations and financial systems. The introduction of the African Continental Free Trade Area (AfCFTA) will strengthen African economies further and allow new value chains to emerge.

However, the narrative about how successful or unsuccessful supermarkets have been in their quest for capturing market opportunities in Africa has precluded the contribution of other businesses that make this retail revolution possible. This chapter addresses this void using the value chain as an analytical tool. It explores aspects of services and support to analyse stakeholders that enable the multinational supermarket chains to run their operations effectively. The literature on supermarket value chains in Africa has predominantly concentrated on the tensions created between supermarkets and local producers and suppliers.

African supermarket revolution in context

In the early 1970s, there were already discussions about a different kind of retail system in the developing world, resulting in suggestions of introducing supermarkets (imagined at the time as large, modern, and low-priced food stores to cater for the growing population of the urban poor (Goldman, 1974, p. 8)). However, the emergence of supermarkets in the developing world, including Africa (with exceptions to South Africa), only started in the 1990s (cf. Reardon and Gulati, 2008). As observed by Crush (2018), this made Africa responsible for adopting the supermarket-style retail model and later catapulting it into the continent, sparking a South African-based supermarket revolution.

This was possible because by the mid-1990s the supermarkets in South Africa had already consolidated their operations into big corporate and supermarket chains with significant control of the food system in the country. With this consolidation came the appetite for growth into the neighbouring countries in the SADC region, which was made possible, as mentioned earlier, by the fall of Apartheid. This also explains why the rate at which the revolution occurred was faster in Africa than it was in other regions of the world (Weatherspoon and Reardon, 2003). For example, as early as 1995, Shoprite Holdings entered Zambia, and by 2001 and 2003 the company entered Egypt and Ghana, respectively (Shoprite). The limited amount of time and geographic spread are worth noting here.

Another thing that puts the South African supermarket achievement in the spotlight is the fact that South African supermarkets have faced unique challenges relating to the unfamiliarity of the concept of my other countries and lack of formal retail infrastructure, to mention just a few in the early years of this supermarket revolution. This raises further questions as to how retailers have been able to deal with operational challenges.

South Africa supermarket expansion strategies

South African supermarkets have been able to enter and operate in different African countries using the following strategies: franchising, wholly-owned subsidiaries, joint ventures, and acquisitions (cf. Dakora and Bytheway, 2014). The use of some of these expansions or market entry strategies has been challenging because of limited formal retail infrastructure, limited acquisition targets, and the like, especially in the early years. Some supermarket chains such as Shoprite had to adapt or change their strategies as they gained more experience and learned how to obviate some of the challenges (Games, 2013).

Apart from the entry, other strategies employed by South African supermarkets in direct response to the challenges include building a local supply base, investing in distribution centres (DCs) in strategic locations to support their operations, investing in retail properties, and dealing with competition from local informal, independent retailers and other international supermarkets (das Nair, 2018). The implementation of these strategies naturally demanded collaborations with other companies (mostly South African) for critical services, which they would not easily find in the host countries.

The danger with this sort of collaborative strategy is that they could create barriers from entry and unfair practices for other competitors. As argued by das Nair (2018), this can easily lead to the vertical integration of supermarkets into the value chain to preclude the threat of competition. According to das Nair, the South African retail industry is characterised by exclusivity in lease agreements with proper developers and exclusive agreements with key suppliers, even to the point of colluding with suppliers to fix prices.[2]

These factors have been troubling South Africa for years to the point of almost preventing new entrants into the industry. The alarming rate of small retail failure caught the attention of the South African Council of Retailers, which believes that this may result from price discrimination, excessive pricing, and exclusionary conduct by major retailers and property developers (Joubert, 2003). Another reason for the troubled retail industry is the excessive development of shopping centres, especially in South Africa and the rest of Africa. As reported by Hartzenberg (2018), 1,950 out of 2,082 shopping centres in Africa are located in South Africa, ranking it sixth in having the most shopping malls in the world. There is evidence to support the argument that shopping overdevelopment is partly responsible for the failure of some retailers in South Africa (Hartzenberg, 2018).

Furthermore, the same big retailers, which are said to be colluding with shopping centre owners in South Africa to the demise of 95% of small retailers, are at the forefront of the Pan-Africa expansion (Joubert, 2003). This is a potential problem as South African supermarkets such as Shoprite continue to make deals with retail property developers such as Actis Africa to roll out shopping malls (e.g. Accra Mall in Ghana) in which Shoprite and Game are the main anchors. The continent is rapidly being 'malled up' in the South African style. The consequences could be more devastating than in South Africa, as most sub-Saharan countries have predominantly small-scale retailers and have a limited regulatory framework. Table 10.1 shows some major malls in Nigeria.

Literature review

The concept of supermarket value chain analysis

The concept of value has evolved and has been used for more complex analysis than has originally been conceptualised by Micheal Porter. Furthermore, the study of value chain analysis has assumed a more sophisticated focus to enable us to understand the human condition. Porter's value chain is based on an input–transformation–output process, and on primary and support activities within an organisation (cf. Porter, 1985). Furthermore, Porter built the value chain concept on the premise that products and services are an outcome of a coherent and systematic arrangement of primary activities (inbound logistics, operations, outbound logistics, marketing and sales, and after-sales service), and support activities

Table 10.1 Major shopping malls in Nigeria

Development	City	Retail m²	Year opened	Anchor tenant	Retail tenants
Palms	Lagos	20,000	2005	Game, Shoprite, Genesis Cinemas	Hugo Boss, Mango, Nike, Puma[36]
Ikeja City Mall	Lagos	22,000	2011	Shoprite, Silverbird Cinemas	Mr Price, Nike, Max Fashion[37]
Polo Park Mall	Lagos	27,000	2011	Shoprite	Puma, Swatch[38]
Ado Bayero Mall	Kano	25,000	2013	Shoprite, Game	Adidas[39]
Delta City Mall	Warn	13,800	2015	Shoprite	Mr Price, Jet[40]

Source: (Uqalo Research, 2016)

(infrastructure, human resource, technology, and procurement) to deliver superior value worthy of competitive advantage.

Subsequently, value chain analysis has been used to help us understand the complex arrangement of activities in the production of products and services in different industries and sectors within industries. This analysis has also led to the development of regional value chains (Pasquali, Godfrey, and Nadvi, 2020) and global value chains (Baglioni, Campling, and Hanlon, 2020). Kaplinsky and Morris (2002) provided the most comprehensive framework yet for the study of value chains in their handbook on value chain research. Kaplinsky and Morris (ibid.) maintain that value chains are useful in their different forms and provide more insights into the accumulation of income and distribution among the various actors along the chain. Moreover, the relationships and power struggles between actors may contribute to more nuanced outcomes such that the value chain requires some degree of governance for it to be effective (Kaplinsky and Morris, 2002). The earlier expansion of South African supermarkets into the rest of the African continent appears to have occurred with the assistance of various stakeholders who assisted in highly unstructured ways. The analysis of the supermarket value chain provides us with tools for a better understanding of the contributions of these stakeholders to the retailers (cf. Dakora, 2012)

The chapter explores the support provided by stakeholders in the effective functioning of the supermarket value chain across borders. The primary activities of a supermarket include sourcing for fresh produce, other hard food and non-food items from suppliers spread over different geographic regions, repackaging, and distributing these products to others stores. However, heightened competition and customer demand for quality products have compelled supermarkets to take a keen interest in establishing a better relationship with suppliers to the point of making investments upstream (cf. das Nair and Landani, 2020). The expansion into other African countries took these supermarkets into new geographical spaces, though with limited formal retail infrastructures and to some extent with non-existent support organisations to provide the required technical installations and logistics. It is, therefore, no accident that there has been some reliance on other South African expert organisations to provide the necessary support services (banking, logistics, design, and technical installations).

There is ample analysis of the supermarket value chain in Southern Africa, revealing how it is controlled, and used as a competitive tool by the large supermarkets to the exclusion of small and independent competitors (das Nair and Chisoro, 2016, 2018). This development calls for governance in the value chain. A similar situation is reported by the Grain Report of 2014 titled 'Food Sovereignty for Sale'. This report looked at how 'supermarkets are undermining peoples' control over food and farming in Asia' (Grain, p. 1). Like most parts of Africa,

> Asia's small traders sit at the front end of the local food systems that ensure the procurement and distribution of food grown on millions of small farms across the region. Traders typically procure their fresh fruit and vegetables, meat, eggs, and fish from wholesale markets where nearby farmers bring their produce daily.
>
> (Grain, 2014, p. 7)[3]

This situation is at odds with formal or modern supermarket operations, which run on individually controlled and integrated supply and distribution systems from farm to the table.[4] The Grain Report contends further that small farmers cannot participate in the integrated supermarket supply chains, as they demand adherence to food safety standards, which are impossible for them to meet (Grain, 2014, p. 7).

There are, therefore, calls for the supermarkets to be regulated as they are buyer-led with numerous suppliers of similar products supplying to fewer and larger supermarkets (Dannenberg, 2013). This allows supermarkets to impose their standards and requirements on suppliers to the exclusion of small suppliers and/or demand further concessions from them, as we have seen in the case of the South African led supermarket revolution (das Nair, 2018; Weatherspoon and Reardon, 2003).

This relates to the African conditions and the situation in which South African retailers found themselves. Previous scholars have made some critical observations; for example, as Miller (2008) argues, South African supermarket retail investment in the continent has followed a colonial approach.

Managing stakeholder relations in the value chain

The complexities of supermarket retail internationalisation in Africa require that South African supermarkets engage and forge partnerships with individuals and organisations to facilitate and assist in the process of entering and establishing themselves in different African country markets. These partners often include logistics companies, property developers, banks, consultants, and even governments. It is interesting to note that these partners in some cases have to internationalise themselves from South Africa in order to provide the needed services to their retail clients. These stakeholders are predominantly South African businesses. As Van Dongen (2015) discovered, South African retailers mostly seek to establish a relationship with local government officials in the host African countries rather than local business stakeholders.

Moreover, in a good interpretation of Porter's (1985) work, Dekker (2003) observes, in a value chain, different types of relationships and/or linkages exist between activities, business units of the firm, and between the firms and their suppliers and customers. A good example of a collaborative and partnership project is that of Massmart Group and Dimension Data (an information services company), whereby the former approached the latter for assisting them with an innovative backup and data virtualisation application. The outcome was the implementation of a new programme that puts Spar in the lead with virtualisation.[5] Another success story is the Massmart supplier development programme, which started with a 200-million-rand fund to support South African SMMES who are either existing or potential suppliers to Massmart.[6]

Methodology

The research approach

This study was guided by the interpretivism paradigm as it sought to understand the subjective interpretations of the phenomenon under study from the involved subjects (Creswell, 2007; Bhattacherjee, 2012). Value chain analyses are in themselves complex; this is especially true when they extend beyond specific organisations and geographies that are sometimes uncharted. The earlier expansion of South African supermarkets into the rest of Africa developed complex value chains in the process, with activities and role players of a diverse nature. To understand the nature of the supermarket value chain in this context, a qualitative analysis of the activities and role players is required; hence the interpretive design was adopted for the study reported in this chapter.

In-depth interviews were conducted with managers in businesses that provided support services to South African retailers operating in the rest of Africa. The study on the international supermarket value chain in Africa is within the ambit of international business, which is influenced by other agencies and actors, thereby lending itself to complex phenomena. It was therefore important to explore the phenomenon through qualitative interviews with the respondents closely associated with the phenomenon. This allowed for a more in-depth engagement on the issue at hand more locally and in the appropriate context (Qu and Dumay, 2011).

Data collection

The study was conducted using a snowball sample in which referrals were made to approach potential candidates based on their in-depth knowledge of the phenomenon (Bhattacherjee, 2012)

These services are diverse and range from banking, logistics, to property development and supermarket installations. This made it difficult to identify a representative sample to administer interviews. In this regard, contacts in the South African industry were based on previous studies that made specific references to organisations that assisted them in navigating around the challenges facing supermarkets in Africa. This initiative led to accessing organisations and contacts who have directly worked on the projects involved in assisting South African retailers in their expansion expedition in the African region. Table 10.2 provides a summary of these organisations and the interviewees. The interviews were conducted face-to-face, recorded on a voice-recording device, and transcribed for coding and analysis. Participants were e-mailed interview questions with the background to the study and appointments were made for the interviews. This allowed interviewees to prepare themselves for the interview, which also contributed to the reliability and validity of the data collection process.

The interviews lasted for an average of one hour, and the responses were recorded using a voice recorder with the permission of the respondents. The interview style was more conversational but directed through probing. This approach allowed for an interactive process in which both the researcher and the respondents participated in a discourse (Qu and Dumay, 2011), generating data through the synthesis of verbal interaction and reflection (Krauss et al., 2009).

Analysis of the interviews and reporting

The data were analysed by means of content analysis in the style originally espoused by Schutz (1959). The content analysis technique allowed the transcribed data to be broken into specific items, evidencing first-order constructs, which were then categorised using second-order constructs in order to build an

Table 10.2 Profiles of the support service providers

Support service providers			
Company	Description	Services to Supermarkets	Number of participants
Consulting	Business development and consulting	Advisory services, Business linkages and market lead	1
Banking	Banking and financial services provider	Banking and advisory services	1
Interior design and fixtures	Retail design specialist	Creating retail brands, concepts, and strategies, store interior specifications and installations	1
Shipping Company	Logistics and Transportation services provider	Provide sea freight services	1
Architects	Shopping centre/mall and supermarket design	Designing supermarket installations	1

understanding of the phenomenon (Bhattacherjee, 2012). The interview analysis centred on the following categories, which were used to structure the analysis:

- Nature of relationships and services provided by the supermarkets
- Understanding of supermarkets' strategy for expansion
- Supermarkets control and management of the value chain

The points listed above are discussed in the next sections.

Nature of relationships and services provided to supermarkets

The relationships and the kind of services provided by the support service providers to the retailers seeking market opportunities in other African countries appear to be essential to the strategic success of the retailers. The most evident and relevant instances of the support service providers' engagements with the retailers, as depicted in the interviews, are presented in the following remarks, which were in response to the question on the operational relationship between these stakeholders and the retailers,

> Okay, we are essentially a retail store design business that is what we were founded on, creating retail concepts for the market place. And, we have extended our service over the years. I think over 17 years now, our business has expanded from not only creating retail brands but also to doing all the concept and strategy work around a brand: retail concept, the store interior design, and doing the architectural detailing of all the elements that go into a store [Retail interior design and exhibition].
>
> Yeah, in Africa, the first one was in Namibia, and from there we moved to Mozambique and then to all the East African countries, Tanzania, and then Uganda. In Uganda, we did two big developments for Shoprite ... Accra [Ghana] mall is a case in point, where the developer there was Actis. And, in that specific installation, we were the Shoprite architects; in other words, we worked with the Actis architects. They did the centre, we did the Shoprite, and we fitted it into it [Architecture and Supermarket installation services].

The kind of services described by the design and architecture company representatives here suggest that the supermarket expansion of their modern retail operations in the rest of Africa would need their services at the entry stages, as they expand within those countries and into new countries. This is because, as indicated earlier, one of the challenges facing these supermarkets is the lack of formal retail infrastructure, which forces them to invest in retail property development (Dakora et al., 2016; Dakora et al., 2010). However, getting into a property development partnership provides the supermarkets with the opportunities of gaining preferential and favourable lease agreements from the property developers to the disadvantage of their competitors (informal, independent supermarkets, and even other international supermarkets) (das Nair, 2018). Another dimension to this relationship or partnership is that some of these South African service providers were internationalised by virtue of being contracted by the supermarket to go and work elsewhere in the continent. This has contributed to the diversity of the South African corporate continental internationalisation project.

The above quotes indicate that retailing is not just about providing products and services to consumers; it is also about creating shopping experiences. This is where retail strategy seems to meet the design. As can be seen in the quotes, retailers rely on the service providers such as architecture and design companies to design their stores and to create concepts and designs that would enable them to offer holistic shopping experiences. Moreover, once the design is complete, the products have to be delivered to the right stores and where trading begins, and of course the money has to be banked. The following remarks shed more light on these aspects:

> So, from our side, we'll offer to big companies and their agents like traders in-between; they have brokers, who look for best prices, and they have buyers who go into those markets, who work on trade deals. Then after they have negotiated and agreed on a price deal, they then approach a company like us to provide the logistics. That is where we then come in to discuss what we do here and to provide the service every week with the sailing [Logistics services].
>
> Each country has a different level of requirements some very big and others may not be as big, and that can slow things down. However, we always encourage the client that his agent is very, very important, and there are specialists, and customs clearing and forwarding agents who are fully aware of what documentation is needed. And we like to encourage them to use these guys who are in the profession and have a good office there, who know exactly what is needed [Logistic services company].

A crucial part of supermarket operation is the control of their supply chain and distribution (Grain, 2014) and more so when it comes to the border crossing, as reflected in the quotations above. South African supermarkets have established DCs and, in some cases, vertically integrated into the value chain (das Nair, 2018) and to distribute globally sourced products to their stores. The service supermarkets get from logistic companies is critical for them to be able to deliver produce from farm to table, as pointed out earlier in the Grain Report.

> What we suggest doing is introducing new business to South African companies, and the new business happens to be Africa. Therefore, I think what I am doing is creating the next avenue for the growth. So all of a sudden these companies are not reliant on the economic situation here in South Africa, because that is where a lot of them are [Consulting services].

What this consulting services company brings to the equation is new market knowledge to assist the supermarkets in making their next moves. This is important because the new market knowledge can facilitate the internationalisation process and minimise the risks. Concerning the retailers' strategies for expansion, the retailers seem to be testing, learning, and adapting their strategies as they go along. The support service providers observe that the supermarkets commit strategic mistakes by not acquiring appropriate market knowledge. As can be seen in the remarks above, the support service providers reveal, in some cases, new perspectives, which might not have been noticed even by the retailers themselves. This is so because the service providers also operate on the continent.

> I think from a banking perspective, what the retailers want from a banking partner is somebody who can provide them with a uniform service across very diverse countries. Very diverse in terms of the nature of dealings, some of the problems are around systems and telecommunication. One of the problems with the banking environment for us is that we made acquisitions in different countries, and we have to convert all those different platforms into one single view for a Shoprite to be able to see across Africa, and control ... from one central point. Now that development is costing the bank significant sums of money [Banking services].

As indicated in a wide range of cases, various kinds of services are offered in different ways and in varying degrees to the retailers as they expand their business across Africa. Moreover, these services are not provided without challenges, and the service providers have to expand in some ways in order to accommodate the demands of their retail partners. The case of the bank having to make acquisitions across Africa is an excellent example of the complex nature of retail internationalisation in Africa. Given the challenge of multiple currencies and different tax and financial regulatory systems, a partnership with a bank that understands the dynamics of the business would be necessary.

Stakeholders' experience in working with the supermarkets

This category reflects the experience of service providers (stakeholders) in working with the supermarkets in the retail expansion drive. These experiences are expressed in ways that relate to the different strategies employed by the supermarkets for entry and for scaling up the markets. Their views revealed some interesting insights on the manner in which the retailers have expanded into Africa, and still increasing their hunt for market opportunities within the African continent. In this regard, their independent views on the retailers' strategies are presented as follows:

> It is very cautious and calculated, and I think quite a costly approach to the end point. But it does take effect; the rewards have been very, very high, the rewards, because of these difficulties, it probably gives you slightly higher returns than you might get in some of the other markets, if you get it right. If you get it wrong, then obviously it's a cost [Banking services].

> ... there is a lot of homework and a lot of learning to do, but I think some of those big guys like Pick n Pay and Shoprite can afford to do the learning. And they can afford to fail once or twice before they get it right. Other brands, if they fail once or twice you wouldn't see them again; they will disappear [Retail interior design and exhibition].

The two quotes above from stakeholders put the complex and difficult nature of the supermarket expansion projects in perspective. These extracts relate to the possible lack of market knowledge, especially in the early years. However, it is market opportunities, which are acknowledged to exist in the continent despite the challenges, that explains the cautiousness and willingness to fail and learn. Cautiousness and learning approaches have emerged as useful strategies.

The following quotes depict some of the strategic moves employed by the retailers. It is not surprising that a lot has been said about Shoprite in these reports, as it has aggressively pioneered the South African led supermarket revolution. Therefore, most of these service providers have possibly gained their own continental experience through Shoprite.

> I mean, the interesting aspect of that, and we report to Shoprite about it as well, is that their model is 100% owned; they don't want partners. That's not necessarily sustainable in the long run. And I'm sure they are thinking about that in the back of their minds, to say when they reach a certain critical stage actually they might have to start relinquishing some of their own stores [Banking services].
>
> The problem with doing it all yourself is that you need to upskill your people quickly. I think if you take Shoprite, for example, I don't know Shoprite intimately, but my sense of what Shoprite has done, Shoprite and Game, is to put South African management onto the floor with the local workforce [Consulting services].

Due to the challenges highlighted earlier, it is possible that Shoprite could not find any franchise and partnership potentials, compelling them to open wholly-owned stores. As the stakeholders note, it can be a concern in the future, but it also appears it is a deliberate strategy to safeguard their investment.

Furthermore, the supermarkets seem to be testing, learning, and adapting their strategies as they go along. The support service providers observe that the supermarkets are making strategic mistakes by not acquiring appropriate market knowledge. As can be seen in the remarks above, the support service providers reveal in some cases new perspectives, which might not have been noticed even by the retailers themselves.

Supermarkets' control and management of the value chain

The stakeholders were asked to comment on the supermarkets' control of the value chain and how they source and deliver products to their stores. The product mix of the various supermarkets and the manner in which they get them to the marketplace is discussed. Below are some of the highlights of products mix and logistics issues emerging from the interviews.

> Yeah, all I know is that in the case of Shoprite, they will try and procure especially fresh products and meat; they will try and procure in that country [Architecture and Supermarket installations].
>
> You are going to have to make sure that the product mix is right to begin with [Retail interior design and exhibition].
>
> I don't think in the short term they can do very much for products beyond the fresh foods. You know if you are selling electronic goods, televisions and so on, you are going to import them from a non-local supplier based somewhere [Banking services].
>
> You have to admire Shoprite; I mean they really are pioneering. And they do the job. Their supply chain is superb, so yeah they really do a good job [Consulting services].
>
> Well, I won't want to mention the retailers, but for the products particularly we see, both for East Africa and for West Africa, and for Central Africa, particularly Rwanda, Burundi, Zambia, which you go in via Dar-es-Salaam on the East Coast. But for West Africa, a lot is building materials, you find that fancy hotel groups are building and they need a lot of glass, crockery, furniture, chairs, fixture, roof panels, air conditioning systems go there, irrigation sprinklers for the garden, a lot of printed material, documentation, and books, and so on [Logistic services].

As the interviews suggest, the sourcing and supplying of products by the supermarket are important components of Africa expansion. It involves making the product mix relevant to the communities in which they operate, as well as improving efficiency in the supply chain to allow for local smallholder participation. This then also links to the scrutiny of the contribution that the retailers make to the local economies of the target countries of the African investments outside South Africa.

Summary and conclusion

As presented in the analysis of the interviews, it is clear that the expansion of a retail business into other countries in Africa requires more than business strategies, products, services, and renting of shop space. The process is far more complex and requires the services and support of other stakeholders such as banks, logistics companies, consultants, architects, and engineers. This also influences the level of commitment to invest not just in capital projects but also in building relationships with key stakeholders.

The study also reveals that stakeholders themselves have to be prepared to expand their businesses in some ways in order to meet the unusual requirements of their partners. In the same vein, the intricacies of these relationships are potentially problematic. As highlighted earlier, there is shopping centre overdevelopment, collusions between retailers and other partners (Joubert, 2003), and the neo-colonial approach to exploiting the opportunities in the rest of Africa (Miller, 2006; Miller, Nel, and Hampwaye, 2008; Miller, 2008). However, the stakeholders studied appear to understand these nuances about the continent better than the retailers do and therefore creating the potential to influence better decision making among their retail partners.

According to the interviews, these stakeholders provide them (the retailers) with services that are critical to the internationalisation process, especially in the initial phases. The identified stakeholders include government, property developers, the banks, business partners, labour organisations, and insurance and advisory companies. These partnership and relationship issues serve to indicate that internationalisation is far more complicated than the movement of products to the markets, due to dependencies of various kinds and levels, and on different stakeholders.

The organisational or instructional arrangement of South Africa to support its corporate investment in the rest of Africa might mean that South African supermarkets would continue to dominate the continent. Future research should look into how South African retailers benefit from the AfCFTA in comparison with other countries on the continent.

Notes

1 cf. D'Haese and Van Huylenbroeck, 2005. The rise of supermarkets and changing expenditure patterns of poor rural households case study in the Transkei area, South Africa. Food Policy, 30: 97–113.
2 For more detail on these isse, cf. das Nair, R. 2018. The internationalization of supermarkets and the nature of competitive rivalry in retailing in southern Africa. Development Southern Africa, 35(3): 215–333.
3 Also cf. Uqalo Report on Formal Retail in sub-Saharan Africa, February 2016. www.uqalo.com for more details of level informal trade on the continent.
4 Grain Report, Food Soverignty for Sale. February 2015.
5 Damention data success story
6 Massmart Supplier Development Fund. https://www.massmart.co.za/sustainability/supplier-development/

References

Allison, S. (2018). Africa's free trade fairy tale. https://mg.co.za/article/2018-03-22-africas-free-trade-fairy-tale [25 March 2018].

Baglioni, E., Campling, L. & Hanlon, G. (2020). Global value chains as entrepreneurial capture: insights from management theory. *Review of International Political Economy*, 27(4), 903–925.

Bavier, J. (2018). Massmart to open 20 stores in African expansion – chairman. https://www.reuters.com/article/us-africa-business-massmart/massmart-to-open-20-stores-in-pan-african-expansion-chairman-idUSKBN1H22FK [30 March 2018].

Bhattacherjee, N. (2012). Social science research: principles, methods, and practices. *The Global Text Project*. A free textbook published under the Creative Commons Attribution 3.0 License.
Creswell, J.W. (2007). *Qualitative Inquiry & Research Design: Choosing Among Five Approaches*. 2nd ed. SAGE Publications, Thousand Oaks.
Dakora, E., Kalitanyi, V., Mutematemi, E., Gyogluu, S., Bagui, L. & Mason, R.B. (2016). Expansion of South African retailers' activities into Africa. Project 2014/05, For Wholesale and Retail Leadership Chair, Cape Peninsula University of Technology, Cape Town.
Dakora, E.A.N, Bytheway, A.J. & Slabert, A. (2010). The Africanisation of South African retailing: a review. *African Journal of Business Management*, 4(5), 748–754 [May 2010].
Dakora, E.A.N. (2012). Exploring the fourth wave of supermarket evolution: concepts of value and complexity in Africa. *International Journal of Managing Value and Supply Chains*, 3(3), 25–37.
Dakora, E.A.N. & Bytheway, A.J. (2014). Entry mode issues in the internationalisation of South African retailing. *Mediterranean Journal of Social Sciences*, 5(4), 194-205.
Dakora, E.A.N., Bytheway, A.J. & Slabbert, A. (2010). The Africanisation of South African retailing: a review. *African Journal of Business Management*, 4(5), 748–754.
Dannenberg, P. (2013). The rise of supermarkets and challenges for small farmers in South African food value chains. *Economia Agro-Alimentare*, 15(3), 15–34.
das Nair, R. (2018). The internationalisation of supermarkets and the nature of competitive rivalry in retailing in southern Africa1. *Development Southern Africa*, 35(3), 315–333.
das Nair, R. & Landani, N. (2020). New approaches to supermarket supplier development programmes in Southern Africa. *Development Southern Africa*, 18(June), 4-20.
das Nair, R. & Shingie, S. (2016). The expansion of regional supermarket chains and implications for local suppliers: a comparison of findings from South Africa, Botswana, Zambia, and Zimbabwe. WIDER Working Paper 2016/169.
Dekker, H.C. (2003). Value chain analysis in interfirm relationships: a field study. *Management Accounting Research*, 14(1), 1–23.
Games, D. 2013. Africa's Business Landscape. The state of Play. Compiled in Games, D. *Business Africa: Corporate insights*. Johannesburg, Penguin: 1–13.
Goldman, C. (1974). Outreach of consumers and the modernisation of urban food retailing in developing countries. *Journal of Marketing*, 38, 8–16.
Grain Report. (2014). *Food Sovereignty For Sale: Supermarkets are Undermining People'S Control Over Food*.
Hartzenberg, L. (2018). It's not an apocalypse, it's a retail revolution. https://www.iol.co.za/news/south-africa/why-95-of-small-retailers-in-sa-fail-109704 [20 May 2018].
Joubert, M. (2003). Why 95% of small retailers in SA fail. https://www.iol.co.za/news/south-africa/why-95-of-small-retailers-in-sa-fail-109704 [20 May 2018].
Kaplinsky, R. & Morris, M. (2002). *A Handbook for Value Chain Research*. IDRC
Kearney, A.T. (2014). Global retailers: cautiously aggressive or aggressively cautious?. 2013 Global Retail Development Index. https://www.atkearney.com/consumer-productsretail/global-retail-development-index/2013#sthash.3haRrPQM.dpuf [25 March 2018].
Krauss, S.E., Hamzah, A., Omar, Z., Suandi, T., Ismail, I.A., Zahari, M.Z. & Nor, Z.M. (2009). Preliminary investigation and interview guide development for studying how Malaysian farmers' form their mental models for farming. *The Qualitative Report*, 14(2), 245–260.

Leke, A. and Signé, L. (2019). Africa's untapped business potential: spotlighting opportunities for business in Africa and strategies to succeed in the world's next big growth market. https://www.brookings.edu/wp-content/uploads/2019/01/BLS18234_BRO_book_006.1_CH5.pdf. [18 November 2019].

McKinsey Global Institute. (2012). Urban world: cities and the rise the consuming class. file:///C:/Users/Apprentice/Downloads/MGI_Urban_world_Rise_of_the_consuming_cla ss_Full_report.pdf [14 July 2019].

Miller, D. (2006). Changing African cityspaces – regional claims of Africa labour at South Africa owned shopping malls. *Africa Development*, XXXI(1), 27–47.

Miller, D. (2008). 'Retail renaissance' or company rhetoric: the failed partnership of South African Corporation and local suppliers in Zambia. *Labour, Capital and Society*, 41(1), 34–55.

Miller, D., Nel, E. & Hampwaye, G. (2008). Malls of Zambia: racialised retail expansion and South African foreign investors in Zambia. *African Sociological Review*, 12(1), 35–54.

Pasquali, G., Godfrey, S. & Nadvi, K. (2020). Understanding regional value chains through the interaction of public and private governance: insights from Southern Africa's apparel sector. *Journal International Business Policy*, 4, 368–389.

Porter, M. (1985). *The Competitive Advantage: Creating and Sustaining Superior Performance*. Free Press, New York.

Qu, S.Q. & Dumay, J. (2011). The qualitative research interview. *Qualitative Research in Accounting & Management*, 8(3), 238–264.

Reardon, T. & Gulati, A. (2008). The supermarket revolution in developing countries: policies for 'competitiveness with inclusiveness'. *International Food Policy Research Institute Policy Brief*, 2(June), 2.

Reardon, T. & Hopkins, R. (2006). The supermarket revolution in developing countries: policies to address emerging tensions among supermarkets, suppliers and traditional retailers. *European Journal of Development Research*, 18(4), 522–545.

Reardon, T., Timmer, C.P., Barrett, C.B. & Berdegue, J. (2003). The rise of supermarkets in Africa, Asia, and Latin America. *American Journal of Agricultural Economics*, 85, 1140–1146.

Schutz, W.C. (1959). On categorising qualitative data in content analysis. *Public Opinion Quarterly*, 22(4), 503–515.

Uqalo Research. (2016). Formal retail in sub-Saharan Africa. www.uqalo.com [15 June 2019].

van Dongen, K. (2015). The internationalisation of South African retailers in Africa. Thesis (unpublished).

Weatherspoon, D.D. & Reardon, T. (2003). The rise of supermarkets in Africa: implications for agrifoods systems and the rural poor. *Development Policy Review*, 21(3), 333–355.

11 Supermarket retailing in Africa
Lessons learnt

Felix Adamu Nandonde and John L. Stanton

Introduction

This chapter briefly presents the lessons learnt from different countries on supermarket retailing in Africa. We understand that the dynamics in Africa make it impossible for each finding to apply to all countries on the continent. However, we confidently trust that investors and policymakers can benefit from the research on consumer preference, ICT usage, and proper retailing formats on the continent and from the remedies for strengthening supplier and retailer relationships.

This chapter highlights some of the issues that may help African governments design and implement policies that nurture supermarkets and promote investment in the retail business. Similarly, the chapter helps retailers formulate strategies to help them attract customers and build relationships with suppliers. Without affecting what has been presented in the previous chapters, we believe that some of the recommendations presented in this chapter will help investors in the supermarket business on the continent.

In practice, retailers aim at getting profits by designing strategies that attract customers and suppliers to work together. For retailers to manage and attract customers to visit their stores, understanding consumer behaviour is very important. Based on the fact that supermarket retailing is at an infant stage in Africa, there must be initiatives by the African governments to support retailers in research and access to the research for the improvement of their operations. Research conducted in areas such as consumption patterns and trends, demand forecast, consumer preferences on packaged foods, and ICT tools may enable retailers to navigate through a number of challenges in the African business environment. We understand that what is good in one country may be bad in another; therefore, we encourage case-based studies.

In theory, policies could be guided by encouraging supermarket retail to benefit from ICT, the growing middle class, and connect producers with markets on the continent. Chapters 5 and 6 show that ICT tool usage by supermarkets in Africa and particularly in South Africa, Tanzania, and Uganda is very low due to the many macro-environmental challenges. This means policies of stimulating the use of ICT tools need to be formulated. Nevertheless, we also need to understand the perception of customers, employees, and owners towards using these tools.

DOI: 10.4324/9780367854300-11

All these need research, and retailers cannot afford to invest in research in such domains due to their infant nature.

As mentioned in Chapter 3, visiting supermarkets is influenced by socio-economic factors, such as friends and loan availability. This shows that investors have to design strategies that attract customers to their stores. In fact, the impact of supermarket retailing is well known on the linkage of suppliers with the market. Chapter 8 shows that suppliers employ strategies such as social networking, employment of experienced staff, and provision of sales support to link with the market.

Notwithstanding the above suggestion, specific strategies need to be designed by retailers to attract customers to their stores and strengthen their relationship with service suppliers (see Chapter 9). Some recommendations, including those shown below, are likely to be relevant for supermarkets business operations on the continent.

Setting the appropriate retail format

Literature of retail formats shows that retailers prefer to transfer their homegrown retail formats to new markets. However, previous studies reveal that imported retail formats do not perform well in foreign markets. For instance, the failure of supercentres in Europe is related to the imported format from America. In this book, we have indicated that it is very important to consider the culture of the host country consumers on the preference of retail formats if one wants to operate in Africa.

Both Chapters 1 and 2 show that some retail formats perform better on the continent than other formats. Chapter 1 indicates that supermarket formats are performing better compared with discount and supercentre formats in terms of sales and revenue. We argue that retail formats have to be influenced by culture, income, and infrastructure availability in a particular country. For example, consumers in developing economies culturally relate the buying process with socialisation. That means customers prefer to buy from the kiosk or bazaar because they can chat with the owners. Further, by knowing the challenges of infrastructure and city planning in a number of African countries, it is appropriate to consider having some formats within residential areas, which reduces travel costs for consumers. In that regard, it is very important to consider consumer preferences and minimise costs by designing convenience retail formats that fit well with African consumers, as a study from Madagascar recommends in Chapter 2.

Facilitating the use of ICT technologies

Although the supermarket business is on the rise in Africa, online retailing and the use of other technological facilities are not increasing on the continent. For example, some online platforms (Jumia, Kaimu, and Zoom) closed their operations in some countries because they were minimally visited. There are many reasons that limit online retailer operation from using technologies on the continent, and these include infrastructure and transaction costs. African governments can play an important role in facilitating the use of ICT tools in supermarkets on the continent. The areas of ICT application include website, automatic vending machines, outmatch payment machines, and royalty cards for facilitating transactions. For example, if transactions are made using cards, this can be used to easily understand customer purchases over time and allows retailers to predict the decisions and demands of individual customers due to their purchase behaviour through the scanned data.

More effective ICT tools are needed by retailers in Africa to facilitate the provision of services needed by consumers and interaction with suppliers and other services providers. Chapter 5 shows that ICT usage is low in East Africa and Chapter 7 observes that retailers in South Africa face macro-economic challenges in their efforts of using ICT tools. In general, to support retailers' use of ICT for the provision of services, African governments have an important role to play. This can be done by formulating good policies on taxing ICT tools and training human resource experts who are skilled at making sure that supermarkets in Africa become users of technology.

Strengthening related supported industry for the growth of the sector

To support the growth of the supermarket business in the future, it would be useful to support a related industry that works closely with supermarkets on the continent. Chapter 10 illustrates that suppliers of services play a great role in the development of supermarkets in Africa. These suppliers are in property management, finance, security, ICT, and human resources. Generally, supermarkets in Africa rely on the stock market and retain earnings (See Okeahalam and Wood, 2009) and loans from commercial banks (Nandonde, 2021) to finance their operation on the continent. With the growth of the sector, some of the sources of financing supermarket operations seem to be unsustainable. This means African governments have to devise other more sustainable ways of supporting supermarket retail.

Retailers are facing a shortage of the number of services such as malls, suppliers of technology, and human skills, in spite of the fact that supermarket retailing is growing in Africa and has managed to attract international retailers such as Wal-Mart, a US retailer that acquired 51% of Massmart, a South African retailer in 2014; Carrefour, a French retailer that operates in eight African countries, including Cameroon, Ivory Coast, Senegal, Kenya and Tanzania with nine stores in Nairobi and Dar-es-Salaam; and two UK retailers, Tesco with stores in Libya and Sainsbury with stores in Algeria. Due to this, retailers have to invest in areas that are not their core business, such as the property industry, by building malls to reach African consumers.

This lack of related supported industry growth limits supermarkets in Africa to capture the growing middle-income class. In that regard, retailers on the continent have to be constructors too in order for them to access some of the markets. Supporting related industries is very important for the growth of the supermarket business in Africa. Some of these related industries include the construction industry, engineering industry for installation of ventilation, and interior design industry. Chapter 10 urges African governments to identify and support related industries that seem to be the backbone of supermarket business development on the continent. Currently, retailers are required to construct malls and premises as part of their investment in many countries. This limits the growth of the sector, and some retailers fail to grow in some cities due to a lack of facilities. For example, before its collapse in 2017, Nakumatt supermarket had to open its first mall in the small town of Moshi, Tanzania, due to the lack of space in the few and occupied malls in the city of Dar-es-Salaam.

Another important area that is linked with supermarket retail development on the continent is human resource development, which can support the growth of the sector. Supermarket retailing contributes significantly to a nation's GDP; for example, in Nigeria, retail contributes about 18% of the GDP, a similar scenario exists in Kenya, South Africa, and Tanzania; however, only South Africa has a proper plan for developing people to assist this sector to grow. In South Africa, the University of South Africa (UNISA) designed and offered certificate, diploma, and degree courses focusing on retailing. We urge African governments to facilitate the growth of the sector by preparing people with skills and knowledge in retailing to propel the sector on the continent. In its current state, the continent seems unready for this avenue. Although some universities seem to offer retail subjects in business-related courses, this is not enough; there is a need to train people with relevant education from certificate to diploma levels who will be ready to navigate the sector, which is at the take-off stage in Africa.

Promotion of the use of operation research tools to support supermarket decisions

Africa is seen as a hard market to crack in the supermarket business as many retail firms have collapsed in different countries on the continent. For example, Shoprite recently reported closing its operations in many African countries such as Nigeria, Ghana, and Kenya. The retailer also closed its operations in Uganda and Tanzania in 2014 due to different reasons, including consumer behaviour and low visitation to supermarkets. During its operations in Nigeria, Shoprite, a South African retailer, experienced hardship in logistics and the distribution of goods to northern parts of the country in the Kaduna Province, which was fuelled by challenges in infrastructure. The challenges retailer and supermarkets face on the continent suggest that investors have to refine their decisions. For example, the collapse of a number of retail stores was attributed to location and understanding of consumer behaviour.

Chapter 7 suggests that in minimising problems facing the supermarkets business in Africa and supporting investors to make decisions, studies should embrace operations research tools to uncover issues such as consumer behaviour, shelf space utilisation, demand forecasting, inventory control, and location selection. Operations management tools will enable retailers to overcome market failure in their business operations on the continent.

Strengthening retailer–supplier relationship

In Chapters 8 and 9, we drew lessons from the relationship between retailers and suppliers in the supermarket business in Tanzania. The lessons are intended to shed light on the manner in which supermarkets strategic collaboration with local suppliers can ensure consistency in the availability of required food products. Globally, the supplier–retailer relationship has been one of the areas considered to be unfair. Some of the issues that suppliers complain about include late payment, support for the cost of advertising, and lack of compensation on products that get damaged or expire while on the retailers' shelves. Africa is not exceptional in this; although there is no research on unfair practices between retail businesses per se, in this book we argue that this is an area that requires the attention of African governments for the future development of the sector.

For strengthening the supplier–retailer relationship in Africa, there is a need for devising policies that protect suppliers against late payments and against other unethical practices. Previous literature on the modern retailing business in African shows that the growth of the sector depends much on the acceptance of domestic suppliers in working with supermarkets (See Nandonde and Kuada, 2016). In general, Africa's suppliers have another marketing channel, which is the open market that can absorb their products and services with fair treatment. For example, in some countries, informal retail controls more than 90% of the retail business in the country, which implies that sales volumes of supermarket channels are still insignificant. In that regard, suppliers have a parallel market, which can absorb more of their goods and services in large quantities. Thus, without good policies, suppliers would likely prefer to continue working with the open market that seems to treat them fairly, and this may limit the growth of supermarkets on the continent.

We need to acknowledge that some countries in Africa have started to design policies that are intended to foster supplier–retailer relationships. For example, the Kenyan government has initiated a programme to facilitate designing policies for fostering relationships between supermarkets and retailers. The initiative started after suppliers complained that they were intimidated by retailers with harsh trade terms. In Chapter 8, we have indicated that suppliers use different strategies to access supermarkets.

References

Nandonde, F. A. (2021). In the desire of conquering East African supermarket business: what went wrong in Nakumatt supermarket. *Emerging Economies Cases Journal*, 2(2), 126–133.

Nandonde, F. A. and Kuada, J. (2016). Modern food retailing buying behaviour in Africa: the case of Tanzania. *British Food Journal*, 118(5), 1163–1178.

Okeahalam, O. C. and Wood, C. (2009). Financing internationalization: a case study of an African retail transnational corporation. *Journal of Economics Geography*, 9, 511–537.

Website

www.carrefour.com

Index

Note: page references in *italics* indicate figures; **bold** indicates tables.

Aakar Innovations 18
Abebe, G. 129
Abouali, A. 110
Aburto, L. 114–115
Achieng, J. B. O. 75
Ackley, D. 118
Actis Africa 174
Adebambo, S. 73–74
advertising *see* marketing and advertising
African Continental Free Trade Area (AfCFTA) 172, 184
African retail market xiv–xvi, 2, 187–191; features of 118–120; formats 1–15, 188; *see also* Algeria; Angola; Benin; Botswana; Burkina Faso; Cameroon; Egypt; Ethiopia; Gabon; Ghana; Ivory Coast; Kenya; Libya; Madagascar; Morocco; Mozambique; Nigeria; Rwanda; Senegal; South Africa; Swaziland; Tanzania; Uganda; Zambia; Zimbabwe
African Union (AU) 172
agri-food systems 36, 129, 130, 152, 157–161, **158**, 163–167; *see also* supply chain; value chain
Ahmed, Z. U. 55
Ahorbo, G. K. 54, 56
Ahrholdt, D. C. 46
Ajzen, I. 38
Al Othiam 8
Albors, J. 73
Algeria xiv, 2–3, 189
Alibaba Campus 99–100
Aloysius, G. 97
Amazon, Go Stores 100
Anas, A. 106
Andam, K. 136

Angola 3–4
Anku, E. K. 54, 56
Aras, S. 114
Artificial Neural Networks (ANN) model 113, 114–115
Ashikin, N. 26
Ashtiani, M. G. 107
AT Kearney 21–24, 129, 172
Atasoy, Y. 130
Auchan 12, 13
Auto-regressive Integrated Moving Average (ARIMA) model 113, 114
Awasthia, A. 107
Awuah-Gyawu, M. 75
Azam Group 164
Azania Millers 164

Baird, N. 95
Balaji, N. 82
banking services *see* financial services
Barney, J. 141
Basic Element Limited 137, 140
Bednar, M. J. 54
Beltov, T. 112
Benin 4–5
Billon, M. 85
BIM 8, 9, 12
Binu, D. 97
Bo-Jian, L. 117
Bone, M. 94
Botswana 5–6, 76
bottom of the pyramid (BOP) markets 16–32, **22**, **23**, *28*, *29*; *see also* income levels
Boxer Superstores 93
brands 25, 65
Braun, V. 57

Index

Burch, D. 153–154, 159, 160
Burkina Faso 6–7
Burkul, V. 116

Cameroon 7–8, 189
Candogan, O. 117
carbon emissions reductions 74, 94
card payments 49, 91, 99, 101, 189
Carrefour xiv, 1, 2, 3, 8, 10, 11, 12, 15, 189
cashback programmes 93–94
Casino xiv, 4–5, 6–7, 9, 12, 13, 14–15
certifications and compliance 132
Chandarana Foodplus 10, 11
Chapados, N. 112–113
Checkers 93, 95, 99
Chile 55
China 2, 40, 92, 99–100, 154
Choppies 5–6, 11, 14, 36
Clarke, V. 57
Cleanshelf 10
closures, store *see* failure
Cohen, M. C. 112
collaboration 171, 173–174
competition 2, 164–165, 166, 174; between traditional markets and supermarkets 54, 55, 62–66
competitive advantage 25, 52, 55, 73, 76, 83, 84, 119, 130, 175
consumer access 59, 66
consumer behaviour xv, 2, 19, 36, 38–41, 55, 58, 129, 164–165, 187–188; in bottom of the pyramid (BOP) markets 16–20, 26, 30; impact of technology on 91–101; motivation to visit supermarkets 36–50, *41*, **44**, **46**, *47*, *48*; preferences for supermarkets *vs.* traditional markets 52–67, **57**; theory 38–39; *see also* culture; income levels
consumer choice 53, 59–62
consumer credit 49
consumer demographics 40, 43, **44**, 49; *see also* socio-economic status
consumer education levels 65; literacy 63
consumer experiences 65, 66, 94–95, 98
consumer lifestyles 4, 49
consumer locations 49; travel to supermarkets 23, 165, 188
consumer price points 16–17, 23–24, 26, 30, 31, 40
consumer spending 2, 4–15; spending power 20–21, 22, 24, 25, 106
consumption inadequacy 16
convenience factors 58, 95

convenience stores 1, 3, 9; *see also* small businesses
cooperative groups 164
corporate social responsibility 72, 78, 87
Corstjens, M. 109
counterfeit products 20, 25
counting technologies 72
credit: consumer 49; trade 144, 145, 191
Creswell, J. W. 132
culture 2, 65, 66, 188
customer service/s 49, 60, 74–76, 83, 113; additional in-store 49, 93–94, 98–99; support staff 142–143

Dadzie, S. H. 41
Dahari, Z. 55
Dakora, E. 92, 161–162
Daniel, W. 81
das Nair, R. 174
data collection and analysis 75, 76, 77, 79, 80, 82, 96, 122–123, 189
Davies, F. M. 39–40, 49
Day, M. 100
decentralisation 72, 79
Dekker, H. C. 177
Delforce, R. 159
demand forecasting 79, 80, 82, 100, 113–115, 120, 121
Den Boer, A. 117
discount stores 3, 4, 5, 6, 7, 8, 15
discounts 49, 58, 61; *see also* promotions
Discrete Event Simulation (DES) 116
distribution 17, 18–20, 24–30, 31, 145–146, 180; distribution centres (DCs) 75, 94, 122, 173, 180; micro-franchising models 18, 26–27, *28*, 31; *see also* logistics
Dixon, J. 98
Dolan, C. S. 158
Doyle, P. 109
Drezner, T. 106–107
Drezner, Z. 106–107
Dube, C. 75
Duncombe, R. A. 76

EastMatt 10, 11
Eckhardt, J. 73
Economic Order Quantity (EOQ) 110–111
Economist, The 99–100
education *see* consumer education levels; staff: training and development
Egypt xiv, 8–9, 110, 136, 173
Ekene, E. A. 74
Ellickson, P. 116

Emongor, E. 129
employees *see* staff
employment xiv, 27, 77, 145–146, 163
entrepreneurship 26, 31, 76, 152, 166
Envirofit 18
environments, business 1, 4, 36–38, *71*, 72, 79, 87, 132, 187
Ernst, A. 112
Erol, R. 116–117
Ethiopia 76, 119, 129
ethnicity 139, 141, 146
European Union (EU) 73, 129–130, 131, 188
everyday low prices 116
Excel software 122–123
exit *see* failure
expansion *see* growth

Factored Markov Decision Process (FMDP) 116
Faiguenbaum, S. 55
failure/store closure xiv, xv, 1, 2, 8, 11, 14, 17, 36, 70, 120, 145, 174, 190
Fairbourne, J. S. 26
Farahani, R. 107
fast-moving consumer goods xiv, 112, 116
FDI *see* foreign direct investment (FDI)
financial services: consumer in-store 93–94; for supermarkets 181–184, 189
Finland 73
food standards and regulations 159, 176; *see also* certification and compliance; quality
Foot Loose Limited 137, 143
footfall/foot tracking 121
foreign direct investment (FDI) 1, 2, 4, 14, 20, 54, 92, 157, 160, 162, **162**, 171, 172; *see also* multinational companies (MNCs)
Foster, C. 76
Fox, T. 158, 159
franchising 161, 173, 182; micro-franchising model 18, 24, 26–27, *28*, 31
Franco, M. 85
Fraym 120
free trade 172, 184
French retailers xiv, 2, 4–5, 14–15, 189; *see also* Carrefour; Casino; Leader Price; Systeme U; Yves Rocher
fresh produce 49, 52, 59, 133–136, 152, 158, 160–161, 164; *see also* local suppliers; quality
Fromm, I. 161
Fruit & Veg City 3, 4, 5, 6

Gabon 9
Game 1, 14, 15, 52, 58, 63, 64, 133, 174
Garcia, M. 85
Gereffi, G. 160
Ghana 1, 10, 40, 41, 54–56, **57**, 130, 136, 172, 173
Ghingold, M. 55
Giotopoulos, I. 71, *71*, 72, 78
global commodity chain (GCC) 160
global consumer culture positions (GCCP) strategy 25, 29
Global Retail Development Index (GRDI) 21–24
global value chain (GVC) 160
globalisation 53, 54–55
government institutions 141, 143, 145
government policymaking 3, 37, 54–55, 64–65, 87, 92, 131–132, 145–146, 151–152, 163, 171, 187–191; *see also* environments, business
GRAIN 119
Grain Report (2014) 176
Green, M. 133
Grönroos, C. 131
growth, business xv–xvi, 1, 16, 37, 66, 70, 73, 79, 92, 98, 130, 146, 157, 173–174, 189–190; *see also* sustainability
Gudergan, S. P. 46
Gulati, A. 55, 56, 153
Gumbo, V. 75
Gunadi, S. 75

Halinen, A. 131
Hami, A. 82
Hammond, A. 16
Happy Sausage 141
Hartzenberg, L. 174
Harvey, M. 159
Hassan, N. M. 26
Heeks, R. B. 76
Hidalgo, A. 73
Hjort, J. 76
Hodgson, M. J. 106
home delivery 58, 96–97
Hotelling, H. 106
Hsiao, H. I. 137
Huang, S. 110
Huff, D. L. 106
human capital *71*, 72, 78–79, 145
human resources *see* staff
Humphrey, J. 161
Hungry Lion 94
hypermarkets *see* superstores

196 Index

ICT *see* information and communication technology (ICT)
Igwe, A. 116
Ijumba, C. 136
IKEA 12, 94
Imalaseko 133
imported foods 129, 151–152, 163, 164, 165
income levels 1, 2, 4, 15, 40, 43, 49, 56, 60, 91, 94, 95, 99, 133, 164, 188; *see also* bottom of the pyramid (BOP) markets; middle-class consumers
India 18, 92, 146
Inditex 3, 12
Indonesia 40–41, 75, 110, 154
industries, related 190
information and communication technology (ICT) 187, 188–189; artificial intelligence 87; competencies *71*, 71–72, 78; e-sales and procurement 72; impact on consumer behaviour 91–101; incompatible systems 85; machine learning 96; telematics tracking 73; usage in East Africa 70–87, *71*, *73*, 122; wireless technologies 73; *see also* data collection and analysis; internet connectivity; mobile phones; online shopping
infrastructure, retail 21, 173–175, 179–180, 188; facility locations 105–107, 120, 121; *see also* shopping centres/malls
input–process–output model 72–73, 79
Intelligent Artificial Neural Network systems 114–115
internal organisation *71*, 72, 79
International Livestock Research Institute (ILRI) 119
internationalisation xiv, 170, 176, 180–181, 184
internet connectivity 76, 77, 101
Intersport International 3
inventory control 70, 74–75, 80, 110–111, 121, 122
Ivory Coast 189

Jake, W. 81
Japan 108
Jhamb, D. 98
Jiao, S. 116
Jingya, L. 107–108
Joanna, S. 82
John, O. 108
Jorne, V. 112
Just-In-Time (JIT) system 110

Kaplinksy, R. 175
Kaufman, F. C. 55
Kenya xiv, xv, 1, 10–11, 36, 75, 76, 119, 122–123, 129–130, 140, 146, 152, 157, 160, 172, 189, 190, 191
Kenyan retailers 1, 36, 76, 129, 133; *see also* Tuskys; Uchumi; Nakumatt
Kero 3, 4
Kilimci, Z. 115
Kinsey, J. 94–95
Kiran, R. 98
Kitheka, S. S. 75
Kithinji, F. 122
knapsack problem 108–109
Korea 154
Korzeniewicz, M. 160
Kuada, J. 144, 145
Kumar, K. 49

labour unions 99
Lagardère Services 13
Latin America 154
Lawrence, G. 153–154, 159, 160
Leader Price 17
leadership *71*, 72, 79
Li, B. 112
liabilities of foreignness 27, 31
Libya 189
local organisations 27, *29*
local suppliers 25, 27, *28*, 52, 94, 121, 189; participation strategies in Tanzania 129–146, **134**, **136**, **137**, **138**; and supermarkets, relationships between 151–167, **158**, **162**; trade credit 144, 145, 191; *see also* small businesses; smallholdings/farms
logistics 73–75, 79–80, 94, 97, 107–108, 183, 190; transportation problem 107–108, 121; *see also* distribution; inventory control
Louw, A. 151, 157
loyalty cards/programmes 49, 75, 82, 91, 93, 96

McDonald's 9
McGuire, W. J. 39
Madagascar 16–32, **22**, **23**, *28*, *29*
Mai, L. 40
Maki Company 20
Makori, W. 122
Makro 96, 97
Malaysia 26, 116, 154
malls *see* shopping centres/malls

management 65–66, 86, 141; *see also* leadership
management science *see* operations research (OR)
market knowledge xv, 180–182
market research 75, 171
marketing and advertising 16, 25, 27, 31, 49, 96–98, 131–132
markets, traditional 20, 53–56, 119, 152, 153, 159, 165, 166, 188, 191; in bottom of the pyramid (BOP) countries 19, 20, 24, 27, *28*, 30–31, 38, 40; consumer preferences for *vs.* supermarkets 52–67, **57**; *see also* local suppliers; small businesses
Masatochi, S. 108
Massmart 16, 172, 177, 189
Mbamba, U. O. L. 74
Melachrinoudis, E. 113
Melcom 52, 56, 59–65
Meng, T. 40, 49
Metro 8, 9
Mexico 92
Michelson, H. 152
micro-franchising 18, 24, 26–27, *28*, 31
middle-class consumers 1, 66, 101, 120, 151, 171, 187, 189; disposable incomes 92, 95, 151, 172
Miller, D. 176
Minten, B. 92
Misra, S. 116
Mlimbila, J. 74
mobile phones 75–76, 81, 100; shopping apps 91, 95–96
Mohamad, F. 116
Mohammed Enterprises 164
Möller, K. 131
Monnakgotla, M. 99
Morocco 11–12
Morris, M. 175
Moving Average (MA) model 113–114
Mozambique 172
Multi-Criteria Decision Analysis Methods (MCDM) 107
multinational companies (MNCs) 55, 94, 152, 157, 160, 172; in bottom of the pyramid (BOP) markets 16–32, *28*, *29*
Mzomo Services Limited 139

Naivas 10, 11
Nakumatt xiv, 1, 10, 14, 36, 120, 133, 135–136, 140, 141, 142, 143, 162, 190
Namazone Business Centre 139–140, 141
Nandonde, F. A. 41, 43, 144, 145

neighbourhood stores 4, 6, 7, 9, 10, 12, 13, 14, 15; *see also* small businesses
Netherlands, The 137
networks *see* relationships
Neven, D. 129, 157
NGOs *see* non-governmental organisations (NGOs)
Ngugi, K. 75
Nielsen 119
Nigeria 1, 74, 116, 172, 174, **175**, 190
Njoike, C. 122
non-governmental organisations (NGOs) 18, 27, 55, 145
Non-Linear Integer Programming model 110
Nosso Super 3, 4
Nyakango, J. N. 75

Ojanperä, S. 77
Ondiek, G. O. 75
online shopping 91, 95–96, 188; apps 91, 95–96; *vs.* in-store shopping 72–73, *73*
Onzere, S. N. 129
operations research (OR) 104–124, **117**, **118**, **120**, **121**, 190
opportunism 164
opportunity cost 52
organic food options 100
organisational legitimacy 27
outsourcing 137–139, 143

packaging 58, 65, 141–142, 164; unbundling 23–24, 26, 27, 30, 31
Panda 8
Panone 133, 142
Paraguay 98
partnerships *see* relationships
Patton, M. Q. 133
Perakis, G. 112
Perego, A. 74
personnel *see* staff
pharmacies in-store 93
Pick n Pay 5, 6, 13, 14, 91, 93, 95, 96, 100
Planet Retail 2
Plummer, K. 132
point of sale (POS) facilities 75, 79, 80, 84
policymaking *see* government policymaking
Popo, L. 144
pop-up experiences 95
Porter, M. 174, 177
Poulsen, J. 76
poverty xiv, 16, 18, 25, 26, 130, 152, 172; *see also* bottom of the pyramid (BOP) markets; income levels

Index

power 55, 152, 157–159, **158**, 175; *see also* spending power
Prahalad, C. K. 16, 18, 22–23
PrefixSpan algorithm 97
prices/pricing 58, 61, 66, 116–118, 122, 165; in bottom of the pyramid (BOP) markets 18, 20–24, *29*; consumer price points 16–17, 23–24, 26, 30, 31, 40, 41; differences in 61–62, 65; product tagging 61, 65
Prince, D. 39, 49
privacy issues 85–86, 96
Probyn, J. 94
products: expiry dates on 59; information access 83–84; locations 75; mix 183; placement 97–98; ranges 143; shelf space 108–110, 121; unbundled 23–24, 26, 27, 30, 31; *see also* demand forecasting; inventory control; packaging; prices/pricing; quality
promotions 49, 82, 111–112, 116, 121; *see also* discounts
property developers 174, 179, 189

quality, food/product 20, 24–25, 29, 49, 60, 62, 66, 137, 163–164, 175; *see also* food standards and regulations
queuing 79, 81–82, 83, 113, 115–116, 121–122

radio frequency identification (RFID) technology 73, 94
Rantala, J. 73
Rao, V. R. 112
Reardon, T. 55, 56, 92, 151–152, 153, 154, 155, 157
relationships, business 139–146, 191; collaboration 171, 173–174; contracts 144, 152, 163, 164; between local suppliers and supermarkets 151–167, **158**, **162**; partnerships 176, 181–182, 184; strategic alliances 27, *29*; tribal 139, 141
research and development (R&D) *71*, 72
resource based view (RBV) theory 130
restaurants, in-store 94–95
Ringle, C. M. 46
Rom, M. 26
Rotich, G. 75
rural areas 92, 119, 152, 172; *see also* smallholders/farmers
Russia 92
Rwanda 76

SADC *see* Southern African Development Community (SADC)
Saharin, S. 116
Said, A. M. A. 26
Sainsbury xiv, 1, 189
Schmitz, H. 161
Schutz, W. C. 178
security 66, 85–86
self-checkouts 91, 99
Selva, P. 114
Senauer, B. 95
Senegal 12–13, 189
service providers to supermarkets 170–184, **178**, 189; *see also* customer service/s
Shan, Y. 107
Shell 11
Shilpa, P. 107
Shop-N-Save 133
shopping centres/malls 37, 52–67, 98, 174, **175**, 189–190
Shoprite 1, 3, 4, 5–6, 10, 13, 14, 17, 36, 52, 92–96, 152, 172–174, 182, 190; relationship with local suppliers 161–165, **162**; USave brand 99
Simchi-Levi, D. 111
Sindi, J. K. 129
small businesses 24, 25, 27, 30, 38, 40, 94, 98, 99, 119, 165, 166, 174, 188; *see also* local suppliers; neighbourhood stores
smallholders/farmers xiv, 36, 100–101, 119, 157–159, 165, 176, 183
smartphones *see* mobile phones
SMMES 177
SNI 11, 12
Snyder, J. 129
social grants 94, 99
social media 84
socialising 49, 188
socio-economic status 49, 52, 188; *see also* consumer demographics; income levels
Sørensen, O. J. 159–160
South Africa xiv, xv, 1, 13–14, 16, 76, 130, 136, 151, 157, 187, 190; impact of supermarket technology in 91–101
South African Council of Retailers 174
South African retailers 4, 36, 92, 95, 129, 170, 189; service providers to 170–184; *see also* Game; Massmart; Shoprite; Woolworths
Southern African Development Community (SADC) 171, 173
Spar 5–6, 7–8, 13–14, 94, 95–96, 99, 177

spending power 20–21, 22, 24, 25, 106
Spinneys 8
staff: customer service support 142–143; experiences offered by 95; processes 76; recruitment 140–141, 143, 145; scheduling 80–81, 112–113, 121, 122; technology skills 85, 86, 142, 190; training and development of 71, 72, 76, 78, 79, 84, 85, 86, 87, 190; turnover/poaching of 78, 79, 80, 83, 86, 122; working conditions 79; *see also* employment
stakeholders 84, 176–177, 181–184
standards *see* food standards and regulations
Starbucks 16
Steeneken, F. 118
Steinhoff International 14
Stokvels 92
Stone, B. 100
Structure–Conduct–Performance (SCP) framework 73
Succar, L. 116
supermarkets 1, 3–15, 17, 92–93, 119, 171–173, 188; history of 153–157, **155**, **156**; *see also* African retail market
superstores/supercentres 1, 2, 3, 4, 5, 6, 7, 8, 9, 10, 13, 14, 15, 95, 116, 188
suppliers *see* local suppliers; service providers to supermarkets
supply chain 25, 75, 79–80, 94, 151, 160, 176, 180; use of operations research (OR) in 105, 107, 108, 111, 112, 115, 119; *see also* agri-food systems
Surahman, S. 75
Surjandari, I. 109–110
sustainability, business xv, 1, 2, 25, 26, 27, 70, 189
Swaziland 172
Systeme U 4, 5

Taha, A. 110
Taiwan 154
Takealot 96, 97
Tanzania xiv, xv, 1, 14, 15, 74, 76, 119, 120, **121**, 187, 189, 190, 191; consumer motivation in 36–50, *41*, **44**, **46**, *47*, *48*; local supplier participation in 129–146, **134**, **136**, **137**, **138**; local supplier–supermarket relationships in 151–152, 157, **158**, 160, 161–167, **162**
TCCIA 142

technologies *see* information and communication technologies (ICT)
Tekin, P. 116–117
Tesco 189
TFDA 141
Thailand 154
Thomas, L. J. 112
Timmer, C. P. 92
Toiba, H. 40, 49
Total 7, 9, 10, 11, 12, 13
Toyin, A. 73–74
trade credit 144, 145, 191
transaction costs 161, 165, 189
Transkei 157
transportation *see* logistics
trolleys 49
trust 139, 143, 145; in technologies 85–86
Tsai, C. 110
TSN 133
Tuskys 1, 10, 11
Tyme Bank 93

Uchumi xv, 1, 11, 36, 75, 133, 140, 145
Uganda xiv, 1, 76, 120, 129–130, 145, 157, 160, 187
Ukwala 36
unbundled products 23–24, 26, 27, 30, 31
Unilever Ghana Limited 75
United Kingdom (UK) xiv, 39–40, 74, 108, 131–132, 158, 161, 189
United Nations (UN): Sustainable Development Goals 77, 87; World Urbanisation Prospectus 151
United States of America (US) 37, 116, 153–154, 188
University of South Africa (UNISA) 190
urbanisation 56, 92, 151, 164, 172

value chain 25, 76, 98, 100, 131, 152, 159–160, 172; analysis 174–179; control 182–183; global 160; governance 160–161; outsourcing 137–139, 144
Valverde, J. 116
Van Dongen, K. 177
Van Zyl, J. 97
Vietnam 92
Vorley, B. 158, 159

Wagner, J. 122
waiting lines *see* queuing
Walmart 1, 6, 10, 13, 14, 15, 16, 172; *see also* Massmart

warehouses *see* distribution centres
Waweru, E. W. 75
Weatherspoon, D. D. 151–152, 155
Weber, R. 114–115
Woolworths 6, 10, 13, 14, 91, 94, 95, 97, 172

Xian, T. 116

Yum! Brands 4, 6, 9, 10, 12
Yves Rocher 3, 9, 13

Zambia 157, 173
Zhao, H. 40
Zhao, Y. 111
Zhou, X. 116
Zimbabwe 75, 157
Zufryden, F. S. 109